Urban Education 2

Schooling in the City

Edited by

John Raynor and Elizabeth Harris

Ward Lock Educational
in association with
The Open University Press

ISBN 0 7062 3637 8 paperback
0 7062 3638 6 hardback

First published 1977

Set in 11 on 12 point Plantin by
Computacomp (UK) Limited, Fort William
and printed by Robert MacLehose and Company Limited, Glasgow
For Ward Lock Educational
116 Baker Street, London W1M 2BB
A member of the Pentos Group
Made in Great Britain

Contents

Acknowledgments

The Open University and publishers would like to thank the following for permission to reproduce copyright material. All possible care has been taken to trace ownership of the selections included and to make full acknowledgment for their use.

Baltimore Bulletin of Education 41 (2) 1963–4 for 'Strengths of the inner city child' by Leon Eisenberg; Professor Harold Entwistle for 'Working class education and the notion of cultural inadequacy' from *Cambridge Journal of Education* Vol. 6. Issue 3 1976; *Forum*, summer 1976, for 'Community school and curriculum' by Geoffrey Partington; Hart-Davis, MacGibbon Ltd/Granada Publishing Limited for 'Conventional Secondary School practice' by D. Holly from *Beyond Curriculum* by D. Holly 1973; *Harvard Educational Review* 37:1 for 'A proposal for education in community' by Fred M. Newmann and Donald W. Oliver; Hodder and Stoughton Educational for 'Civilized authority' by Rhodes and Boyson and 'A question of quality' by G.H. Bantock from *A Question of Schooling* by John E.C. Macbeath 1976; Holt Rinehart and Winston New York for 'What is urban about an urban school?' by Mario D. Fantini and Gerald Weinstein from *Making Urban Schools Work* by Mario D. Fantini 1968; Hutchinson Publishing Group Ltd for 'Children who are "vulnerable" or "at risk"' by Mia Kellmer Pringle from *The Needs of Children* 1974; Jossey-Bass Publishers Ltd for 'Educational models for the disadvantaged' by V.C. Cicerelli, and 'Middle-class teacher and lower-class child' by Bruno Bettelheim from *Rethinking Urban Education* by Herbert J. Walberg and Andrew T. Kopan (eds) 1972; Professor Alan Little for 'The performance of children from ethnic minority backgrounds in primary schools' from *Oxford Review of Education* Vol. 1 No. 2 1975; Methuen and Co Ltd for 'Cultural revaluation' by Gabriel Chanan and Linda Gilchrist from *What school is for* by Gabriel Chanan and Linda Gilchrist 1974; New Beacon Books for 'What the British school system does to the black child' by Bernard Coard from *How the West Indian child is made educationally subnormal in the British school system* 1971; *The Northern Teacher* Winter 1973 for 'The school and cultural development' by Malcolm Skilbeck; NUS Publications for Racist textbooks Parts II and III by Chris Proctor; The Open

University for Education and the crisis of the urban school' by Stuart Hall from *Issues in Urban Education* by John Raynor (ed) (E 351 Block 1) 1974; *Peace News* August 1975, for 'No alternatives to truancy' by Val Hennessy; Penguin Books Ltd for 'Education and black children' by David Milner from *Children and Race* by David Milner 1975; Pitman Publishing Ltd for 'City schools' by Neil Postman and Charles Weingartner from *Teaching as a Subversive Activity* by Neil Postman and Charles Weingartner 1969; Wayne R. Robbins and Wyn Williams for 'Community education'; Routledge and Kegan Paul Ltd for 'The community school – a base for community development' by George and Teresa Smith from *Community Work One* by David Jones and Marjorie Mayo (eds) 1974; and for 'The "problem" of the urban school: some radical and Marxist formulations' by Gerald Grace from *Teachers, Ideology and Control: a study in urban education* by Gerald Grace 1977; and the Gulbenkian Foundation for 'Declining pupil performance and the urban environment' by Alan Little and 'A counter view' by Peter Newsam from *Education and the Urban Crisis* by Frank Field (ed) 1977; Sage Publications Inc. for 'The city as educator: how to be radical without really trying' by Edgar B. Humbert from *Education and Urban Society* Vol. 4 No 1; Schools Council publications for 'Aims and the educational covenant' from Working Paper 53, *The Whole Curriculum 13–16* 1975.

General introduction

Three companion volumes of readings: *The City Experience; Schooling in the City* and *The Political Context*, have been prepared for the third-level course *Education and the Urban Environment* offered by the Faculty of Educational Studies at the Open University. As many people will now know, the Readers form only one component of Open University courses which also include correspondence texts, BBC radio and television programmes, personal tuition and summer schools. In the preparation of these Readers we have deliberately excluded material which will appear in other components of the course. This accounts for the non-appearance of names and materials which might otherwise be expected.

Taken together the three Readers are designed to provide students with:

1 a sample of perspectives on the city and of the social processes at work within urban settings
2 a survey of some of the principal debates encountered in urban schooling
3 an introduction to a variety of political and economic issues in urban education.

It is only four years since the previous course, E351 *Urban Education*, was prepared with its two Readers: *Cities, Communities and the Young* and *Equality and City Schools* (Routledge and Kegan Paul 1973) and in that short space of time it is interesting to note the differences in emphasis between the two course. In the earlier course, one of our central concerns was the problem of urban poverty and the disadvantaged learners in our city schools, and the course preparation period coincided with the Educational Priority Area and the Community Development Programmes. Again, we were writing against a background of high truancy rates, high teacher turnover, and the reported crises taking place within many of our large secondary schools. Not surprisingly therefore, our attention came to be focused on the process of institution-building within schools, on community relations and on alternative strategies for education. Today's educational picture has changed, and the new course reflects that change.

As might be expected at a time of cutbacks and economic stringency, considerable time is given to examining resource implications for urban schooling. Again, though the earlier course gave some attention to an understanding of urban processes, the new course contains even more material reflecting our greater awareness of the way the city serves as a distributive agency; of the plight of the 'inner city' areas, of cultural dislocation within different groups and the implications all of these have for urban schooling. Further, we are, today, much more conscious of the difficulties of searching for a multi-cultural education in a period of economic recession and unemployment, when the racism which lies so close to the surface manifests itself in hostility towards minorities.

This is not to suggest that Urban Education is nothing more than a loose collective title for a number of disparate topics conveniently gathered under one heading susceptible to whim, current concern or the crisis of the moment. In any course on urban education, one would now expect to find students examining some, if not all, of the following issues:

1 *the urban setting* covering the main urban processes, not only in terms of location and structure but also in terms of interests, community and culture
2 *urban politics* introducing students to the questions raised by the priorities, activities and judgments of urban decision-makers in terms of physical planning, city governance and educational policies.

From these two basic considerations a whole number of issues branch out. Among these can be identified:

(a) *issues of equity* – the debates, the research and the programmes for equal educational opportunity; compensatory programmes, multi-cultural education; bi-lingual education and affirmative action.
(b) *management, finance and government* – the structure, plans, methods and budgetary considerations of urban education.
(c) *institutional issues* – the most appropriate kinds of provision for education for different groups at different ages in different parts of the city. Here, too, is that debate on the nature of the curricular objectives that are being pursued in urban schools and the way they relate to parents and to community.

The three Readers in this series reflect the issues outlined above. They have been compiled to enrich the course which starts from a study of the urban experience, considers a number of issues in urban schooling, and concludes with an experience of various political and economic questions. However, each volume can be read separately from the course and gives the reader a useful introduction to the field of study.

In Reader 2, we look directly at a variety of issues within city schooling.

Section I presents papers across the spectrum of the debate which is in progress about the so-called crisis of the urban school; pupil performance, authority and control, and community schooling. The second section is concerned with curriculum issues, with special focus on the extent to which the cultural contexts of schools should affect what is taught within them. The third section examines the impact of schools, their curricula and attitudes and the materials they use, focusing especially on the black child. Finally, in section 4, we present papers on the strengths and vulnerability of city children and conclude with an examination of the consequences of the current dilemmas facing the urban teacher.

1 City Schools

Introduction

To what extent is it meaningful to talk of a crisis in urban schooling? Certainly we must acknowledge that all is not well, either within the educational system in general, or in city schools in particular. It is not easy to judge the extent to which the difficulties of the urban school can be termed 'a crisis'. On the one hand, the system and the schools are assailed by critics on a whole variety of issues – discipline, pupil performance, types of teaching etc. – for a whole range of motives. The assailants often generalize beyond the evidence but the defenders defend by reacting as though there is nothing wrong and, if there is, all that is needed are a few minor changes here and there.

The papers gathered in this first section review *some* of the criticisms offered against the urban school. Hall (1.1) examines the historical, political, social and cultural dimensions of urban schooling in Britain in order to understand the nature of the current crisis. Fantini and Weinstein (1.2) approach the problem from a different point of view; they see the density, diversity and discord of the modern city bringing particular stress into the urban school. This stress is exacerbated by the practice of many urban schools of turning their back on the urban experience which is fundamental to the child's life. Fantini & Weinstein argue for an urban curriculum which would incorporate rather than eject urban phenomena. Little (1.4a) and Newsam (1.4b) debate the issue of declining pupil performance in urban schools.

Possible ways out of the crisis are discussed in the papers which follow. Postman and Weingartner (1.3) present a case for the community control of schooling, with both children and parents participating in learning together in efforts directed towards community improvement. This view is echoed by Smith & Smith (1.5) who consider the case for using schools as the basis for community development, and by Robbins and Williams (1.6) who look at the wider issue of community education. The section closes with a paper by Rhodes Boyson (1.7) who outlines his philosophy as a former Headmaster of one of London's large comprehensive schools.

1.1 Education and the crisis of the urban school

Stuart Hall

Clauswitz once called war the pursuit of diplomacy 'by other means'. Education might be thought of as the pursuit of politics 'by other means'. Such an observation runs right against the grain of the English mode of thought, which shows a persistent tendency to take as many issues of public interest as possible 'out of politics', as the saying goes. Education, we are told, should not be made 'the plaything of party politics': education is 'about personal development'; it is about 'self-fulfilment': it should be pursued 'for its own sake'. Of course, there is more than a grain of truth in all this. The error lies, rather, in the way in which the 'development of individuals' is always set off in opposition to the social nexus, the latter providing a somewhat shabby and illegitimate – though necessary – route to the achievement of the former. In fact, of course, education is precisely the means, in modern societies, by which men and women are formed and shaped as *social individuals*, who are not born but rather *become persons* within and by means of the social nexus which locates them (family, school, community, work and production, the State). It is not therefore by chance or in error that every major change in the education structure needs to be understood as being intimately connected to a shift in power; and, consequently, that reforms have frequently been both proposed and resisted in those terms, on those grounds. Despite this, the debate about education in England has always exhibited a double structure: on one side, the debate about education 'for its own sake'; on the other side, the debate about education's social and political function.

It is worth saying again, therefore, that the education system is one of the central mechanisms by which societies reproduce themselves. It

Source: E351 *Urban Education*, Block 1, pp. 49–55, The Open University Press.

distributes knowledge and skills as between different groups and classes. It is the 'gatekeeper' between the school population and the world of work, of occupations. It shapes men and women into 'citizens'. It transmits the dominant values and beliefs of the cultural order. The more complex such societies become – socially, technically and politically – the more the education system provides them with a central spine. The point at which parents pass their children, compulsorily, into the school system, is also the point at which the private sphere of the family intersects with the public world. Teachers are the guardians of this crucial transition. The formal content of the knowledge they transmit is only a part – the most visible, but perhaps the least significant – of the process of social and cultural formation which constitutes their task. And yet, the history of English education has been marked by this effort to carve out or reserve an area where education could be pursued and discussed 'for itself', freed from the web of surrounding pressures and interests. This latter emphasis has certainly been well-intentioned: but there is some question as to whether it was well-advised. It may have served, not – as many liberals think – to protect education from the inroads and pressures of power, but rather to mask and mystify its real connections. A good deal of what has passed for the 'philosophy of education' has been nourished on the basis of this illusion. Its days, however, must now be numbered.

The modern problem of education began at that moment when a section of the English nineteenth-century intelligentsia persuaded itself that it would have to 'educate its masters', if society were not to split irrevocably apart into two warring (not simply separate) nations. The notion of 'gentling the masses' placed education once and for all at the pivot of the social question: the struggle for power. This recognition was the product of long and deep secular shifts in English society which culminated in the nineteenth century. The great movement of population from the land into the towns, from village to factory, proved irreversible. The 'formation' of the English industrial working class, and its characteristic environment – the industrial city – was accomplished in the wake of this revolution in the countryside. Industrial capitalism made England the 'workshop of the world': but by the same movement, it created the working classes as a massive social, political and economic presence. The inhuman and brutalized conditions of life in the industrial factories and towns were then only painfully and slowly unearthed throughout the century. That discovery pointed clearly to the limits of the market as a mechanism for 'invisibly' securing the greatest good for the greatest number: it pointed to modification, reform, improvement – and, thus, necessarily, social intervention. There were more urgent priorities than learning, such as sanitation, poverty, child labour and disease: yet the modern education system followed in the wake of other kinds of social intervention, and some of the toughest battles between gradual reform and last-ditch laissez-faire were conducted over the issues of education. At the same time, there was more than a touch of self-interest behind the urge to reform. Trade, capital investment, technical innovation, expansion – the essential ingredients of industrial progress – could not forever be sustained on the backs of an unskilled and illiterate workforce. Intervention there was: but for long a minimal literacy, as required by the needs of the productive system of industrial capitalism, was all the education the great urban masses got. The slow expansion of the education system was, however, part of this improving 'progressive' response to the world that industrial capitalism had created.

The city in its modern industrial form provided the living space for the 'industrious poor'. It was also, however, the home of the 'mob', the breeding ground of crime and immorality, of social anarchy and rebellion. The cities had to be improved: they also had to be controlled. The growth of a regular police force and the expansion of the school system were not as unconnected as they might at first appear. Social control and public order, enforced from the outside, were not a sufficiently organic solution to this latter problem. Some way had to be found to create, within the ranks of the urban-industrial masses, an inner attachment to society's goals, a positive commitment to the social order. Respectability, thrift, sobriety, self-discipline were required, to form – as it were from inside – an impulse, a 'formed sentiment', among the masses to adapt to the logic, rationale and mores of industrial capitalism. Thus, education took its place, alongside chapel, tract, self-improving societies, temperance movements, improving popular fiction, as a major cultural force reshaping the inner sentiments and aspirations of the masses. Like the other missionary crusades, it was only a partial success.

The gradual expansion and reform of the education system through the century was, therefore, promoted by what can only be called very mixed motives. The Victorian governing classes were visited, from time to time, by two persistent and recurring dreams. The first was that of the self-improving 'working-man', or rather, of society arranged in an endless series of social stations, each level linked to the preceding one by the impulse towards respectability. The second, however, was a nightmare – the descent of the 'industrious poor' into the abyss, the spectre of the 'unruly mob', the 'dangerous classes', rising up to murder decent Englishmen in their beds, claiming with sticks and staves what they clearly were not going to win by franchise and ballot. The English working class had imprinted itself right across the face of the urban landscape. It had begun to challenge and redraw the map of political power. In time, it would reshape the map of English culture, too. It had entered 'political society'. How were the governing classes to negotiate and accommodate this presence? Some of the great Victorian political figures became pastmasters at it – the tactic of eleventh-hour conversions, five-minutes-to-midnight concessions. Their reputations seem, in retrospect, exactly to hang on the nicety of their judgement as to how long to hold out and when to concede, usually at the expense of consistency, sometimes at the price of their parties of parliamentary majorities. Peel, Palmerston, Disraeli, even the redoubtable Gladstone, were men who knew how to 'give a little' at the strategic moment. But it was men somewhat removed from the immediate tactical struggle, the formative minds, the intelligentsia, who most articulated a response. We might think here of two representative figures, John Mill and Matthew Arnold. It was Mill's task to persuade society to yield, by gradual stages, to the change in the political balance without a showdown between the classes. The main mechanism was electoral reform, leading ultimately to universal adult suffrage. Mill could recommend this with a clear spirit – he worked untiringly for it – because he also had a complementary strategy. Power would ultimately pass to the great mass: but not yet. First, the masses must be formed, shaped, 'educated to power': remade and remoulded into citizens of an enlarged social order. The mechanism for *this* part of the process was education, leading ultimately to the universal compulsory school system. The political and cultural-educational strategies complemented one another.

Mill is one variant of the English compromise. Arnold was another. He started, speculatively, from even more exalted heights than Mill, but descended as far as the administration of the reformed educational system itself, and became one of the creators of that great instrument of gradualism, the school inspectorate. It is salutary to remind oneself that one of the sounds which that great, cultivated, author of *Culture and Anarchy* had ringing in his ears as he composed this text was the din of a section of the militant urban working class rattling the Hyde Park railings. The dream and the nightmare of the collective Victorian middle-class unconscious, as well as the contradictions of the English educational debate, are beautifully captured in Arnold's paradoxical prose. For 'persons ... mainly led, not by their class spirit but by a general humane spirit', the 'best self' was active, and could be led to perfection, to 'sweetness and light' through keeping company with 'the best that had been thought and said'. *But*, if 'our playful giant' was going to 'hoot, bawl, threaten, rough and smash', then it would have to be disciplined by 'fire and strength'. Throughout the century, educational reform advanced by way of these delicately balanced options.

Yet that is only one side of the picture. The urban masses were not, after all, merely the 'objects' of social policy and reform. They had become 'historical subjects' in their own right. If the education system, in its formal and informal ways, seemed to have designs on them, they, in response, had designs for it. Education may often have been conceived as a mechanism of social control, moral containment and spiritual restraint: but it also provided a means and a language by which whole classes of men and women could struggle 'for themselves', and thus become something more than the instruments of the productive system. Time and again, the major movements of working-class agitation and politics through the century discovered, at its heart, the educational cause. Nevertheless, in its overall impact on the society, education remained a mechanism for operating what Lawson and Silver (1973) have called 'the distribution of privilege and underprivilege as well as a system of learning and teaching'.

Thus there has never been, in England, anything remotely approaching a 'common' or 'comprehensive' school experience for all classes of children. Each kind of school has been absorbed into its socio-geographic segment, and taken on something of that imprint. The most privileged schools – like so much else in the structure of social privilege in England – have remained essentially outside the city, surrounded by ample playing fields, as the great country houses and the ancient (and new) universities remain embedded in their fields and commons. The great grammar schools – often the creations of the rising bourgeoisie – have arisen within the city, but as annexes to the more spacious middle-class suburbs: the playing-fields abut on their lawns. With the more recent expansion of the professional middle classes and technical strata, there has developed an intermediary band of city school: the lesser grammar schools, the new comprehensives and the handful of true technical schools. Their spirit and purpose is reflected in their functional architecture: glass and prefabricated slab. In and around the inner city stand the urban working-class schools, the beacons and landmarks of working class education. Only a high brick wall separates their concrete playgrounds from the paved streets.

In one sense, these inner-city schools have become an integral part of the urban working-class landscape. Alongside the terraced houses, corner shops, local pubs and chapels, the dense network of streets, they have helped to define a crucial social space in English culture. In turn, these living spaces have shaped and supported what Cohen (1972) has called 'the close textures of traditional working-class life, its sense of solidarity, its local loyalties and traditions. And this in turn is underpinned by the extended kinship networks of the traditional working-class family'. The school was an integral part of this typical kind of locality and neighbourhood, forming an ecological area of a quite distinctive kind. Such neighbourhoods were and are certainly not self-sustaining. Either the great majority of men and women leave them each day to go to work; or the neighbourhoods run right into the entrances to factories, small workshops, packing yards and storehouses where the heavy day's work is done. Occasionally – just to point the contrasts – the pylons of the local football ground rise up directly out of this matrix. Work, then, sets boundaries to the 'neighbourhood' and its schools on one side. And though the neighbourhood has its own corner shops, there is usually, not far away, the great, crowded, bustling commercial high street, where the main week's shopping or the important purchases are made. The neighbourhood is also bounded, on the other side, by trade, by consumption. Yet the working-class neighbourhood formed a relatively independent 'communal space', somewhere between the private intimacy of the family and the totally public spaces of work and high streets. These are spaces which working-class people have 'won' or rescued from the surrounding culture, and over which an intricate web of rights and obligations, intimacies and distances, and informal social controls have been established. Over these places, working people have come to exert something approaching the rights of 'sitting tenants', the rights of territorial possession. They belong, not by right of ownership or of force but by customary occupation. They represent *negotiated* cultural spaces. The dense, closely-webbed solidarities of English urban working-class life have enclosed them. These solidarities have not prevented, over time, their slow erosion (drift of population, changing character of local work available etc.) or more rapid disintegration (by property speculation and redevelopment): but they have delayed the impact of these forces on the local population and culture. And these horizontal social networks have also linked the local school to neighbourhood and locality. If we think of such areas, we understand better what Thompson (1963) meant when he said that, though the English working class has not often been able to confront directly the social and economic power and cultural hegemony of 'the governors', it has succeeded in *warrening* the society and culture from end to end. The patterns of life, values, kind of social meeting and interaction which characterize such localities are radically distinct from those which prevail in other parts of the city and for other classes, even though at another level they share with other parts of the city some underlying shared experiences and values. The balance between continuity, variation and opposition which characterizes this negotiated, corporate culture is extremely complex: and the local school belongs to it.

From another point of view, the urban school did not 'belong' to this working-class space at all. In terms of vertical networks, this school had quite other connections, served other purposes, was serviced and administered by quite different people. It stood, in essence, for values, for kinds of learning, for types of discipline and authority, it affirmed experiences altogether at variance with its natural environment. Through its selective mechanisms – streaming, tracking, eleven plus – and its knowledge boundaries, it linked the urban working-class zone to the wider society in ways which were connective but also *dis*connected. In this sense, the local urban school is a paradigm case: an institution which in its global meaning and vertical networks can clearly be seen, in however complex a way, to be a dominant institution, the institution of a dominant culture: but which, in its horizontal connections, in its local and neighbourhood context, was *at the same time* part of a negotiated class culture. This mismatch between where these schools stood, and what they stood *for*, was always a glaring one – part of a larger contradiction. Yet some general consensus of values held the unequal parts together. A few of the lucky ones – mostly boys – used the school to clamber, vertically, up and through the divisions. Characteristically, this represented both a personal gain, even a growth, for them, and a loss to their class and neighbourhood. This, too, was part of that larger contradiction: one in which the very nature of the institution, and its cross-ties to locality and to society, forced on the minority the classic choice between individual advancement and community solidarity. It is not by chance that the *ladder* has provided English education with its most powerful metaphor. The rest – the great majority – took what they could and departed. Later in life, they would remember 'school days' with affection, particular masters, friends and enemies, local characters etc.: but it is doubtful whether most of them thought of the school as providing the means to their 'personal growth and development'. In any real sense, they had been educated by the 'university of the street' and graduated into the even larger 'university of life'. Among their number is to be counted the working-class intellectual who 'stayed at home'; but he or she was the product, not of the school, but more often of night class, adult education centre and public library. Yet the school system as a whole seemed for long stretches to hold together: if not in its experienced reality, then perhaps in the sense that proper and necessary reforms *could* be conceived as leading to a wider and fairer distribution of the 'educational goods' at present available only to the privileged few. Indeed, this aim – to win for the deprived classes the best the education system had to offer, to redistribute educational chances more equitably – formed the principal strand in English educational reform. There was nothing basically wrong with education: the trouble was, only a minority really got it. We might call this the 'social democratic' strategy for educational reform.

Gradually, in more recent years, however, an alternative strategy has been emerging. In part, this is the product of an extremely complex shift in political mood and direction in the whole society. In part, it is the product, more directly, of the growing crisis of the urban working-class school itself. The more the major political parties became alternative potential governments, and the more the connections of locality and class through into political parties has decayed, so the more the pattern of political life has assumed a 'localist', community basis, and adapted itself to a strong decentralizing impetus. The varying forces promoting this kind of secular change in the political culture of the society are too complex to sketch in here. They form the background to the emergence of an alternative educational strategy. The crisis of the city – and thus of the urban school – on the other hand, is very much in the foreground. The social-economic system of the modern industrial city has slowly begun to crack apart. London here demonstrates the crisis at its worst, but is not as untypical as we are sometimes inclined to think. The movement of population to the suburbs, the closing down of traditional occupations in the inner urban zones, the pattern of post-war redevelopment and rehousing, above all the penetration of these areas by speculative development and the private property market, have seriously disrupted the organic life and 'natural economy' of the urban working-class neighbourhood. This process has also left the urban school visibly stranded – beached – above the retreating social landscape. The position and logic of these schools have thus been ruthlessly exposed to public view as never before. What, after all, are these schools doing there? What are they *doing*? Who is teaching in them, and who is being taught? What is being taught – and why? Who is benefiting?

This is the matrix of the emergent 'radical' stream in educational thinking. It has been fed by the experience of radical educators working in other, backward, economically-deprived and often 'underdeveloped' parts of the world, who have asked – about the education normally offered to such people – whether it is really a form of advancement, or simply a part of the 'pedagogy of the oppressed' (Freire, 1970). We used to think that the 'oppressed' only existed 'overseas'. But the fact is that, in the areas of multiple deprivation such as our present social system has successfully constructed in all our large industrial cities, the 'culture of poverty' (Lewis, 1966) does not seem all that different from conditions in a Latin American village, and the plight of the 'oppressed' at home is no more tolerable for developing in a society which, elsewhere, is galloping rapidly through 'booms' and 'standstills', 'affluence' and 'inflation'. Consequently, the focus of the 'radical' stream in educational thinking and action is the politics of the classroom, rather than the reform of the system as a whole. It reflects the blunting and containment – though not the breakup – of an older, urban working-class politics, and its partial replacement by the politics of the locality, the strategies of community action and power, and the thrust towards decentralization. The pace of this development has been accelerated by the famine of good teachers for these kinds of school, by the descent into poverty of whole sections of the less manually skilled, and by the influx of immigrant children, which further compounds the situation. 'Radical thinking' in education points towards the relocation of conflict in the urban setting. Its aim is the radicalization, indeed the politicization, of educational practice as a whole. The urban school is now seen, not as a 'sop' but as a 'threat'. Its unintended consequence might well be further to denude and erode the urban working-class community of its necessary defences. It fragments the resistance by such communities to incorporation into the wider dominant culture. The counter-strategy, then, is not to 'school' the urban classes better, but to 'deschool' them.

There may not, yet, be many teachers in such schools who fully subscribe to this interpretation; but it is clear that the very situation itself has already had the effect of undermining the young teacher's confidence in what he is supposed to be doing. Just as the organizing and politicizing of claimants has made many social workers understand better the way in which they often are obliged to negotiate their 'clients' into and through the welfare system, so young teachers are coming to see the way they have been made to act as 'gatekeepers' to the working classes. Such an awareness is tending to polarize and politicize the teaching profession as a whole, especially the men and women who, on behalf of the wider system which rewards them very badly comparatively speaking, nevertheless keep the urban school going.

This crisis really began in the 1950s. The network of family, neighbourhood, street and class always provided the real 'educational' environment for the majority of working-class children. But in the 1950s, this set of local solidarities began to be eroded. Simultaneously, the city itself – but now in the form of a spreading youth culture – began to offer an alternative education, as commanding, and perhaps more relevant than anything being offered in the classroom. The great disenchantment, on both sides of the blackboard, so to speak, began here. I remember the day I first walked into an urban classroom as a young supply teacher. The school itself – a 'secondary modern' – was twice creamed. Those who passed the eleven plus went to the 'local grammar': those who 'failed well', went to a rather better school up the road: we got the rest, and I had 1J. I remember the section head of a junior school, who travelled up from Dulwich or somewhere every morning, and left every afternoon at five minutes past four, telling a boisterous 2B one morning that, if they didn't behave, he'd 'take away their French'! There was an unofficial list in the staffroom of when the worst troublemakers in 4FX (what I believe used to be called Fourth Remove!) reached their fifteenth birthday and could be statutorily released on to the job market. The boys in the back row were clearly already reading the 'Jobs Vacant' page in the local newspaper. A third of them were black. A good school: no violence, no gangs, no knives in the playground, few elder brothers waiting outside the gate ... still, patently, a school – a culture – *in crisis.*

Dedicated teachers, generation after generation, have done their utmost for children in such schools, trying to draw down a little illumination from the high, Dickensian windows, endeavouring to give the chaotic experience some coherence and shape. Many of them – without adopting anything so explicit as a 'pedagogy of the oppressed' – simply, quietly, renounced their earlier aspirations for a distinguished career crowned by a headship, and settled down in or near the school for life. They adopted the local school, and the school 'negotiated' them into its culture. Patient, backbreaking work. Few teachers of this kind had any notion of the 'politics' of the situation they had entered. Yet, in a quiet way, their dedication touched lives, made links, occasionally changed lives, year after year. Until the educational millennium comes, what indeed is to become of the majority working-class school and who is to teach its children? More pertinently (it is a question the 'deschoolers' must answer), can the deprived classes ever win power in the system if they are educationally unprepared and unequipped for the struggle?

On the other hand, the most dedicated teacher in the urban classroom must ask himself the question whether, unwittingly perhaps, he or she is not in fact colluding with the system: an agent for the dismantling of a set of real defences, and their replacement by a lukewarm, poor man's version of the dominant culture in which their pupils have no allotted place. It is possible to train a limited number of children to *mimic* an educated language which has no real connections to their experience, feelings, position, life-situation or prospects. Indeed, this question of language has focused the problem in the sharpest way. The fact is that the dominant education, and indeed the technical complexities of any modern society, are conducted in elaborated codes of expression, to which a middle-class training and upbringing gives access. It seems to follow that, if the working classes are not only to enter society, but to assume power in it, they must learn the dominant educated language and its modes: and that the role of their allies and supporters is to win for that class the right and opportunity to appropriate knowledge of the modern world in the mode in which it is elaborated. The fact is, however, that this legitimation of certain kinds of language has had the effect of *de-legitimating* the natural speech, language and modes of expression in which that majority already speaks: a language which has been formed in and by a real connectedness to life-situation and experience, and without which the young working-class boy is literally 'speechless' (that is, he has no language for his own experience of the world) – and is therefore open to be labelled inarticulate. By contrast, a good deal of throttled, formalized speech is sanctioned because it approximates to what teachers think of as 'educated talk'. Labov's (1973) experiments with black and working-class language in the United States should have a powerful effect in dispelling at least some aspects of the myth of verbal deprivation.

There is more than one kind of speaking: and it is not by chance that education favours some varieties and degrades others. It may be better to give a child confidence in whatever language he has rather than to train him into a language in which he cannot name the things he needs to know to survive. What is more, he needs to name things – above all, the sources of his own deprivation – which our kind of education screens out. The most difficult questions of educational practice and politics thus emerge from these scattered reflections on the crisis of the urban school. The point where power and the urban school intersect is also the point where the struggle for power is in the cities, and thus the fate of a class will be decided. It was ever thus.

References

ARNOLD, Matthew (First published 1869) *Culture and Anarchy*

COHEN, Philip (1972) 'Subcultural conflict and working-class community', University of Birmingham, Working Papers in Cultural Studies, 2, Spring 1972. See *Urban Education 1: The City Experience* Ward Lock Educational, pp. 236–48

FREIRE, Paulo (1970) *Cultural Action for Freedom*. First published as a monograph by the *Harvard Educational Review* © Center for the Study of Development and Social Change, Cambridge, Mass.; Harmondsworth, Penguin Education (1972)

LABOV, W. (1973) 'The logic of non-standard English', Nell Keddie (ed.) *Tinker, Tailor: The Myth of Cultural Deprivation*, Harmondsworth, Penguin Education

LAWSON, J. and SILVER, H. (1973) *A Social History of Education in England*, London, Methuen

LEWIS, Oscar (1966) 'The culture of poverty', *Scientific American*, 215 pp. 19–25

THOMPSON, E. P. (1963) *The Making of the English Working Class*, London, Gollancz

1.2 What is urban about an urban school?

Mario D. Fantini and Gerald Weinstein

If we were to choose the one characteristic of an urban context that has priority for schools it would be stated as follows:

The urban context is one in which there is *persistent stress imposed by intensely concentrated social realities*. Although all schools operate in a context of social realities, those that are in smaller more homogeneous communities have much less tension because the schools reflect a reality that is more parallel to that of the surrounding community. In addition, in those communities there is not the intense concentration of so many varied realities – so many different slices of life. The urban school, located in an area of great density and diversity, finds itself at a convergence point of a whole array of realities.

While most schools have devotedly divorced themselves from direct confrontations with social reality, the urban school stands out as most absurd in its emulation of the way reality is reflected in suburban schools. But, before we go into what the school is or is not doing, we must take a hard look at the urban social realities and the stress they impose.

Although there are numerous ways to describe and diagnose the persistent press of social realities in urban areas, time and space force us to limit this particular discussion. However, from reading what some of the 'experts' in urban diagnosis have written and by using our own perceptions and experiences, we would like to single out those aspects that have a clearer (for us) relationship to educational prescriptions.

It will be necessary to describe briefly some of the concepts that shape our perceptions and help us diagnose the urban scene. Our general

Source: Mario D. Fantini and Gerald Weinstein, *Making Urban Schools Work*, (1968), New York, Holt, 3–10, 24–9.

framework for examining the urban scene is this: How does the press of urban social realities affect certain basic human issues?

Human beings have a combination of personal issues with which they continually attempt to deal in some satisfactory manner. Many of these issues are common enough to be designated as a pattern – '*human* issue.' Although these human issues have been labeled through the years in a variety of different ways (needs, wants, concerns, drives, and so forth), all of these different labels have something in common.

Although these issues are usually integrated and less distinct as discrete personal arenas in individuals, we think it is helpful to keep them separate as we now examine some of the social realities of the urban context and their relation to these issues.

These human issues can generally be grouped into issues revolving around safety, security, or survival, which include most of the physical needs – food, clothing, shelter, health – as well as the emotional needs for safety and security. A separate grouping can be made of those issues dealing with the psychosocial needs of love, recognition, status, affiliation and potency, agency or effect. In addition a third grouping may be made: one dealing with aesthetic, knowledge-seeking, spiritual, and self-actualizing issues. Once some of these issues are described, one can look at the cities with the question: What are the physical and psychosocial characteristics of city life and what effect do they have on its inhabitants in their attempts to work through the issues just described?

For the purpose of this writing we intend to deal with the middle range of issues described, the psychosocial group, and to limit even those to the issues of identity, connectedness or affiliation, and power (potency – agency – effect), and then to proceed to outline some of the effects of urban life on these issues.

By *identity* issues, we mean those aspects of a person's behaviour which aim at providing him with a sense of worth. This area includes all the questions pertaining to the process of self-evaluation and the consequences of these evaluations. It is referred to by such terms as self-image, self-concept, identity, self-awareness, self-esteem, ego, ego-strength, and the like. All of these surround the basic questions: Who am I? What am I worth?

By *connectedness* issues we mean those aspects of a person's behaviour which aim at providing him with a sense of positive affiliation with others. This is the relations-with-others domain, ranging from the primary face-to-face relations to secondary relations with less direct groups. Connectedness issues involve the questions: To whom does the individual feel an allegiance? To whom does he feel he belongs? What are people to him? Who are the significant others? How does he relate? With whom does he *integrate*?

By *power* issues we mean those aspects of a person's behaviour which aim at providing him with a sense of control or influence over what is happening and will happen to him. Does the individual feel that he has a significant part to play in the construction of situations that will affect him? If he does, does he act in accordance with these feelings?

Density and loss of identity

To what extent do the urban realities contribute to the identity crisis of the city dweller? Do I really count? Do I have any importance? Am I being lost in the massive shuffle of the big city life? These are often the unverbalized questions of the city dwellers – all of which may be condensed into: How does the city affect my perceptions of myself?

Everyone knows that cities are crowded, that space is at a premium, that it is difficult to get away from crowds of hustling, bustling people. Everywhere there are lines of people waiting. Subway trains provide for some of the most physically intimate rides obtainable anywhere. But what is the persistent stress on the individual confronted with great numbers of people? We would contend that the result is greater depersonalization, less empathy, greater feelings of loneliness and anonymity, and a general hardening or mechanization of relationships with people.

Varied comments of urban dwellers reflect this description:

> I don't feel sorry for nobody. When you been around this town as long as I've been and ya seen all the nuts and kooks, it just runs off your back like water.

> How can I possibly count as anything important when I've never felt more lonely in my life than when I moved to the city? Everyone seems to be in such a hurry to get to his own hidden little world. Strange to feel so lonely when there are so many people around.

People living in extremely close physical contact with one another and highly dependent, yet remaining isolated in general from one another – a sea of unknown faces – is just one of the paradoxes of the urban social reality of size and density. Impersonal relationships are numerous here, and the brief casual contacts between persons allow in most instances for the communication of only superficial information. Yet, on the basis of this limited information, people evaluate and rank others. Standardized, superficial criteria for stratifying people thus evolve according to address, speech, manners, skin color, dress, and so forth.[1] There are too many people to absorb as individuals; therefore, a categorical depersonalized shorthand becomes reinforced.

Within the urban school itself, depersonalization is dramatically evident. Class size has rarely been pared down, in spite of 'average' numbers issued in board of education reports. Having *every* child study the same thing at the same time for the same length of time is the rule. Teachers rarely live in the same community in which they teach, and thus parents and teachers are strangers. Because of the great numbers of children, cumulative records and reports in effect become the 'children' about whom standardized decisions are made. Personalizing education would mean fouling up the machinery of the organization and by all means the machinery comes before the individual or else we would have chaos.

This problem of depersonalization brings us to our next major social reality of the urban area.

Bureaucratization and powerlessness

In spite of Mayor Lindsay's pronouncement that New York City shall be known as Fun City, living there has been like being a member of 'Strike-of-the-Month-Club'. In the last three years the city has had subway, newspaper, hospital workers', teachers', garage, taxicab, and, most recently, garbage workers' strikes. Many of these caused considerable inconvenience to the urban residents. What struck us the authors, however, was the degree of nonchalance with which the citizens endured these events with an 'Oh, well, it will be over soon' attitude. It was almost as if people were being reminded that this was the price they had to pay for living in Fun City – or for that matter, in any large city. James Reston, in an editorial in *The New York Times*, was astounded at the complacent and passive reaction of the New York citizenry. 'The force [the bureaucracy] is so powerful,' he writes, 'that they are beyond reason or persuasion or control. Power will tell in the end, they seem to be saying, and the people are merely spectators and victims in the struggle.'[2] 'You can't fight City Hall' is the dominant theme. The bigger the city, the less feeling of control, so why bother?

Many people question public institutions as to who serves whom. The verdict rendered most often is that in reality the client is at the service of the institution. Thus 'You can't fight City Hall' has become 'You can't fight the Board of Education'. As cogs in a gigantic machinery, administrators, teachers, children, and parents are rendered powerless in persistent ways.

The following statements help to sum up this powerlessness vis-à-vis bureaucracy and urban living: 'For satisfaction and growth, people need to engage in active interchange with their environment; to use it, organize it, even destroy it. ... [their] physical surroundings [and institutions][3] should be accessible and open-ended ...'[4] The present urban social reality is very far from this ideal.

Diversity and disconnectedness

To which extent does the city create a context for connectedness between different people? Does it engender a sense of community in which its variety of people see each other as important and related to one another? Does it create a sense of belonging?

Of all the social realities faced by the urban dwellers and especially the urban school, the tremendous diversity of people looms as the most crucial distinction. Because so many different kinds of people, attitudes, perceptions, values, and habits are concentrated in a limited geographical area, this may be cited as one of the most unique aspects of an urban environment.

It is one thing, however, to know that diversity is a fact of urban life; it is quite another to realize how diversity is viewed by the urban resident. To a few, diversity provides an exciting possibility for enrichment and expansion of one's own perceptions and experiences through a kind of cross-fertilizing interaction between different groups of people. These are the few who thrive on variety and find it nourishing. But we think that this attitude is not the one prevalent in the city. More often diversity is viewed as threatening, and at best as novel or interesting but certainly not anything one would consciously seek to develop. It is in the city, typically, that the great potential for cross-fertilization lies and yet the distinct ethnic and racial turfs are entered by others only when absolutely necessary. It seems as if the only meeting ground between these diverse groups is in the restaurant – but then only recipes and foods cross-fertilize, not the people. Physical and psychological boundaries that keep people disconnected and alienated from one another are as well maintained as the Berlin Wall.

The urban school, meanwhile, has always considered itself the great homogenizer. It has taken great masses of diverse people and acculturated them to the middle-class mainstream. Whether or not specifically articulated as such, this is what the mission of the school was and is. Only *now* something seems to be going wrong. The acculturation mission is having tremendous bumps and wobbles. Many of the processes established by the school are intended to stamp out diversity, both cultural and individual, so that the urban school actually alienates diverse pupils and keeps them disconnected from the school. Until recently, for example, it was illegal in New York for a teacher in a school to speak in Spanish to Spanish-speaking pupils except in foreign language classes.

If we now go back to our initial characterization of the urban milieu – which was stated as 'the persistent stress imposed by intensely concentrated social realities' – we can summarize in this way: density and size, bureaucracy, and diversity are social realities which persistently lay stress on the individual's concern for identity, power, and connectedness.

Certainly there are other ways to select and categorize social realities; however, we think this will serve our present purposes.

The stresses we have been discussing also imply that a city dweller has less opportunity to ignore social realities. He is exposed to them whether he wants to be or not. He is close to crime, riots, poverty, muggings, alcoholics – they are constantly making themselves felt – and he cannot remain totally impervious to them. So it is with children in the urban school. The urban school has attempted to shy away from things going on in the real world which are part of an urban child's experience. Thus there is dichotomy and tension between the child's urban curriculum and the school's more antiseptic curriculum – a dichotomy that usually leads the urban child to label the school's curriculum as 'phony'.

We have been saving a final descriptive characterization for last in order to emphasize it. What we have been discussing up to now are some of the effects of urbanization on the 'average' resident – who could very well be middle-class and white. Depersonalization, anonymity, isolation, powerlessness, can be and *are* felt by people whose bellies are relatively full, who have steady incomes, and who have not been discriminated against by society. Now, however, it is becoming more evident that increasingly the 'average' city dweller is more likely to be poor and discriminated against. Public schools in large cities are basically the habitat of the socioeconomically disadvantaged and will become more so. Therefore if the characteristics of urban stress are felt by those who are relatively well-off, we must magnify those stresses, perhaps double or triple them, when applying them to the disadvantaged resident. We must also magnify those stresses when applying them to the urban public school itself. The urban school thus finds itself in the center of a situation where the black demands for power, identity, and connectedness are hammering on its doors with ever-increasing insistence.

A model of an urban school

After all this description of urban realities and analysis of their effects, what kind of prescription for the urban school is possible? According to the diagnosis given thus far, we shall offer a suggestion for a beginning model of an urban school that is directly connected with the issues we have raised. Therefore, corresponding to the limits we have given ourselves, the model would have to meet the following criteria:

1 Social reality and the school's curriculum have to be intrinsically connected.
   (a) The school must acknowledge the realities by setting up a structure in which children are engaged in the examination of these realities.

(b) Children will learn the skills and behaviours needed to influence social realities.
(c) The skills and behaviours for social change will be applied by the children to the social realities.

2 Power, identity, and connectedness have to become a legitimized basis for curriculum with the aim of expanding the repertoire of responses children have in dealing with these concerns.

3 Diversity, both cultural and individual, and its potential for cross-fertilization has to be encouraged and expanded through educational objectives and organization that allow and legitimize such an aim.

4 The school and the community it serves have to exist less as separate entities and instead develop responsibilities and lines of authority that are more integrated and shared.

Our construction of the model will have four major directions: (1) to consider an expansion and change in form of educational objectives; (2) to chart succinctly what a school that follows through on these objectives would look like organizationally; (3) to explore more fully some of the unique aspects of such a school; (4) to consider the relationship of this school to what society demands. In addition, after constructing the model we will address ourselves briefly to the questions of scheduling, staffing, and teacher training.

The objectives

'A' objectives

For a starter we can begin with four kinds of objectives, only one set of which is presently legitimized in the schools.

The legitimate ones ('A' objectives), as we have repeatdly indicated, are those that are geared to the attainment of academic skills and subject matter content. These are the objectives that rule the educational roost (in spite of the fact that they have not succeeded in achieving many of our broader educational aims). These are the objectives that almost all educational 'innovations' are turned into. When these are the sole objectives of education all descriptions and diagnoses of any group of people or of any area (for example, urban) become very difficult, because they must be squeezed into subject-matter goals. If we discuss power, identity, diversity, connectedness, and all the other issues we have mentioned, it becomes quite a challenge to try to fit those issues into teaching tasks that have as their aims getting children:

1 to read, to compute, to outline
2 to know the causes of the Civil War
3 to become familiar with the geography of Latin America

4 to know the parts of speech
5 to know the material that constitutes the Earth's crust.

We certainly do not intend to deny the value of such tool skills and knowledge, but we find it difficult to relate sociopsychological descriptions to such objectives. In fact, we think this is a major reason for so many urban teachers becoming annoyed with consultants and with special resource people who feed teachers descriptions and analyses of their pupils. For they, the teachers, are constantly being put in the position of implementing a description when none of their teaching tasks have any intrinsic relation to those descriptions.

We have consistently had our knuckles rapped for the off-handed way we treat 'A' objectives. However, we did not care much, because the objectives we were most interested in have been, and still are treated in an off-handed way by those in the educational power structure. It was not until we were reprimanded by our colleague Bruce Joyce that we began to reconsider. Joyce, in his book *Alternative Models of Elementary Education*, has cogently spread out a menu of academic strategies from which objectives might be derived.[5] He lists as educational strategies those that deal with:

1 Symbolic-technical proficiency (reading, arithmetic, and so forth).
2 Information from selected disciplines (commonly, history and geography).
3 Structure of knowledge (concepts from disciplines).
4 Modes of inquiry (how scholars think).
5 Broad philosophical schools or problems (aesthetics, ethics, and so on).

It is fairly clear to us that, in reality, schools concern themselves largely with Strategies 1 and 2, 'Symbolic-technical proficiency' and 'Information from selected disciplines'. Given *only* these two strategies, we can reiterate our frustration in trying to relate sociopsychological description to them. However, using a combination of the last three strategies on the list makes it easier to relate them to our diagnosis. If we use Strategies 3 through 5 in order to develop academic objectives we would begin by raising such questions as:

(a) What *concepts* from what disciplines, or what *philosophical schools of thought* have the greatest priority for the urban issues as we have defined them?

or

(b) What *modes of inquiry* from what kinds of scholars would have the greatest priority?

Thus, while still acknowledging the importance of and including skills and subject achievement objectives as a portion of the schools' responsibility, we would like to suggest three more sets of objectives:

'B' objectives

1 to have the children acquire the skills of negotiating with adults
2 to have the children devise a variety of strategies for getting something they want
3 to have the children learn to identify the real power sources in their community
4 to have the children develop the skills of organizing people in order to create some change in their immediate social realities
5 to have the children learn to use all forms of media in order to gain support for some social action they intend to take
6 to have the children develop general skills for constructive social action such as:[6]
   (a) the ability to define clearly the objectives of social action
   (b) the ability to evaluate the existing situation, to identify obstacles to the goal, and to identify the available resources for overcoming these obstacles
   (c) the ability to analyze and to generate alternative measures for action, and to predict the various outcomes of each alternative
   (d) the ability to select the most valuable of these alternatives and to test them through action
   (e) the ability to evaluate the tested procedure and to revise strategies, thus beginning the cycle again.[7]

If curriculums were developed with these types of objectives as their focus, we would begin to see a more intrinsic linkage between a teaching task and descriptions of powerlessness.

'C' objectives

1 to have the children become aware of how with whom they live and where they live influence how they perceive themselves
2 to have the children learn how society's definitions of groups of people affect the way they judge themselves
3 to have the children analyze the criteria they are using for self-judgement in terms of its objective base
4 to have the children become more capable of predicting their own behaviour
5 to have the children expand their repertoire of responses to situations
6 to have the children see themselves as more differentiated 'subselves'[8]

7 to have the children discover strengths, talents, and interests within themselves of which they may not now be aware.

Although these objectives are crudely stated, we hope that one can begin to see their relationship with the descriptions of the urban dweller's concern for identity.

'D' objectives

1 to expand the child's repertoire for interaction with others
2 to expand the child's repertoire for interaction with more kinds of others
3 to expand one's capacity for self-disclosure to others
4 to expand one's capacity for taking the risks in going out to others unilaterally
5 to expand one's circle of significant identifications
6 to expand one's ability to 'experience other people as they really are, i.e., to become able to really listen, to really develop a kind of third ear for the music that he's playing as well as the particular notes and words – what he's trying to say as well as what he is actually saying in words."[9]

One can begin to see the relationship between 'D' objectives and a concern for connectedness. Moreover, this set of objectives is particularly poignant in a society that has been diagnosed as 'white racist' by the President's Commission on Civil Disorders.[10]

When one thinks of all the energy that has gone into the curriculum reform movement without even considering curriculum that might achieve the types of objectives listed in these last three categories, one begins to wonder if we are really serious about dealing with the basic concerns of our society...

Notes

1 See BESHAR, J. M. (1962) *Urban Social Structure*, New York, Free Press, p. 46.
2 'New York: The city that quit,' editorial by James Reston, *The New York Times*, 22 October 1965.
3 Authors' insertion.
4 From the chapter by LYNCH, K., 'The city as environment' in *Cities* (a *Scientific American* book), New York, Knopf-Random House, 1966, p. 194.
5 Boston, Ginn, 1969.

6 These are basically problem-solving and scientific method skills, but here they are applied directly to social action.

7 FANTINI and WEINSTEIN, (1968), *The Disadvantage: Challenged to Education*, New York, Harper & Row, p. 436.

8 Briefly, a subself may be thought of as one of the many characters of the self, each of which plays different roles and whose interaction with one another constitutes a unified self-image. The concept of subselves is derived from Dr Stewart Shapiro, whose article 'Transactional aspects of ego therapy,' *Journal of Psychology* (1963), pp. 487–9, explains the term more fully.

9 MASLOW, A. H. *Eupsychian Management*, (1965), Homewood, Ill., Richard D. Irwin and Dorsey Press, p. 168.

10 *Report of the National Advisory Commission on Civil Disorders*, 1968, New York, Bantam Books.

1.3 City Schools

Neil Postman and Charles Weingartner

City schools as they now exist largely confine students to sitting in boxes with the choice of acquiescing to teacher demands or getting out.

Although it seems easy to disparage the observation that teachers with conventional middle-class attitudes cause most of the problems that they themselves deplore in schools, the testimony provided by students, both verbally and behaviourally, requires that this criticism be met. In the case of white teachers and black students, the dismissal of this criticism merely requires the dismissal of reality.

The very form and substance of conventional city schools, especially for 'disadvantaged' students, *produces* the most commonly perceived problems. The problems are real, but they are not inevitable, because the process which produces them can be modified.

At present, the conventional school is a hostile place, especially to urban 'disadvantaged' children. They do not learn what the school says it 'teaches,' and they drop out – or are thrown out – of it as soon as they reach the age where this is legally possible.

These 'failures' do not disappear. They remain in the community, and they comprise an endless and growing population dedicated to 'getting even' with the society that has reviled and rejected them in the school. The cost – just in dollars – we pay for dealing with these drop- or push-outs far exceeds virtually *whatever* cost would be entailed in modifying the school environment so as to produce attitudes and skills in these young people that would help them to become participating and contributing members of the community rather than its enemies.

However 'impractical and romantic' the following suggestions seem, they are certainly no more 'impractical' than the existing city schools which now contribute to the development of the greatest source of threat to

---

Source: *Teaching as a Subversive Activity* (1969) Pitman Publishing Ltd.

the existence of the city as a viable community – its 'disadvantaged' youth.

It is possible to view the 'school' in the city, particularly in 'disadvantaged' areas, more as a *process* than as a structure. There are many reasons for taking such a view, not the least of which is that of changing the connotations that the school conventionally elicits. Furthermore, if the process is viewed as having its primary objective the provision of direct and immediate service to the community, a number of otherwise 'invisible' potentials become apparent. For example, the process could be structured around (1) identifying community problems, (2) planning possible solutions on a variety of levels, and (3) carrying out a plan the objective of which is to produce some immediate and palpable amelioration of the problems. In a way, such a school process permits the school to function as a kind of local 'think tank' with the intellectual activity focused on problems the staff (students) identifies, and with all of this reinforced by the physical activity entailed in carrying out the solutions.

Such a school process has the immediate community as its 'curriculum.' School, in this sense, becomes a primary instrument for dealing in services and products which the community needs.

There are no 'subjects'. in the conventional sense; the community and its problems and the students working to develop possible solutions embody all 'subjects'. The students – across all of the age ranges now found in school – are the primary action agents, and they are paid (rewarded) not merely with 'grades', but with currency they value, including public recognition.

Adolescents, especially male dropouts, should have leadership responsibility throughout, with 'teachers' playing a consultant or advisory role.

One of the functions of this kind of schooling is to open an avenue of constructive, responsible participation in community affairs to adolescents and young adults who are now usually denied such opportunity, and who, partly as a consequence, turn to anticommunity activities as an alternative.

This kind of schooling need not confine students to sitting in a classroom. The whole city can – and should – be a continuous 'learning laboratory', with the immediate community as the source of immediate reward for all activity.

The services such a 'school' might use as a vehicle include:

1 community planning and action programmes, running from information services that could include newsletters, magazines, and films, to rat extermination, with a bounty paid for each rat killed, and awards for better approaches to the problem

2 a range of services geared to immediate daily problems, including repair services for household appliances and equipment
3 a range of 'cultural' services, including student-produced musical and dramatic programmes, puppet shows, films, television programmes, etc., on a continuing basis; there could be a city-wide talent programme with the best performers and performances being showcased on a weekly TV programme, or in other community facilities
4 a range of 'athletic' services (possibly adjunct to the 'cultural' programme again on a city-wide basis; this might be of an 'intramural' type, possibly under the aegis of a City Athletic Club, with a continuing roundrobin series of contests; placing participants on an Olympic team might be one of the objectives of such a programme
5 a range of services in or to city agencies – hospitals, police, fire, sanitation, parks, museums, etc. (this might be extended into private business).

The school might also get into the production of stuff including clothing, food, and household and personal decorations. These products could be sold – or otherwise distributed – in the community. Students could operate vegetable and flower gardens as well as bakery, toy-repair, junk-conversion (even into 'art'), millinery and dress, ceramics and jewelry, and photography shops, for example, with the whole merchandising process being added to the production process. Animal shelters and 'pet libraries' could also be operated. The school process might even include a kind of *kibbutz* experience on public or privately owned land both inside and outside the city. The point to all this is to give kids something constructive to *do* – and it could be on a continuing year-round basis, just like the rest of the community. Not only would the range of their kinesthetic experiences be widely increased, but the consequences of this would permit the development of 'literacy' in a variety of ways conventional schools do not even admit exist. It probably needs to be emphasized that the foregoing is not a restatement of a plan of 'vocational' education. We are suggesting here examples of a spectrum of activities addressed to community needs which could comprise a vehicle for a total education.

Private business and industry might be induced to provide 'awards' in various forms to the students who participate in ways that ought to be recognized beyond the performance itself.

Arrangements could probably be worked out with public and private colleges and universities to admit students from such a school system on the basis of performance in these activities rather than on the basis of 'grades' in conventional 'subjects'.

Arrangements could also be made with various business enterprises in the city and state to provide some kind of "apprentice" opportunity at various points in the programme. It might not be necessary to send students out in all cases, since business and industry could provide some "consultants" to assist students engaged in some activity they need help with.

Such a school process, then, has as its primary function the development of responsible community leadership through providing students with the opportunity for substantive participation in the invention, initiation, and implementation of programmes intended to improve the community. This, in turn, produces various effects, including (1) freeing students from detention in a school that virtually insures their alienation from the community at large, and (2) minimizing the continuation of bureaucratic agencies populated by functionaries who are not part of the community ostensibly to be served. Such a process also would have the effect of channelling the energies and abilities of young (particularly male) adolescents into constructive rather than destructive directions. It could also produce a viable political network by maintaining direct communication with the community through its youth, thus minimizing the proliferation of competing 'spokesmen' and organizations, especially from sources outside the local community.

A school system of this type has the potential for becoming one of the most useful social-political instruments possible for dealing fruitfully with the problems of the city as they presently exist and as it seems they will probably develop in the future.

In such a system you do not need school structures as they presently exist, nor school 'curricula' as they presently exist, nor school faculties as they presently exist. Whatever the reasons were for the present form of public schools, they have little or nothing to do with the problems that the city faces now, and so they need to be changed. If *any* publicly supported institution does not help to resolve problems as they really exist, why have it at all?

1.4a Declining pupil performance and the urban environment

Alan N. Little

As far as schools situated in inner city areas are concerned, there have been many studies of school performance. A recent example is an attempt of Barnes, in which he compared backward readers in primary schools throughout the equivalent of the ILEA in 1952/54 with 1968/71 and more limited comparisons in the area within which an EPA study took place. In 1953 the LCC took a sample of schools from which they derived a representative sample of children; of this sample 14 per cent of the eleven-year olds were described as backward (using the criterion of a reading score below 85). In 1968 a cohort of eight-year olds contained 27 per cent with a reading score of 85 and below and the same cohort three years later yielded a similar percentage. Assuming a normal distribution the expected proportion scoring below 85 is 16 per cent. Therefore, it is possible to argue that in the early 1950s LCC primary school leavers were performing at a marginally higher level than expected and that by 1968 they were doing significantly worse than the national average. At this point it is worth noting that the mean score of all ILEA pupils aged eight in 1968 was 94.4 (equivalent to a six-month retardation in reading age) and at eleven 94.2 (equivalent to a ten-month retardation in reading age). The important observation is that in the early 1950s roughly one pupil in seven was defined as being backward: by 1968/71 one pupil in four or nearly twice as many could be categorised as backward.

These figures relate to reading and to primary schools, but a wealth of information exists to show a high correlation between reading and other skills taught in primary schools and between primary and secondary school performance. Therefore reading can be taken as a fair indication of basic skill performance. Given this a further point can be made using reading scores; the ILEA developed an index of educational priority areas (i.e.

Source: *Education and the Urban Crisis* (1977), ed. Frank Field, pp. 64–72.

socially disadvantaged), based upon the type of criteria suggested by Plowden. A recent study has related reading scores to the EPA rank of the school. When schools were divided into quartiles, the mean reading score of pupils in the least privileged quartile was 89.2, compared with 100.4 in the most privileged quartile. Translated into reading ages this means that pupils in the beginning of the second year of junior school in the most privileged areas had a mean reading score well over a year above their age peers in the least privileged areas. It also means that inner city areas contain a variety of schools which can be differentiated in terms of pupil performance.

Concern about behavioural standards covers a wide canvas. For some it relates to specific behaviour like truancy, delinquent behaviour, vandalism and violence within the school. Most of this is anecdotal and impressionistic, but it certainly gives a picture of the inner city school being more difficult to teach and learn in than the outer city counterpart. Undoubtedly some of the descriptions of what is going on and, perhaps more important, predictions of what will happen, derive from looking at the current UK situation through a series of preconceptions derived from experiences within the USA and therefore of questionable usefulness in the UK context.

Nevertheless, concern about the prevalence of maladjustment in city schools is confirmed by the work of Rutter and others. Rutter has developed a scale of pupil maladjustment based on teacher ratings of individual pupils. An extreme comparison is instructive for the purpose of our debate. Using Rutter's own operational definition of maladjustment the percentage of pupils rated as maladjusted in the Isle of Wight was 10.6 per cent. By contrast, the percentage in primary schools in an inner city borough in the ILEA at the same time was 19.1 per cent. As a result of this finding a special survey was undertaken of one in ten pupils aged 11-plus in the ILEA: these were scored by their classroom teacher on the Rutter scale. This indicated that 21.6 per cent were maladjusted. It seems safe to conclude that the incidence of 'maladjustment' is twice as high in inner city areas as in small towns in Britain. In this context it is worth noting that the reading scores of maladjusted pupils were of considerable educational interest: whereas the mean for pupils classified as normal was 96.6, those considered to be maladjusted had a mean score over ten points lower (86.2). Put another way, whereas 'good readers' had a mean behaviour rating of 2.3, for poor readers the comparable figure was 7.6. Therefore the inner city school is likely to have more maladjusted pupils and they are more likely to be poor performers in school. This point about relative performance of pupils 'at risk' is worth making in relation to social disadvantage. Again, to cite literacy data and the EPA index: pupils were ranked according to the level of their own exposure to social disadvantages and grouped into low-risk (no disadvantage) and high-risk (exposed to five or more disadvantages). The mean reading score of pupils with no disadvantage was 103.8; with five or more disadvantages 81.5. This is a gap of more than 22 points and is the equivalent of more than two years' reading age at eight or nine. Put simply: disadvantaged children do less well than advantaged, and inner city schools have more disadvantaged children than other schools. Maladjusted children do less well than adjusted and inner city schools have more maladjusted children than other schools. The dynamics of this relationship are analysed in a recent study in the ILEA which indicates that 'educational failure' precedes and gives rise to behavioural difficulties, rather than the other way round. Further, that other factors (class, family size, immigrant status) which are related to maladjustment 'do so to a considerable extent only through their effects on academic performance'. On this analysis social factors cause poor performance, which in turn may generate maladjustment: further, regardless of social factors, poor educational performance is seen as a cause rather than a consequence of maladjustment. However, this behaviour is not peculiar to the inner city schools: it is the high incidence that is.

Concern about teachers and teaching is made up of three separate points: the difficulty of recruiting teachers in inner city schools; the difficulty of retaining teachers in inner city schools; the difficulty of recruiting/retaining experienced teachers. The scale of the recruitment problem facing a large urban educational authority is illustrated by a study completed five years ago in the ILEA. The size of the teaching force was under 20,000, and in a single year 4,775 teachers resigned from the authority's service; this is 23.8 per cent of the stock. The broad magnitude of teaching turnover has been confirmed by a DES enquiry in 1972/73. Amongst primary schools teachers in the ILEA, the overall turnover level was 33.4 per cent of the stock and in secondary schools 25.9 per cent. Nevertheless, the turnover for all LEA was 17.6 per cent and 15.3 per cent respectively.

Therefore, an authority like the ILEA has nearly twice as high a turnover rate as the rest of the country, and is confronted by the problem of recruiting 5,000 teachers every year. The difficulty facing individual schools in retaining experienced teachers is well illustrated by an earlier ILEA survey: of the permanent teachers who resigned, 77 per cent of the men and 87 per cent of the women had been teaching in their last school for less than five years. Inevitably, individual schools (and especially primary schools) are faced with the joint problem of high staff turnover and few teachers with more than a limited amount of teaching experience. Again, the ILEA index of educational priority areas is relevant. One of the criteria was a measure of teacher turnover; namely the percentage of teachers who had been in the school for less than three years. National data suggested that the average figure should be about 25 per cent: in the school ranked first (i.e. most disadvantaged in terms of the index) three-quarters of the staff had been at the school for less than one year. In the school ranked 50th the proportion was two-thirds, and in the school ranked 100th it was nearly half.

There is no doubt that a case can be made advocating the special needs for inner city schools. However, we ought to be considering a further set of questions: how far the difficulties facing the inner city school are the result of the character of the inner city area and how far they are the product of more general changes throughout society and the educational system. Three general changes are worth examining in this context: the effect of earlier maturation; changes in authority relationships; modification of educational objectives and practices. The common element of these points is to suggest that the concerns people have about inner city schools are in part the result not of changes within the city but of the sort of factors outlined above. That pupils are maturing earlier is accepted: for example the age of menarche has been reduced by nearly a year in a generation. Young people of both sexes are maturing physically far quicker than previous generations, allied to which certain aspects of psychological and social development have also accelerated. Much behaviour (both socially approved and disapproved) once associated with late adolescence and early adulthood is now common amongst early and mid-adolescents. It is tempting to illustrate this with behaviour that is frequently disapproved of (smoking, drinking, sexual experimentation, etc.). Equally relevant is behaviour (ranging from political participation to sophistication in styles of dress and other patterns of consumption) to which the adult generation reacts in a more neutral and approving manner.

Allied to this, changes in authority relationships generally may well have influenced the relationship between pupil and teacher. Traditionally both age and class hierarchies were clearly established and widely accepted. Children deferred to their elders (especially parents) and social deference (working-class towards middle-class) was commonplace. A variety of macrosocial changes have at least modified these relationships. The cult of youth among both adolescents and adults implies a change in the relationship between age hierarchies, and the frequent demonstration of changing income differential between certain grades of manual and non-manual work might indicate a changing relationship between class hierarchies. On both levels the 'teacher' is in a potentially vulnerable position; as a representative of the adult generation relating to the young at a time when young/old relationships are changing and as a representative of non-manual activity particularly exposed to the types of changes in income and status alluded to above.

A third set of changes is within the educational system itself. Raising the statutory leaving age first to fifteen and then to sixteen has meant the prolongation of the educational experiences of all pupils. Parallel with this, profound changes are taking place in educational objectives, methods and structure. There can be little doubt that the range of objectives of schools has been broadened to include a variety of social and psychological objectives that were either nonexistent or ill-defined a generation ago. Similarly the introduction of progressive methods into primary and secondary schools (unstreamed classes, team teaching, subject integration, etc.) has advanced considerably. The reorganisation of a secondary school system on comprehensive lines is a further illustration. It would be surprising if changes as fundamental as this did not affect the characteristics of pupil and teacher relationships throughout the system.

But even here special attention might have to be paid to the inner city school, not because the consequences of these changes are peculiar to it, but simply because they are either more visible or less tolerated in these areas. Forms of behaviour (or types of performance) hidden in the past or tolerated in smaller communities might have higher visibility or low tolerance in the current urban situation.

Let me give an illustration: authorities like the ILEA are currently administering a parallel system of secondary schools, a proportion (it differs from authority to authority but in most LEAS still as many as one pupil in ten is entering a selective school) going to grammar schools and an increasing proportion of the remainder attending comprehensive schools. If we take a situation in which the brightest 12 per cent of pupils enter grammar schools, what is the entry to comprehensive or non-selective schools like? In London a secondary school to which 240 pupils entered each year would have around forty pupils with a verbal reasoning score of below eighty and another fifty between 81 and 89. Roughly translated into likely performance on a reading or arithmetic test an eight-form entry school would have well over one class of eleven year olds performing perhaps three years below their chronological age and nearly two other classes perhaps a year and a half below their age. Nearly 40 per cent of the intake would require considerable remedial support and included in that would be 17 per cent performing at a level frequently associated with ascertainment as ESN.

Why labour these points? I do so because I want to suggest behaviour (in this case educational performance) that was invisible or tolerated in some instances may well be becoming intolerable or highly visible in urban centres because of social and educational changes. Poor performance of a fourteen-year old in a higher elementary school a generation ago might have remained hidden or taken for granted. Keep him on at school until he is 16, accelerates his physical and certain aspects of social and psychological development by a year and perhaps the situation is different. A 2- or 3-form entry higher elementary school might be able to cope equally well with ten or fifteen very backward pupils per year: I wonder whether an 8- or twelve-form entry school could cope equally well with its 40 or 60 such pupils. Evidence put forward by Henry Hodge suggests they cope less well. Further, we ought to discuss the question whether or not an inner city school is able to cope with such numbers as its counterpart in smaller towns. For the typical inner city school, with reorganisation, is likely to be large.

I think two types of changes within the city are relevant to our discussions: first, changes in the population base; and second changes in the physical base. Changes in the birthrate and migration patterns over the past decade have had a profound effect on the number of people living in certain inner city areas. Again to cite the ILEA: 4,536,000 people lived in the old LCC area in 1901; in 1961 this had fallen to 3,200,000 and by 1971 to 2,775,000. Put in most recent educational terms, in 1960 56,642 births took place in the equivalent of the ILEA, five years later 38,143 pupils entered schools and at the time of transfer to secondary school the size of the 11-plus age group had fallen to 32,366. This is the result of differential migration patterns, and in the future school entry numbers will be affected by recent falls in the birthrate. In 1965/66 nearly 60,000 births took place in inner London, in 1970/71, this had fallen to just over 42,000. The joint effects of migration and fertility will mean that between 1974 and 1981 the projected size of the primary school roll is likely to fall from nearly 200,000 to around 123,000. Peter Newsam considers some of the educational implications of such a change (see page 42).

Concurrent with such changes two other points have been made: one related to ethnic composition of inner city schools, the other to their socio-economic composition. The first point is relatively easy to document. Probably between one-fifth and one-quarter of all pupils in the ILEA have parents born outside the UK and Eire. Although the fact of central areas containing many immigrants is not new, the scale and type of this immigration in the late 1950s and early 1960s is new. The majority of these immigrants come from the New Commonwealth (Asia, Africa, West Indies) and in so far as the fact of racially and ethnically mixed schools raises different educational issues (and these outlast the newness of the migrant) then there has been a significant and sudden change in the educational needs in areas like inner London. In passing it should be pointed out that the decline in performance in ILEA schools is not the result of immigrants: the mean reading score of pupils born in the UK was under 96 and therefore below national norms. More difficult to assess is the changing socio-economic situation of the inner city areas: considerable discussion has taken place on the extent to which inner city areas have become either single-class communities (containing only rich or poor) or have lost the middle part of the social spectrum and become cities of rich and poor. Recent research on the 1966 and 1971 censuses suggests that as far as inner London is concerned, its population has not become less educated or lower class. Nor is it becoming a city of the rich and the very poor. In fact, as Hamnett has noted, there has been 'an overall upward shift in the socio-economic composition of inner London'. Further, this is true not merely on an authority level but also on the level of a ward analysis. Hamnett's concluding sentence is worth quoting: 'the problems manifested in the inner city represent a larger social problem not an urban problem, and purely urban solutions are likely to remain inadequate'.

1.4b A counter view

Peter Newsam

It is hard enough to understand what is happening in one school; to generalize about many hundreds of urban schools is that much more hazardous. Part of the trouble lies in the information we collect. So far as the quality of education is concerned, this is of two kinds. The first consists of the information derived from such general sources as standardised tests of reading and other skills or from records of examination passes. Where these tests are repeated at the same points in pupils' school careers the results can be used to compare the performance of successive year groups. In the ILEA this monitoring is carried out when children are in the last year of junior school. The second type of information is derived from the performance of individual children over time. These longitudinal studies remain rare but, without them, the effect of teaching in particular ways or types of school cannot be accurately assessed. This means that in our present stage of knowledge even obvious-sounding questions like 'are standards rising or falling?' or 'is this kind of school better than that?' cannot be answered without hedging the answer round with a host of qualifications. Any such qualifications are ignored in public discussion. This in itself makes those who are at the receiving end of most of the misunderstandings, principally teachers and administrators, wary about the whole process.

It is worth exploring a little further how the simple measures which are sometimes all we have can obscure the complex reality they seek to interpret. One actual example will be sufficient. A group of twenty-three children were tested for reading attainment in their third year in the junior school. During the year, three things happened: three of the best readers moved away; the twenty remaining children made some useful progress in their reading; three new children with virtually no English entered the class, and these in turn began to make progress. From the point of view of the teacher, the year's work reflected a high degree of professional skill:

Source: *Education and the Urban Crisis* (1977), ed. Frank Field, pp. 72–9.

everyone's standard had improved. But the mean reading age of the fourth-year children was rather lower than a straightforward comparison with the third-year results suggested would be possible. In that sense, standards were down. This objection would be overcome in studies like the ILEA literacy survey where comparisons are made between the same pupils at different ages and not just between schools, age groups or classes regarded as comparable from year to year. But in the actual situation described it is impossible to answer, in a simple yes or no form, the question 'have standards in this class risen or fallen?' Whose standards? More important than the answer is what someone might try to do with it. In this instance, for example, it would be wrong for someone in a position of authority to conclude, from a look at the results from the two years, that there is something wrong with the teacher's methods or that greater concentration on reading is needed. This may or may not be true but it cannot be derived from the evidence provided by the tests.

In qualitative terms, there is not much in the way of general statements based on evidence that can be said about urban schools. This is not intended to sound defeatist. It is anyway easy to put too much weight on the usefulness, other than to publicists, of general statements about standards.

Although the question 'what is happening in our schools?' cannot in qualitative terms be directly answered, some useful indicators can be designed. For example, from the various surveys the ILEA has conducted two findings show how what happens in school is being affected by the nature of population movement.

On a sample of some 30,000 pupils, aged eight in 1968 and eleven in 1971, it was found that despite a considerable movement of population, the social class distributions for all pupils in 1968 and 1971 were similar; if anything the distribution in 1971 was less skewed towards the bottom than in 1968, although the nature of the data means that this finding must be received with caution. Here is at least some counter to the argument heard from time to time that the 'better' people are moving from the inner city and are being replaced by those lower down in the Registrar-General's categories.

Secondly, the mean SRB (reading) score in 1971 of pupils (26,205) who had also been in the 1968 survey was 94.9. The mean score in 1971 of the newcomers since 1968 (5,555) was 90.5. This finding, unlike the previous one, confirms the common assumption. It is after all not surprising that people coming into a system, many from overseas, do less well in it than those who have been here longer. The results went on to show that the mean score of all the pupils in 1968 was 94.6. In 1971, with the numbers leaving balanced by the new-comers, the mean score for all pupils was 94.2. This could be regarded as a fall in standards as the pupils went through the schools or, as London teachers would understandably see it, as a very creditable effort to integrate newcomers while maintaining standards overall. The 1973 stage of this survey, when the children were in the third forms of secondary schools, shows an improvement, in a mean score of 98.0.

Information of this kind helps to interpret what is happening. The paragraphs that follow look first, essentially through London eyes, at other factors affecting schools and then go on to look directly at what is happening within them.

The most important feature of the inner city is the fall in population that is now beginning to be experienced. The ILEA September roll projections illustrate the point:

ILEA (September rolls)	1974	1978	1980	1984
		(thousands)		
Pupils in: primary schools	201	159	140	126
secondary schools	179	173	161	128

Is the fall in numbers to be seen as helpful or otherwise? The point has rightly been made by David Eversley that planners have tended to assume, wrongly he argued in the case of London, that moving people out means more space and other good things for those who are left. Educational planners have often made the opposite assumption and may be equally wrong. Educational planners find increasing numbers, to which they have grown accustomed over the years, both convenient and comforting. They like to build and develop their services. Yet falling numbers may bring educational benefits if properly used.

The outstanding advantage of falling numbers is that they can be used to increase the amount of space available to each teacher and child. The degree to which urban schools are still overcrowded is not widely understood. For example, a recently built London school for 1,700 pupils is on a site of 4½ acres, much of which is taken up by the building itself. This compares with an area of 9¼ acres laid down in the building regulations. The degree to which overcrowding contributes to stress is difficult to measure but easy enough to observe. Conversely, where there is enough room for people to move freely, intractable educational problems appear easier to resolve. This can happen quite suddenly; numbers are somewhat reduced, there is somewhat more room and the change becomes apparent. As a community, the school may begin to live and work in a more relaxed and effective way.

A fall in numbers can have important side-effects. Historically there have always been more primary children than secondary ones, sometimes overwhelmingly so: we have grown used to this. As the London figures show, by 1980 this will have changed. Increasingly this will affect teachers; at the moment, numbers of primary and secondary teachers are nearly in balance; but if pupil/teacher ratios in 1980 are, as they are at present, about 1:20 for primary schools and 1:15 for secondary schools, approximately preserving the present differentials, the balance of inner London's teaching force will have changed markedly. Instead of being approximately in balance, there will be 10,600 secondary teachers to 7,200 primary ones. There is, of course, far more to a change of this kind than the number of different kinds of teachers employed. For example, reduced numbers of primary teachers could reduce their influence on an area's educational thinking. Conversely, sufficient primary teachers may move into secondary schools to make their influence more directly felt there than it now is. Either way, this must affect what happens within schools.

One of the most sensible developments authorized by the DES in recent years has been the idea of 'off-programme' building; new school building financed by the sale of old premises. Falling numbers mean that children remaining now have a chance of schools with better physical standards. Already two major developments are planned in London, and there is a chance here for inner city areas to break out of the present deadlock whereby new school building goes to the places where population is rising, and children remaining in areas of static or declining population have to stand by and watch their position relative to others worsening year by year.

Against the one overriding benefit of more and perhaps better space for those who remain there are at least four problems that falling numbers bring. The first is financial. As numbers fall, unit costs tend to rise. London's experience of a fall of 12,000 in the primary school population is that the pro rata saving of £2.75 million that might have been expected in a full year will become an actual saving of £1.6 million in a full year. Schools with somewhat reduced rolls still have to be heated, the rates have to be paid, the roofs mended. In this situation, an education service cannot act abruptly. It cannot suddenly close down plant, as it were, in these participating days even if on educational or financial grounds it was thought desirable to do so. The second problem brought by falling numbers is its effect on the whole planning process; on the possibility of planning itself. The whole tradition in educational planning is based on rising numbers. Schools are built; they become full, and other schools have to be added.

Always there is a programme, a looking ahead and a race not to be left too far behind. But the process cannot be reversed when numbers fall. Falling numbers mean a situation that is in principle unstable and to a large extent unpredictable. If it is known now that in five years numbers in an area will have fallen so far that one or more schools in bad premises could close, it ought to be possible, the planners think, to say so and plan accordingly. But life is not so simple. To discuss officially and in advance the closure of a school is like talking about devaluation. Either the discussion brings it about too soon, because there is a run on the currency or away from the school, or promises have to be made that it will never happen at all. So the drift continues until there is room to spare in several schools in the area and a growing uncertainty about what is to happen next.

This uncertainty seems essentially an urban phenomenon. Cities will never be the same since events in Paris in 1968. The third problem some would say is the effect of parents and of parental influence in an open market. Students of law look to the Education Acts to find out how schools are closed. In the new situation parents will be able to close schools as easily as education authorities can. If a school, however irrationally, becomes unpopular when there are empty school places near by, it can effectively be shut by an absence of entrants. This can happen quite suddenly and serves to emphasize the irrelevance of most of the talk of legislation or vouchers to give effect to parents' choice of school. When schools are full, legislation is ineffective; one person's preference can be met only at the expense of another's. When schools are empty, legislation is redundant; no one can be prevented from sending a child to a school where there is room.

In the inner city, falling numbers reduce stress and provide new opportunities by improving spatial standards; but these other uncertainties are already arising and their force and effect make for structural instability.

What is happening within the schools themselves? One thing is evident: there is no problem that is not somewhere being successfully tackled. The work of educating in the inner city can be done by ordinary, skilful human beings. The implications of this are important. There is a fashionable disillusion with education which argues that factors outside school are of such importance that what happens within schools can be of little effect. The attitude is catching. It is not unknown to hear people go on to suggest that 'you can't expect much of children with that kind of background'. The refutation lies in the excellence of the work done in some of the schools with, so far as measurement can take us, some of the greatest problems. It is crucial that this should be recognized. It is idle to look for elaborate reasons unrelated to school for the inability, to take one example, of eleven-year-old children, suffering from no physical or mental defect, to learn to read when very similar children learn to do so perfectly well in the school down the road. Herein lies the problem. There are wide variations in the quality of inner city education which any averaging process tends to obscure. These variations appear to have little to do with the size of a school or any of its physical characteristics. It is simply that in some schools the ordinary processes of learning and teaching have all but broken down. The picture is familiar and well publicized. Children move in and out, so do the teachers. There is no stability anywhere and the school tends to start each day without any sense of continuity either with its own past or with the whole tradition of teaching that has developed in this country over the past hundred years. In other words, just as there is no problem, however difficult, that is not somewhere being solved so there is no procedure, no obvious element of what constitutes a school, that cannot somewhere be found to be missing. But the essential point is that there are people now in schools showing how the job can be done. Their skills need to be recognized and transmitted to others.

There are some hopeful signs. One development is the growing recognition that a school, primary or secondary, can be seen as a group of teachers with varied skills just as much as a vehicle for transmitting a curriculum. The implications of this are profound for the way improvement is brought about. Increasingly such groups of teachers wish to improve their professional skills in each other's company. The school itself becomes a self-educating community with influences from the outside brought in where necessary.

This is the opposite of the traditional in-service notion which regards training as something that happens to an individual when removed from his working environment. The effect of this thinking on the – in some way opposed – notion of hierarchy will be evident. Management principles, the salary structure, the expectations of parents and the outside world all see the school as in some way hierarchical. Not all schools now feel like this from the inside.

If the skills of a group of teachers are the essence of a school the curriculum loses at least something of its primacy. So too, in the face of falling rolls, does the idea of the entirely self-contained school. Co-operative arrangements between schools are developing fast. These range from consortia of up to ten schools, as in Birmingham, to the joint sixth form arrangements now being initiated in London. Ideas developed from the geographical necessities of Oxfordshire are now very relevant to the inner city. Within schools themselves there are a number of contrary notions at work. First, there is the reluctance to do overmuch measuring of pupils' standards except in their own terms. Thinking in Mode 3 as it were. Meanwhile, from the outside, the desire to hold teachers accountable grows. This is part, perhaps, of the disillusion with education already referred to. Some people concerned with education never have believed it could do much except for their own children in their own schools. Others thought it could and now are less certain. Both groups wonder whether the educational system is giving good value for money and intend to try to find out. Unfortunately, the more resolutely one presses people to be accountable the more they tend to try to define precisely what it is they are accountable for. The danger is that they will then concentrate too narrowly on achieving these definable measurable objectives to the neglect of others. Hence renewed moves towards defining exactly what the teacher's day should be. A related issue is the way the desire to hold schools accountable, to ensure that they run in a way closely related to clearly defined purposes, is opposed to moves to devolve more and more responsibility for allocating resources in the way best suited to the school itself.

Again there is the tug between what is done within school and what is done outside. There is a general desire to bring more children, however difficult their problems, within the ordinary school. At the same time, as pressures on schools have increased, there is the contrary desire to be rid of those who cause trouble, not just for the problems they themselves represent but also for the effect they have on other children's learning. These two contrary forces are being interestingly combined, in London and elsewhere, in a number of off-site arrangements. For example, at one school a volunteer worker has taken a house near the school and gives accommodation to a teacher who then takes in small groups of eight to fifteen children recommended by the school for full or half-day sessions for varying lengths of time depending on the children's needs. Elsewhere a teacher within a council estate works with children who are reluctant to go to the main school and eventually brings them back into the main school with her. It is the quality of the relationships established within these proliferating arrangements that is their outstanding feature. Though their aims may differ, in this respect they share something of what the free schools represent.

Extended day arrangements are also developing. On the one hand there is the move to define more closely the nature of the teacher's day, its length and the conditions of service under which it is to be worked. On the other, there are a whole range of activities extending in many schools beyond the end of afternoon school. This is not just a matter of games and clubs; the actual development of learning can be impressive.

To sum up: whatever else urban education in England may be it is not static and it is not dull. It cannot be static because the fall in numbers, which in some ways is coming to the rescue, imposes structural uncertainties on the situation and these affect teachers, pupils and administration alike. It cannot be dull because within schools and within the administrative system there are powerful opposing forces at work. These generate tension. Wherever synthesis may lie it is not in the immediate future.

The quality of education in our cities is patchy. Indisputably there are areas of outstanding and largely unrecognized success. So the job of educating inner city children can be done. Where there is failure the reasons are complex and mostly to be found within the school itself. Neither success nor failure can be deduced from the size or type of the school concerned. The quality of something cannot be deduced from its form in education or elsewhere.

1.5 The community school – a base for community development?

George and Teresa Smith

In the final report of their action-research programme (Halsey, 1972), the Educational Priority Areas projects called for six major educational developments in EPAS.[1] With the publication at the end of 1972 of Mrs Thatcher's White Paper, *Education: A Framework for Expansion*, it looks as if the score after the first round is – two positive, three doubtful, and one nil response to these proposals. On the positive side is the expansion of pre-school education with priority for EPAS, and the acceptance of the principle of 'positive discrimination' and its extension to certain rural areas, small towns and new housing estates as well as the inner city. Successful implementation will not be easy; the White Paper says nothing about the criteria for identifying EPAS, and is vague about how to ensure that parental involvement on a wide scale becomes a characteristic of pre-school education. It is encouraging that research will monitor the expansion.

On the negative side, the White Paper has nothing to say on another of the EPA recommendations – the development of 'community schools'. This is perhaps not unexpected. Pre-schooling has a long history of development, a relatively clear-cut institutional form, and a powerful lobby of supporters. Even with the addition of parental involvement it could without difficulty be translated into administrative proposals – what more radical educational reformers have dismissed as 'an addition to the system', though, we would argue, none the worse for that. But 'community schools' are a very different animal – one that implies new directions and changing roles for existing institutions. Despite the claim of the EPA Report to have developed the idea of the 'community school' from the sketchy and restricted description in Plowden – 'a school which is open beyond the ordinary school hours for the use of children, their parents and,

Source: *Community Work One* (1974), eds. David Jones and Marjorie Mayo, pp. 186–98.

exceptionally, for other members of the community' (para. 121) – the concept still remains vague, a long way from any neat administrative package. Perhaps the very different 'community school' experiments set up by various EPA projects have increased the confusion; what looked like a simple proposal to extend school opening hours is shown to be complex and far-reaching.

In this paper we want to re-examine the idea of the 'community school', using evidence from the EPA programme, in particular the setting up of a multi-purpose education centre, Red House, by the West Riding project. By placing description of a practical development against a background of more general debate, we hope to show some of the reasons for the slow, and, for many, unsatisfactory development of 'community schools' so far. It is not our purpose to specify in detail what a community school should be like; over-concern with detail rather than broad objectives may be one reason for the lack of progress. A major lesson of EPA was the importance of tailoring developments to fit the local situation. Thus the aim of writing on 'community schools' should be to set out general guidelines, and a range of possible institutional forms, rather than a single model.

With feet in both the EPA and Community Development Project (CDP) camps, our concern is with the question of how far education, in the shape of 'community schools', can become a base for wider community development; the focus is on institutions that seek a wide range of involvement with the community, not merely the extension of their opening hours. Clearly with such frequent use of the word 'community' and phrases like 'community development' and 'community school', we cannot slip by without offering some indication of what we mean by these terms. This is not the place for a strict definition, even if one were possible; we suspect that the strength and attractiveness of 'community' to us and to others, lies partly in its Protean character, unlike some of the more precise, but short-lived, technical concepts that social science proliferates. Sociologists who plead for a moratorium on the use of 'community' have, like Canute, clearly got it wrong; they need instead to analyse how 'community' is used in social situations and by different social groups.

In projects like EPA and CDP, terms such as 'community' and 'community development' imply a number of related assumptions, even though these may not be well articulated. First, 'community' refers to a relatively small area, characterised by a high degree of face-to-face interaction, with some degree of shared value patterns. Second, it implies concern with the total group in any category, rather than a selected sub-group. Schools in EPAS, for example, clearly fulfil a creaming function, still formalised in some areas with selective secondary education for a minority; community education, in contrast, aims at the complete group, developing a curriculum relevant to the needs of those likely to remain in EPAS. Third, it emphasises a broad, non-specialist approach to the services in the area; social or individual problems are seen to be the result of a complex set of factors, and therefore not best tackled by a series of unco-ordinated and highly specialised agencies. Fourth, for the same reason it emphasises linkage and integration among organisations servicing an area; and fifth, it stresses the importance of participation and development of the community's own institutions on the basis that the community is a viable entity, independent of the administrative structures created to service it. Community development, then, is the broad process which embodies this approach, rather than the bit of social life that is left over, when education, health, social services and the other big battalions have been taken out.

With the 'community school' we are on a well-trodden path. Usually four or five types are identified – each article on the subject perhaps stepping out a little further to add something extra to the final, most attractive variety. First, it can apply to a school which serves an entire neighbourhood; most primary schools and more and more secondary 'neighbourhood' schools would qualify. A second definition is a school which shares its premises with the community. This has been a long-standing arrangement in many areas, and in the West Riding EPA one of the primary schools had been carefully designed with this purpose in mind – in 1893. Large modern comprehensive schools obviously have bigger and better facilities to offer, such as swimming pools and libraries. But size can be a problem, as the catchment area of the school will also be large, and this may conflict with the need to develop links with a relatively small area. We would also like to place a query against a strategy which attempted to draw the community into the school as its main objective. Sharing buildings may be economically sound, but both groups may function side by side with comparative autonomy: school content and organisation do not necessarily become more community-oriented or responsive by opening the doors to community-run activities for adults.

A third possibility is a school which develops a curriculum of community study, arguing for the social and educational relevancy of local and familiar material. Much of the work of Eric Midwinter in the Liverpool EPA (1972) has centred on this theme. To the charge that this type of education will produce increased conformity and second-class citizenship, Midwinter replies that 'community education is about moving on, not standing still'; the aim is to produce 'constructive discontent'. Yet there is plenty of evidence that curriculum is nearly always used in ways unintended by its authors. The problem remains of ensuring that socially relevant material is used to weaken rather than confirm social divisions.

A fourth type is a school where there is some degree of community control. This is familiar in the United States, particularly following the Ford Foundation-supported programmes for community control of inner city schools in the late 1960s; but less so in this country, outside a few Free Schools and LEAS experimenting with greater community participation on governing boards. A fifth and final possibility is a school which seeks to involve itself directly in promoting social change within the local community. This type incorporates some of the earlier varieties, as it could well include longer opening hours, community use of buildings, and community participation. Schools have considerable advantages in taking the initiative in social change. First, they are institutions acceptable to the community, in contrast to other social agencies which may be stigmatised by their association with problem groups. Second, there is the sheer number of schools and teachers which are already present in the area. In the West Riding EPA, as an example, there were 130 to 140 teachers at eleven separate primary and secondary schools, yet the social services had no base in the area, and there were perhaps two or three social workers, part of whose territory included the EPA. Such considerations make the idea of the community school as an agent of social change within the community powerfully attractive. Yet the problems of turning this into a reality have hardly been examined at all.

Most practical examples of 'community schools' have been of the first four types, and though there are examples of the last type, these are often drawn from developing countries, where the relationship between school and community is likely to be very different. Examples closer to home often cite activities such as surveys of the neighbourhood and similar studies, but these by themselves hardly constitute an adequate community school programme. There is a wide gap between these practical examples and the attractive theoretical picture of the school as an agent of social change. We can all accept the proposition that 'community minded and community-competent teachers are essential at all levels ...' (Olsen, 1963), but the problem is to translate into practice the exhortation typical of writing on community schools. Further training is a favourite suggestion. But first we need to examine whether the problem is more basic than mere lack of training. As S. M. Miller argues (1967), more education tends to become the standard panacea for a number of problems, 'whether those of racial prejudice, sexual unhappiness or economic conflict'. Even in education itself the belief that further training will bring about change is often an illusion.

A basic problem which has been overlooked by those anxious to develop the idea of the school as an agent of social change, is the gulf between the way an ordinary school functions, and that required for community work. Even in its most progressive format, schooling remains a highly structured activity; there are set times of day, week and year when schools operate. Pupils are divided into class groups and work with specific teachers for set periods of time; the content of what is done may be defined by outside bodies, external exams and so on. Community work is at the other end of the spectrum: there is no fixed group of clients, place or time of operation, and the type of work may change dramatically as new groups or problems crop up.

The difference is underlined by looking at the experience of workers who attempt to span the gap. A youth or community worker attached to a school has to develop a flexible programme to deal with events outside the school, but may be constrained by the within school requirements of class groupings, timetables and school organisation. A study of secondary school teachers running community service projects (Smith, 1969) demonstrated the problem of conflicting interests. Despite differences of organising community service in academic and non-academic schools, teachers saw it primarily in terms of benefit to their pupils – a way of developing a sense of responsibility, self-confidence and maturity: the work was defined in individual moral terms, as a problem which 'one had to do something about' in personal action. It was not clear whether teachers in the study failed to see the significance of community service for the role and position of the school in the community, or whether they rejected this approach because it would have taken time from what they saw as their main objective, the development of individual children. 'Free Schools' could be another response to the same problem. Frustration with the inability of existing schools to develop a suitably flexible programme for the local community was a major reason in setting up the Liverpool Free School, which has planned extensive community development work linked to the school.

Though we need more evidence about the problems of developing community work from a school base, these examples show that not enough attention has been paid to conflicts that emerge as schools attempt to balance their traditional concern for individual children against their new role in community development. This ought to be the type of problem that action-research experiments investigate – can the organisation of schools tolerate the kind of relationships demanded by community work, or do they require new organisational forms? Are schools or other educational institutions in fact capable of initiating programmes of social change, or is the growing pessimism about the role of the school as an agent of change justified? Practical experiments of this nature might be more useful than further exhortations to teachers about the importance of 'community orientation', or even training courses to develop new attitudes.

As a first shot at what such experiments might be like, we turn to a description of the education centre set up by the West Riding project, and the experience gained in running it over three years.[2] It is important to make clear that the centre was not developed as a 'community school'; in fact the label was resisted – it was not a 'school' in the accepted sense, and those who ran it tried to avoid identification with community schools whose objective was to absorb the community into the school building. The project area was a small, socially isolated mining community in the Don Valley – a community in the strong traditional sense – a stable population with shared experience in the work place and in social life. Roughly 60 per cent of the men worked in the local pit, and there was a close-knit pattern of friendship and marriage within the area. But the decline of the mining industry meant that the driving force of the community was gradually running down. The general picture of a stable area was underlined by the schools, where in contrast to many other EPAs there was an extremely low level of teacher turnover: many teachers had also taught the parents of their present generation of children.

The EPA project focused on education. Though it could analyse the more basic changes threatening the area, it was clearly powerless with its small resources to make any impression on them directly. In the educational field, the programmes set up by the project were of two types: first, specific pieces of action meeting an obvious need – the provision of preschool places, or a remedial reading scheme; second, and more fundamental, there was a need for more general exploration of the ways schools could be stimulated into change, and for ways of extending the role of education.

The project team saw a multi-purpose education centre as one possible strategy for change in the area. But different groups had different expectations about how this could be realised in practice. First, there was the idea of a centre attached to a school with short-term residential accommodation for children during periods of crisis in the home put forward by the Chief Education Officer of the West Riding, Sir Alec Clegg (Clegg and Megson, 1968). Second, some schools were anxious to have a centre outside the area, partly for residential purposes and partly as a base for project work: their concern was to remove the child at least temporarily from his environment. Third, the aim of the project team was to set up a multi-purpose base, linking schools, the social services, and the community.

The objectives would be broad ranging, and mainly institutional in form. The centre would work closely with schools and colleges as well as with parents and the community. It would act as a demonstration and resource centre which could experiment with pilot schemes, cutting across the age grouping which characterises most educational institutions, and trying out schemes that involved children of different ages, and adults from different sources – from schools, colleges, or the local community. It would be able to operate outside the normal school day and term timetable, offering courses in the evening, at weekends, and during the holidays. The centre had to be accessible to the community at all times, and therefore locally based. Community involvement was to be a high priority. This did not mean the formal trappings of participation – committees of local people – but an institution that could respond to local needs and had flexible enough resources to meet them. For this reason, staff and facilities could not be tied to a strictly specialist role, but had to adapt rapidly to radically different demands. Residential provision was to be one of a range of facilities available to the community.

The actual development of Red House was a combination of these various strands. With the help of the West Riding, and a generous grant from the Rowntree Trust, a large house in the community was bought and converted into an education centre. This included limited residential accommodation and space for a resident warden and family.

Red House opened in January 1970. In describing the work of the centre since then, merely to list the activities set up would not be helpful for our purposes: it has become characteristic for the centre to be used throughout the day and evening by many different groups of children and adults. One activity grew out of another: we propose to concentrate on these growth points. Activities have almost always been organised for limited numbers, ranging from three or four children in residence to a school class or pre-school group of twenty-five to thirty-five children; over the school year large numbers will have taken part in various courses. The purpose was to act as a 'demonstration' centre, to show what could be done and what additional resources could be tapped: success therefore depended on how far other groups took up ideas developed at the centre.

The first stage was to develop local confidence and show that the centre could meet school and community needs. The 'intensive courses' were designed in response to requests from local schools for a programme for junior age children. Initially, groups from three separate schools came to the centre every morning for half a term. At the centre the children were mixed up and split into groups of four or five, each group working with a teacher-training student, following its own programme in the centre, or making field trips to collect material for environmental study. A problem found in the first year was that class teachers could not be fully involved. In the second year, the scheme covered complete school classes instead of groups from different schools: class teachers could work alongside students with small groups from their own class, giving advice where necessary. At the same time, a pre-school group was set up. The policy was to make places available to all children in a particular age range and school catchment area, to avoid problems of selection; to ensure that everybody was approached, home visits to all families with young children in the area were made and the scheme explained. Parental involvement was encouraged from the start, at first by operating an open door policy.

The pre-school programme and its parental involvement sparked off a series of further developments. Early on, the main objective of this form of pre-school work came to be seen as strengthening the educational resources of home and community rather than merely getting parents into schools. This resulted in a shift of emphasis in the pre-school group itself, towards the role of parents as teachers, or the training potential for this purpose of the pre-school group. As some parents gained confidence in teaching skills, they were able to take control of groups of children, and the teacher could spend time working with other parents. Confidence gained here increased awareness among parents of their role as educators outside the school context. Out of the pre-school have grown parent groups meeting in the evenings as a general discussion group rather than with invited speakers.

Raising the level of educational resources in the home and the community led directly to the development of home visiting. This had become part of the pre-school programme, with the teacher taking materials into the home to work with parent and child together. It was also turned into a separate programme. Here the home visitor worked with younger children and their parents, making weekly visits over a year or more: with suitable educational material she could show the skills that young children develop, and equipment was left in the home for parents to experiment with. A weekly stall run by the project, selling educational books and toys, was another way of adding to the area's resources. A pitch in the local open market was a place to display children's work, to show films and slides of projects such as holiday schemes, and to serve as an advice point on education and welfare rights. These developments placed the project in a position to improve support for the growing number of playgroups in the district with advice, materials, and training courses.

Another growth point was the development of schemes using one group in a learning situation to help another. A new form of the 'intensive courses' was set up for infant children, using fourth and fifth-year secondary school pupils instead of students to run the small groups. Similar aged pupils had worked in the pre-school group, and in other courses at the centre where they could develop practical skills such as cooking and serving a regular meal for old people or pre-school children. In the evening, week-end, and holiday courses, the project relied heavily on the help given by students and local volunteers.

Residential work had to develop slowly if the community was to accept that the centre had a broad role to play. The accommodation was useful for other groups such as students on placement, but its main purpose was to provide short-term residential care for children during periods of difficulty in the home. The centre had no statutory powers. As the centre was local, children in residence continued to go to their local schools and maintained contact with their families. Most children were already familiar with the centre, where they had attended various courses. This contact meant that a system of 'self-referral' developed, as children and parents became aware that the centre had residential space available for a crisis such as a parent going into hospital. Relatively small numbers of children have stayed in the centre. Short-term residence was not seen as a way of 'curing' the particular problem, but one of a number of strategies the centre could adopt to strengthen contact with a child or his family. For some situations, a residential stay was not appropriate; in others, it could be a support for the child at a time of acute family crisis; or it might put the child in contact with adults sympathetic to his difficulties. It might produce information about the family situation which enabled the centre to call upon the other services for specialist support. Children who had been in residence could and did return to the centre, which was within easy reach, for example for a weekly meal or evening course.

More important, perhaps, than a brief description of the programmes are the underlying trends. First, there is a clear shift from the educational starting point to social and community work, though from an educational perspective. This is a logical development. If the child's experience outside school influences classroom performance, then clearly the field of education has to be extended. In many cases this must go beyond merely visiting families, or making parents welcome in school. Residential work at the centre emphasised the need for wider involvement as it brought staff into more intensive contact with families and the community. The growth points at the centre are now social and community work. At a more tentative stage are explorations of work and employment, the idea of a community workshop – perhaps a future growth point.

A second theme is linkage – reducing the distance between different age levels and levels of education as well as between education and related social and welfare services. This is partly a matter of unused resources which can be realized by linking levels or institutions – students can staff courses for junior children, or secondary school pupils work with infants; parents or other community members can develop teaching skills. Not surprisingly, some of these links had their organisational problems, which underlines the importance of an independent group or institution whose role it is to create such links. Similarly there is the reinforcement that one programme can provide for another: for example, the market stall supplying a need stimulated by the home visiting or pre-school projects.

A third and related theme is the type of role that this method of working demanded from the team at the centre – one with no clear boundaries but with overlapping functions of teacher, social worker, counsellor, as the situation demanded. There was also the creation of 'intermediate roles', when students, secondary pupils, parents, and others adopted teaching positions. This meant that although the team at the centre numbered only six or seven, the effective number was always far larger. The role of the central team was to organise and plan for the use of these resources as well as to work directly on the courses.

The final point and most important is the changing conception of the relationship between school and community. Instead of trying to improve the educational process in school by encouraging parental involvement, the direction was reversed: the aim should rather be to strengthen the educational resources of home and community. This meant that the centre increasingly became a base for programmes extending out into the community, rather than drawing the community into the centre as an end in itself.

We have deliberately kept this outline of the work at Red House at a general level. Obviously in practice there were successes and failures: schemes were piloted, modified with experience, and launched on a larger scale. In general the approaches adopted were shown to be viable in practice, and the response from schools and community encouraged the centre to continue along its path. For the two years of the centre's running by the EPA project, it was supported by a group with independent resources and the flexibility to use them as it decided best. Since 1972, the centre has been taken over by the West Riding LEA though largely retaining the same staff and continuing with similar programmes.

In this final section, we turn back to some of the general questions set out at the beginning, using the development of Red House as an example. First, the assumption that education is a well-placed starting point for wider social and community development is supported. Though research may emphasise the gap between home and school values in working-class areas, nevertheless, in contrast to other services which are selective and associated with problem groups, education is universal and an accepted institution. The logic, too, of extending work from an educational base into the community is easily understood; for the objective of improving educational standards remains the same, though the field of operation is enlarged.

Red House, however, is not a school; and though education in its broadest sense may be the starting point for community development, we cannot say from the example whether a school could undertake a role of this kind. Comparing the centre with a small school on the five elements we identified as characteristic of a community development approach, we find a number of differences. Both may service a small area, and try to avoid any selection, except that demanded by age or catchment area; but on the remaining three characteristics the flexible organisation of the centre clearly gives it an advantage: it had no statutory obligations or set programme, and its resources could be committed where appropriate. It was thus better placed to develop a flexible role to meet changing needs, and to stimulate links among other institutions. As the centre was small, and staff limited, there was an incentive to tap community and other resources, and develop work out in the community rather than attempt to get the community into the building.

As we argued in examining the fifth type of community school – one that seeks to act as an agent of social change in the local community – the central problem is one of institutional form and its related roles. We identified the wide gap between the typical role of teacher and of community worker. The set-up at Red House can be seen as an institution intermediate between schools and community, with obligations to both groups. Clearly this was a feasible role, though one which at times brought almost intolerable shifts of style to deal in rapid succession with, for example, a teacher planning a course, a social worker following up a case, a class of children working on a project, a youth in trouble, and a visitor wanting an account of the centre's operations. These shifts of role meant inefficiency in traditional terms, though this may be a necessary feature of any multi-purpose centre where roles cannot be highly specialised. Specialisation by restricting the range of problems that a professional has to deal with may seem efficient. But issues are usually complex, and at the local level it is essential to have a group prepared to tackle a wide range of problems, who can bring in specialist help where necessary. Though obviously such roles will be demanding, it may be that the development of a suitable institutional context will provide a measure of insulation and support.

In the same way that Red House developed intermediate teaching roles as one way of breaking down the teacher/learner distinction, we may need 'intermediate institutions' to link school and community. It is important to develop the necessary roles and institutional framework to take advantage of their links with schools, yet provide enough autonomy to prevent them becoming merely satellites. Again, individual appointments such as teacher/social workers or teacher/youth leaders to this intermediate position have demonstrated the problems of individuals in this situation. As Craft suggests for social workers in his account of the school welfare team (1972), the need is to push for the appointment of teams or groups, rather than of isolated individuals.

One of the major lessons of EPA was the importance of tailoring institutions to their setting. Red House was planned and developed in response to what were seen as the needs of an area and its schools, not as a general answer to the problem of setting up 'community schools'. Red House could be one way of developing links between education and community work. But there may well be other, more appropriate forms, more closely linked to an individual school. What is needed is further experiment to try out some of these possible variations. If this were to take place, preferably in an action-research context, then the debate on 'community schools' might be based on more practical examples and increasing knowledge about the problems and possibilities of the community school as an agent of change. Unfortunately, we seem reluctant to experiment. The first director of the Parkway Project in Philadelphia, one of the most imaginative community school developments in the USA – which has no school buildings as such but uses the resources of the city centre, libraries, museums, and firms to provide courses for its students – was asked how as an Englishman he came to be running such a project in the States. In reply, he asked which local education authority in England would have given backing on this scale to such an innovation.

Now that pre-school education is to be expanded on a wide scale, that part of the Urban Programme previously reserved for playgroups and nurseries should become available for other educational projects, as indeed has happened with Phase 9 in 1973, which has funded several similar schemes. If the Urban Programme is to continue its role of piloting future developments, 'community schools' of the type we have outlined ought to be strong candidates for these funds. If so, we should quickly see a more realistic debate about 'community schools', more examples, and more information about the potential of these centres for wider community development.

Notes

1 The recommendations were, in outline: (i) the extension of the EPA policy of 'positive discrimination'; (ii) the expansion of pre-schooling in EPAS; (iii) the development of 'community schools'; (iv) improved home-school relations; (v) improved teaching methods and resources and (vi) more action-research projects. A final non-educational recommendation was for a comprehensive programme of community development to accompany these educational changes.

2 Though we were both members of the West Riding EPA team, the conception of the centre and its development were the work of Mike Harvey, the project director, and Geoff and Lin Poulton, the first wardens. A longer account of the centre and of other project work in the West Riding was published in the project's final report: *Educational Priority*, vol. 4, *The West Riding EPA Project*, HMSO, 1974.

References

Central Advisory Council for Education (England), (1967). *Children and their Primary Schools* (Plowden Report), HMSO

CLEGG, A. and MEGSON, B. (1968) *Children in Distress*, Penguin Books

CRAFT, M. (1972) 'The school welfare team', in M. Craft, J. Raynor, and L. Cohen, (eds), *Linking Home and School*, 2nd ed., Longman

HALSEY, A. H. (ed.) (1972). *Educational Priority*, vol. 1, *EPA Problems and Policies* HMSO

MIDWINTER, Eric (1972) *Priority Education* Penguin Books

MILLER, S. M. (1967). 'Dropouts – a political problem', in Schreiber, D. (ed.), *Profile of the School Dropout*, New York: Vintage Books

OLSEN, E. G. (ed.) (1963). *The School and Community Reader*, Macmillan

SMITH, T. (1969) 'Community service and the school', unpublished thesis for Diploma in Social and Administrative Studies, University of Oxford

1.6 Community education

Wayne R. Robbins and Wyn Williams

Origin of community education in the United Kingdom

Community education has been defined as 'a conglomerate term which includes a school curriculum study of different aspects of community life. The purposes vary with the ideology of the advocates; some emphasize preparation for future community participation; others claim it as a means of achieving social change.'[1] This definition is interesting in that it emphasizes the school's central position in community education in England and the continuum along which supporters of community education can be found. This includes conservatives concerned with the problem of training responsible, participatory adults to radicals concerned with encouraging the study of peoples' 'grim social reality'[2] with a view to changing it.

The way in which these different positions have been reached can be best understood by looking at the different directions from which community educators have come. In the 1920s, Henry Morris, the Director of Education for Cambridgeshire opened the first of the 'Village Colleges'. The Village College was built upon Morris's concept of education as a lifelong process which began in the cradle and ended in the grave. The school was to be the focus for the educational, social, and recreational services needed by rural people living in villages too small and poor to provide all the necessary services. The Village College, therefore, became centred in one village and acted as the focal point for about eight small villages.

The expansion of Morris's idea

Morris's concept, in particular the idea of education as a lifelong process and the idea of a central place for services to be housed, has been taken up

Source: Unpublished paper (1976).

and adapted to their own situation by a number of other local authorities. A Conference in Coventry run by the School's Council in January 1974 led to nine local authorities being invited because of their strong interest in community education. They ranged from the heavily urbanized Coventry and Inner London Education Authority to rural Devonshire and mixed urban and rural Nottinghamshire. Double that number of authorities could have been invited.

The common characteristic of these Authorities who derive their community education ideas from Morris is that the 'secondary school' becomes the community school and its 'district' becomes the boundary for defining the community. Sutton Centre, in Nottinghamshire, which centres on a comprehensive school with 1200 pupils aged eleven years through 18 years, is typical of this strand of community education. The town it serves has a population of 40,000 people.

Educational deprival and community education

The other major educational force which led to a concern with community education was the concern expressed in the Plowden Committee's Report on Primary Education (1967).[3] This concern was over the inability of many schools to provide their pupils with equality of educational opportunity. Plowden reported on 'educational priority areas' in which housing conditions and levels of income on one side and motivational factors like parental lack of knowledge on the other combined to produce 'educationally deprived' children. One of the Plowden recommendations was that the 'community school' be tried as a vehicle for involving parents in their children's schooling. This fairly vague reference was developed in much more detail by the Educational Priority Area project set up in January 1968 to find ways of:

1. Raising education standards
2. Improving teacher morale
3. Involving parents in the educational process
4. Developing in the community a sense of responsibility for the community.

Community education, based on the primary school district of between three and four thousand people, became seen as central to changing the 'grim social reality' and achieving equality by educational means. The rationale for this approach is outlined by the Halsey Report[4] and by Eric Midwinter in *Patterns of Community Education*.[5]

Midwinter, the EPA Director in Liverpool, stresses community education as part of community development and emphasizes the part that a community-oriented curriculum is to play in creating the 'constructive discontent' with their 'grim social reality' that will enable the young together with their parents to change it.

Midwinter's concern has increasingly become with community education as a part of the movement for decentralization. He sees a need for local communities to directly control many services, health, social services, law and order, as well as education. In response to that, his definitions of community now extend to an area of 10,000 to 20,000 people containing four or five 'community schools'.

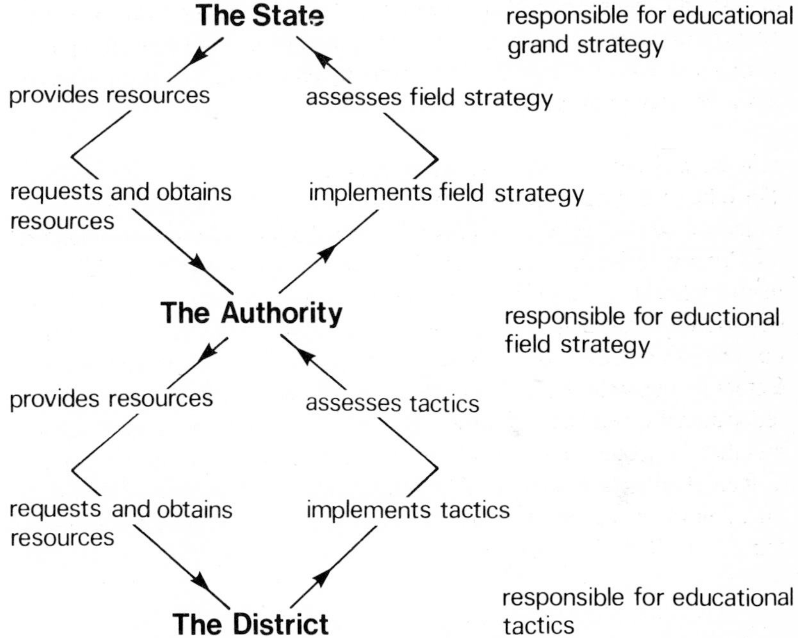

It is clear that the two interpretations of community education differ quite markedly. The Morris concept visualizes the school as a social, educational, and recreational centre providing services for a sizeable geographical area. The Midwinter concept arises from the concern with inequality and has developed into a view that the two major issues to which community education is to respond are the gap between representative and participatory democracy and the gulf between professional (whether teacher or administrative) and the client (whether student, parent or social service recipient).

The 'community' being spoken of is rather small in geographical area; the purpose, to secure participation by the community. It is worth emphasizing that both concepts of community education are undergoing change. In Nottinghamshire, both influences can be seen at work. Practitioners of one brand often borrow the clothes and even the rhetoric of the other. Thus, for example, the 'community-oriented curriculum' has become an issue in Sutton Centre in Nottinghamshire despite the fact that the influence of Morris is apparent in the concept of building a community centre.

Community education and community development

The third major force influencing the development of community education in the United Kingdom has been community development. In 1969 the Home Secretary announced in Parliament the launching of the Community Development Project as a 'neighbourhood-based experiment finding new ways of meeting the needs of people living in areas of high social deprivation'. As the Inter-Project Report of 1973[6] puts it: 'The experiment was originally conceived and planned on a number of basic assumptions. It was assumed that problems of urban deprivation had their origins in the characteristics of local populations – in individual pathologies – and these could best be resolved by better coordination of the personal social services, combined with the mobilization of self-help and mutual aid in the community, even among those who experience most difficulty in standing on their own feet.'[7]

The educational implications of this statement are obvious. The local community's sense of awareness and the social skills of its members have to be developed.

In Coventry, one of its first four community development projects, a Community Education Advisor was appointed in September 1971 to work closely with the already existing Community Development Project. His objectives were:[8]

1 to help disadvantaged people find ways of meeting their needs and aspirations
2 to help people exercise increased control over their own lives
3 to help enlarge the opportunities of disadvantaged people in directions which they themselves see as desirable
4 to increase the capacity of the education service to respond by providing help which is more acceptable, intelligible, and lasting in its effects.

These objectives are almost indentical with those stated by the Community Development Project. In order to meet them, he outlined the following strategies:

(a) an extension of pre-school provision
(b) a programme within schools designed to develop home/school and community/school relationships
(c) an in-service training and support programme for teachers
(d) a curriculum programme designed to introduce community-orientated elements into the curriculum
(e) a social education home-tutoring scheme for immigrant mothers.

This close link between Community Education and Community Development has been strained by changes within the Community Development Projects themselves.

The Inter-Project Report of 1973 stressed that their original assumptions about communities were wrong. 'We are beginning to identify and analyse different strategies of action, and get a clearer idea of what may be expected from the project.'[9] As a result, their view of education's place in the Community Development process has changed as well. They comment that 'emphasis on education fitted with the early assumptions of the Community Development Project's experiment and several of the earlier projects took up ideas developed in the Educational Priorities Areas programme, but others have avoided involvement in conventional education completely, or have experimented with education away from a school base. The central question is whether and in what form educational change can promote wider changes, and the ensuing debate has called into question several of the assumptions underlying the initial importance given to education.'[10]

Thus, within the Community Development Projects, three types of educational work have resulted.

1 Conventional education development where the project has called for the improvement of existing facilities on the assumption that the education system can be effective but needs more resources.
2 Community education in which the Project concentrates on improving home/school links, developing a relevant curriculum, and a community school in order to create 'constructive discontent' through the community school.
3 Emphasis on work outside schools, on informal adult education, dealing with real life situations like unemployment and rents. The object is to stimulate knowledge and awareness and encourage pressure for change among those directly affected.

It is clear from reading the Interim Report that the writers feel approach '3' fits in best with the new Community Development Project analysis based on a conflict model of society. 'It is work in adult education, informal sessions with resident groups and organizations which develop around concrete local issues where Community Development Project can make a distinctive contribution.'

The implications for community education of this new direction in community development has still to be worked out. So far, the Coventry model, closely linked as it is with the Midwinter Educational Priority Areas programme, seems to be spreading.

Midwinter himself, in part in response to his critics, in part in response to the lessons of the EPA project in Liverpool, has moved community education's emphasis away from deprivation alone and towards a concern with community education as a vital process in training people to make decentralization of local government work.

Certainly the tension between community educators and community developers is likely to produce further changes.

The concept as expressed in Nottinghamshire

It is clear there is no agreed definition of the concept of community education. If we look at Nottinghamshire, it is possible to find there major developments which have affected the way the concept is expressed.

SUTTON CENTRE

Sutton-in-Ashfield is a small town of 40,000 people roughly twenty miles from Nottingham. It's traditional employment was mining for men and hosiery mills for women. Recently light engineering has also been developed. It is designated by the government as a 'grey area' – one which needed to attract new industries and was eligible for the special government grants intended to attract such industry.

The town centre until 1970 had become rundown. At that point, the Sutton Council planned a new commercial centre sponsored by them in cooperation with a commercial developer.

In 1971, the County Authority commissioned a feasability study[11] to identify neeeds in Sutton. The subsequent report indicated that the community was a 'wheel without a hub' and recommended the building of a multi-purpose Community Centre to include:

1 education provision for a school for 11 year old to 18 year old pupils, a Youth Centre, and Adult Education section deliberately linking facilities and classes together
2 a sports centre for joint use by the school and adults in the community
3 provision for young children in a Day Care Centre.

4 a health clinic (which already stood on the proposed site)
5 provision for the aged and handicapped, which was intended to 'end their isolation and ensure a permanent opportunity for worthwhile community service for the young people of the school'
6 probation Service at the Centre
7 youth Service accommodations
8 a centre for town functions like dinners, dances, and exhibitions to be held
9 a theatre to be shared by school and community.

The Sutton Centre is clearly intended to provide the town with a 'heart', (a phrase used in the study). It is assumed that the education institution should have an impact upon the town by encouraging maximum use of the facilities and cooperation among providing agencies.

The Authority saw Sutton as a *model* for other such Centres to be developed elsewhere in the county. The emphasis has been put on the provision of educational, social, and recreational services which will provide missing amenities and do away with the 'grey area' connotation Sutton has had.

The school within the Centre was seen as having a key role in this community education experiment. The headmaster, when writing to prospective teachers, said that 'the Centre will be known equally for the quality of its teaching and for its community involvement'.[12] To ensure the latter, the twelve departments were encouraged to examine ways for involving themselves in the community, and four departments were specifically required to involve themselves directly with the community. These were:

1 The Communicative and Resource Department which was to act as the main link between the Centre and the community of Sutton.
2 The Environmental Department which was asked 'to develop in all students a critical awareness of their own environment and of the corporate responsibility of the whole community for the quality of rural and urban life.'[13]
3 The Personal Relationships and Community Service Department was responsible for coordinating the community service work of the centre.
4 The Home Management Department which was asked to involve adults in their programme making joint use of the Centre facilities.

Sutton expresses certain aspects of the community education concept. Particularly cooperation among agencies and the development of awareness of community problems, especially among pupils, through community orientated curriculum. There is a strong emphasis upon the relevance of education. The headmaster has stated as an ideal that 'if education is to have any real meaning to our boys and girls, it must surely be based initially on the community they know and the environment where they live.'[14] But other aspects of the concept are missing. There is no real machinery for involving people in community planning or promoting community leadership and decision-making in the educational process. We will return to this issue later.

The Sutton Centre does express the community education idea of being an instrument for social change, but only in the sense that it seeks to develop a sense of community. Perhaps the problem lies in the inadequacies of the developmental process which we describe later.

NOTTINGHAMSHIRE'S COMMUNITY TEACHERS

The other major educational development affecting the concept of community education stems from the Authority's concern with implementing a policy of positive discrimination in favour of areas suffering from multiple deprivation. The *County Study on Deprivation* (1975) defined deprivation as 'a relative concept, measured not by objective standards but by comparison with the relatively superior advantages of others.'[15] It defined multi-deprivation as 'social groups or areas which experience consistently worse conditions relative to other groups or areas and have relatively less opportunity in relation to such social markets as housing, employment, leisure, facilities, etc.'

The intention of the report was to promote a genuine sense of equity and social justice in the development and review of County Council policies, particularly as they affect the more vulnerable sections of the community. Thus the concept of positive discrimination is developed in association with the notion of equality of opportunity; ideas which are central to the County Councils' Interim Statement of Planning Policy.[16] The principle aim of the work was declared to be that of: 'enlarging mutual understanding between the school and the families and neighbourhoods which it serves and to strengthen the help which they can give to each other, bearing in mind especially those children who need most help and whose parents sometimes seek it least.'[17]

This emphasis upon the home liaison teacher working with 'parents who seek help least' certainly implies a much more limited concept of community education than the one we have outlined earlier. The involvement of parents is really intended only to help them help their children. It is not intended that they and other adults should extend their concern to changing conditions in their neighbourhood. This is confirmed by the stress in the job description upon Home-School links rather than community links and on 'avoiding confusion with established social workers.' The responsibility for creating community schools is given to the community teacher but only as one of a number of objectives. The concept of community school itself is limited – 'if community schools are organized on primary school premises, then the home-school liaison teacher should be closely involved in the evening activities.'[18] The stress is on programmes not on process.

The major emphasis within this approach in community education is on developing changes in the home environment which will result in a positive change in student achievement. It is a response to the evidence submitted by Professor Wiseman to the Plowden Committee in which he argued that 'educational deprivation is not mainly the effect of poverty; parental attitude and maternal care are more important than the level of material needs.'[19] This stress upon motivational causes of deprivation rather than structural has an important bearing upon the definition of community education.

The emphasis is not so much on education for social change, but rather on improving the understanding of the schooling process by the community. The implication is that condemned by the Community Development Project – namely that failure to achieve in the system is a result of individual weaknesses. The concept as defined here is essentially conservative.

NOTTINGHAM AREAS PROJECT AND COMMUNITY EDUCATION

The Nottinghamshire concept of community education which has developed at Sutton and through the community teachers may come to be influenced from a different direction. In 1973 the Chief Constable's Annual Report expressed concern over the rise in juvenile delinquency in the county. Two young unattached youth workers got together with the Probation Department and wrote a proposal for Urban Aid funding. This was successful and five community workers were appointed in July 1974. The areas in which they worked were chosen because they varied and shared in common only 'considerable scope for a worker with an open brief.'[20]

The work of the Project quickly revealed that the agencies serving the neighbourhoods, while full of good intentions, frequently acted as barriers against effective community involvement.

Two incidents were brought before the Management Committee of the Project as illustrations of the problem. Both concerned the Education Department. In one instance, a group of mothers organizing holiday activities for the young children in the flats, found that their primary school was denied to them by the Headmaster. It took six weeks of battle and the intervention of a Councillor to reverse the Headmaster's decision.

In the other instance, the new community teachers appointed by the Authority were told to run Summer Playschemes with paid volunteer teachers. This was after a group of mothers had run an effective Easter Playscheme. As the Project worker remarked bitterly in his monthly report: 'Who did this? Who decided that teachers were the best people to run the playschemes? What say did residents have in appointing these leaders? What encouragement did residents get to apply for the jobs? The answer to the last two questions is "none"! It seems to be the old story about participation ... that it ends as soon as money or influence is involved.'[21]

The community workers in this project are stressing the most basic process of community education – the involvement of the community itself in determining its needs and wants and then finding the appropriate avenues to satisfy those needs. How much effect the NAP will have on community education as defined by the Education Administration remains to be seen, but the project is certainly educating community groups to seek active involvement in tackling their own problems.

THE DEVELOPMENTAL PROCESS

When we looked at Sutton Centre, we commented on the fact that the concept of community education there has not worked out successfully how to involve the local community except as consumers of services. The process of involving community groups in the identification of community problems and their solutions has still to be achieved.

The explanation for this in part arises from the emphasis upon the Centre as a provider of services. However there were major weaknesses in the way in which Sutton was established. The need for the Centre was identified by administrators who tried to consult with community groups. From the start, the important sense of personal ownership of the Centre was really missing. Formal presentations to the school board about the concept of community education and to representative groups within the community were not achieved.

Within the school itself, there was a much clearer presentation to the teachers applying for jobs there. The job description spoke of the 'large numbers of adults who will use the Centre for educational and recreational purposes during the day alongside younger students. Applications are therefore invited from men and women who believe in the community school idea.'[22] Unfortunately it was not made clear which 'ideal' was being spoken of.

Nottinghamshire also decided in the case of Sutton not to appoint or rather involve the community in appointing a Community School Director. The process of contacting and involving the community is therefore in the hands of teachers as a body.

The other major consideration in developing a process of community participation is the Centre Management Board. As we pointed out earlier, such boards have traditionally left matters to the Headmaster to decide and have been composed of people appointed by the Education Committee. The element of direct community representation is through the three elected parents and three elected teachers.

In this vital area for the developmental process of direct community participation in the running and policy making of the Centre, there is still a long way to go. Community schools organized through the community teachers attached to primary schools have not really started at all.

IMPLEMENTING THE PROCESS

It is in this area that the critics of Community Education become most sceptical. The failure in Nottinghamshire to develop a satisfactory process stems from assumptions about the purpose of community schools as well as weakness in developing adequate mechanisms for participation. Byrne and Williamson[23] attack community schools as an irrelevance in the struggle for equality of educational opportunity. They take issue with the evidence of Professor Wiseman who stressed the importance of parental involvement, and by implication, parental inadequacy as the major factor in explaining poor results among working class pupils.

Byrne and Williamson provide strong evidence to suggest that differences in allocation of resources both *between* one local authority and another and *within* a local authority is a more critical factor in explaining the comparative failure of working class children to achieve as highly as middle class children. The requirement for community teachers to concentrate on 'parents whose children need it most and seek it least' would be evidence that the Nottinghamshire emphasis in community education is based on the assumption that the community school is a mechanism for involving parents only in as far as it affects their children's achievements.

Another argument put forward against Community Education was presented to the Conference on Social Deprivation and Change in Education[24] held at York in May 1972. Jackson and Ashcroft criticized Community Education as currently being practiced by the EPA projects and CDPs. They argued that the critical question in the equation social class affects educational opportunity was 'opportunity for what?' They argued that the process of Community Education which stressed parental involvement was based upon a false assumption – namely that 'class' was no longer being used as meaning the differences based upon power and status, but was instead based upon the notion that the 'poor' or 'deprived' were a sub-section of the working class who were significantly different and should be treated as such.

From this perspective, the community educator's concern with finding a 'relevant' community-orientated curriculum, as at Sutton, becomes a means of persuading the community to accept their 'grim, social reality' rather than challenge it.

Jackson and Ashcroft put forward an alternative objective. They want community educators to seek to develop with community groups programmes based upon an examination of issues like unemployment or housing that they define as important. The purpose of such study to develop class consciousness defined as happening when some men 'as a result of common experience feel and articulate the identity of their interests as between themselves, and as against other men whose interests are different from, and usually opposed to, theirs.'[25]

At the moment, in Nottinghamshire anyway, the implementation of the process is still at the minimum level. However, the Nottinghamshire Area Project workers through their emphasis upon enabling groups to identify their needs and find ways to meet them is probably much further along in the developmental process. The Balloon Woods Estate successfully negotiated a proposal for an Adventure Playground to be funded by Urban Aid. As a result, the residents were able to appoint their own workers. As the project worker remarked: 'It (the Adventure Playground Association) has employed workers and it is becoming some kind of institution within the estate.' He goes on to quote Marris and Rein,[26] 'Community organization falters because it cannot offer any future to the neighbourhood leaders it promotes but a lifetime of parochial effort.'

The project worker notes that the developmental process does mean that at the end of community participation in identifying needs must be community control of means to meet them. The new and highly successful Action Group which arose to fight for better housing conditions ran into the problems of success. Of the five original organizers 'two have obtained transfers, one an exchange, and the other two seek a move: in short, the activists have been deprived of leadership.'[27]

This last example of the problems of successful community involvement raises one, perhaps critical, question about the implementation of the developmental process. Should such a process be from the top down or from the bottom up? The answer to this question may well determine the way in which community education will develop both in Nottinghamshire and elsewhere.

The question was raised most effectively by Fantini and Gittell in their book, *Decentralization – Achieving Reform.*[28] They suggest that 'demands for decentralization and community participation are indices of the inaccessibility, irresponsibility, and unresponsiveness of the institutions of urban government in the 1970s.'

The issue then centres upon the way in which decentralization is to be achieved. The developmental process of community education suggests that the community be encouraged to participate in this process. It is basically a political process concerned with the redistribution of power and in particular with the control of recruitment, selection of personnel, and determination of priorities. Fantini and Gittell give examples of the conflicts that have arisen between existing political machines and professionals on the one hand, and community groups on the other. The most famous being the struggle for 'community control' by parents in the 201 school districts of New York in 1966.

In Nottinghamshire, the process of appointing two Advisors for the socially disadvantaged who have responsibility for seventy community teachers, is an example of a system seeking to make more effective links between the agencies, particularly the schools, and the local communities. It is essentially a top-down process.

Further, there are ambivalent feelings about the amount of say local communities should have. This is illustrated by an interesting conflict between the local Authority's Community Development workers employed in the Social Services Department and the Nottingham Areas Project Workers. The Working Party on Community Development suggested that the worker should be 'accountable to his employing agency for the wise use of his time and resources, to the voluntary groups he is seeking support for decisions and tactics and to staff with community work experience for standard operating practice.'[29] In a sharp rejoinder, the Nottinghamshire Area Project workers argue that this is to make community workers 'a tool of theirs (the local Authority) and not residents or community groups.'[30]

The obvious conclusion to be drawn is that the developmental process of community education is going to be the critical area in determining the final goal of community education – a real community participation in identifying and meeting needs – can be achieved. John Benington, the Coventry Director of Community Development, has summed up the issue by saying, 'token participation has the effect of co-opting dissident elements in the community and preempting the threat of more vigorous and successful challenges to their policies in the future.'

THE CONCEPT OF COMMUNITY EDUCATION – WHERE IT IS NOW

The three major forces which have led to the development of community education lay different emphasis on the concept. For those who see it as a movement centred on the secondary school, the major significance is in the idea of education as a lifelong process. That concept implies a concern with 'opening' up of formal education institutions to people in the community and identifying the type of programmes that people will find most meet their needs.

The community education derived or influenced by the concern with 'disadvantaged' or 'deprived' children emphasizes the importance of creating a partnership between adults, children, and professionals in 'deprived' areas to enable them to translate discontent into a unified attack on making the educational system more responsive to the needs of the deprived. The implication is that the political and economic systems can be responsive to the needs of groups who do not get a 'fair' share of the educational cake – provided they develop the skills to use the bureaucratic system.

The community education derived from the new concern within community development emphasizes the concept as raising the level of awareness about the nature of the economic and political system in such a way that those communities that are poor see themselves as being part of a working class that does not effectively control its own destiny in the work or residential structure. The implication is that the conflict model of society, in which groups compete for resources and power, makes most sense in understanding society. Community education should lead to community action. Thus we have a concept of community education which currently rests in three different models of society – a consensus model in which the real concern is with better delivery of education services to the community; the community itself being basically homogeneous. Conflicts can be resolved by better communical and interpersonal relationships.

The second interpretation is based upon the pluralistic model of society which sees society as a competition between groups which have, or can have, a balance of power. The imbalances can be met by more effective participation of those interests who are under-represented.

The third model is the conflict model which sees a fundamental conflict between classes in society. The problems are defined in terms of inequalities and the major tactic is better organization and raising of levels of consciousness.

It is hard to predict which of these models for explaining social change will predominate in the future or what the consequences would be for community education if one did come to predominate.

Let us rather indicate our own preference. Community education ought to be intimately linked to community action. That action is geared to securing a greater degree of local community control over the bureaucratic system that delivers services and a greater say in the definition of what needs those services should be meeting. The concept is concerned with greater community involvement. It is likely to be linked to movements that see the taking of power by the powerless through class struggle as a major goal.

COMMUNITY EDUCATION – THE PLACE WE ARE NOW

In Nottinghamshire, pre-school provision, senior citizen activity, recreation programmes, and adult education programmes are all provided at Sutton Centre. The community teachers are engaged in developing family-orientated activities (like the summer playschemes and the greater use of school facilities in the community) and involving parents in their children's education. On the other side of the reference point, there is evidence of an increasing effort to develop a community-orientated curriculum which uses the community as a laboratory, involves community people as resources, and studies community problems – thereby integrating school with community. *But* there is little community action derived from the community school base and little grassroots democracy in the sense of participating directly in the planning of programmes or the policy making of the school. The programme orientation at the moment clearly exceeds the process orientation.

This issue of local community control over the institutions and staff is related to the wider issue of 'control' raised by the Community Development Projects. They ask whether local communities *can* effectively influence the problems they face – unemployment, crime, poor housing, poor social services. Their scepticism has led them to see 'control' as something only achievable by local communities in cooperation with organized working class institutions (e.g. trade unions) which are themselves class conscious.

WHERE WE SHOULD BE

We feel community education's ultimate goals will be achieved only when local communities take power and involve themselves in the struggle to participate directly in the allocation of resources within their school district and the appointment of staff directly responsible to them. Such a development in our view cannot be achieved by a top-down process however well-intentioned the educational professionals and political policy makers may be. A developmental process has to occur in which the local community comes to feel the need for control and seeks to develop the skills and cohesion needed to obtain this control.

This is not to say that we deny the importance of committed

professionals and politicians. The Fentini model for decentralization by a partnership between local community and central bureaucracy and political machine seems to be a viable and desirable one. Effective community participation comes as a result of this process.

THE DEVELOPMENTAL PROCESS – WHERE IT IS NOW

In Nottinghamshire the process of community education has largely been a top-down one. The County Deprivation Study in emphasizing equity and social justice and a positive discrimination in favour of deprived communities required departments to respond. The Director of Education's response has been to develop community education as a means of achieving those objectives. This technique has been to (a) create a model Community Centre at Sutton, and (b) to appoint seventy teachers under the direction of two Advisors to work on home/school relationships in order to improve parental understanding and involvement in the educational process. The local communities involved have not been prepared for these moves via the developmental process we described earlier.

If we develop a hierarchy of objectives, then we can identify community development and the integration of the total community in all its aspects at the top of the scale. At the moment, we are near the bottom of the hierarchy. There is an expanded use of school facilities and a lifelong learning programme being developed in Nottinghamshire.

To move from one end of the scale to the other will require that community educators keep in sight the integration of community activities. The process by which this will happen is by heavy emphasis upon citizen involvement and decision-making in the policies and running of the local institutions including schools. The greater cooperation and collaboration of agencies providing services will rise from that process. As a goal, it is only truly significant as a logical outcome of increased community participation. It is *not* an end goal for community education itself.

CONTROL AND POWER – AS IT IS NOW

The conclusions we have just drawn about community education as part of community action and a hierarchy of objectives to be reached culminating in the integration of community activities under the control of local communities raises starkly the question of *how* this process is to begin and who is to control it.

It is clear that, at the present, control of the educational institutions and staff working in community education, is firmly in the hands of the existing representative political machinery – (in Nottinghamshire, the Education Committee) and the professionals (the Director of Education, and

Headmasters). This is reflected in the fact that the existing machinery for local community representation is extremely ineffective. In Nottinghamshire, the school boards are being revitalized by the appointment of three elected parents and three elected teachers, but the power to Boards of Schools under the 1944 Education Act have rarely been exercised except to dismiss a Headmaster. Training courses for school governors are almost unknown, and the Boards in no way mean real participation by local people.

However the 'opening' up of the schools to adults in the neighbourhood and parents has increased awareness of the concept that the institutions *belong* to the people. Moreover the Community Centre at Sutton is headed by a confirmed believer in community involvement and both Advisors see community participation in schools as a critical aspect of the work of community teachers. How far this enthusiasm will affect community awareness remains to be seen. At least there is manpower in the form of community teachers, who see themselves as having a commitment to encourage parents, at least, to see the school as theirs.

WHERE IT SHOULD BE

Given the inertia of schools to change and the problems facing teachers in 'deprived' areas, it seems to us probable that any real community involvement may come from the action of the community workers. Here their encouragement of groups in the community has already led to demands being made for the use of school buildings and school support for Mothers' Playschemes by relating curriculum experiences of pupils to activity in the community.

Perhaps a partnership of community teachers and community workers can achieve a more effective developmental process. The former by:

1 extending their work with parents to include adults in the community, and
2 placing greater emphasis upon the idea of making primary (elementary) schools into community schools.

This could work in conjunction with community workers who could:

1 encourage local community groups to extend their concern with rents, housing conditions, and social services into active participation in the community school which could be the meeting place and resources for various groups
2 make local government aware of the community's desire to participate in all matters that affect them whether it be running programmes or planning the development of their area.

WHO IS THE COMMUNITY SCHOOL SERVING?

At present in Nottinghamshire, the Community School is in an ambivalent position. The Sutton Centre, in the desire to avoid equating community education with school, has deliberately avoided the word 'school' and calls itself a 'Centre.' As for the seventy primary schools with community teachers, the task of creating community schools is only one of twelve or thirteen listed objectives for the community teacher to achieve.

As a result, in Sutton, the Centre serves a variety of groups within the town of Sutton – pre-school children, youth, elderly and handicapped adults, and adults who wish to attend programmes or adults who want help in school. The recreation activities inevitably attract people from the neighbouring towns and countryside.

If the community school is to meet the ends of community education listed earlier, then the school has to be the focus for the variety of interest and age groups that go to make up a community.

It has to have facilities available for the Tenants' Association that is organizing against rent increases as well as providing space or programmes for the mothers who want to get together to develop pre-school education.

The ultimate goal of community education is to help create a community in which there is the power to effectively participate in the planning and implementation of decisions that impinge upon people's lives. The community school as a vehicle for achieving that goal will have to be run by the variety of groups that make up the community. The mechanism for that in the United Kingdom will probably be a reformed School Board of Managers/Governors. The power to actually control resources, identify the priority needs of each community, and the ability to employ the staff needed to help implement those needs is going to be critical.

We still have a very long way to go in the developmental process.

LEGISLATIVE SUPPORT

In England, at the national level, there never has been a direct Act in which community education was specifically mentioned. The 1944 Act merely emphasizes the importance of a 'comprehensive service' for each area and the responsibility of the Secretary of State for Education for seeing that authorities provide it. That 'comprehensive' service could and should include community education, but at present, does not.

At local authority level, we do have funds and staff applied and appointed in the field of community education. Inevitably, each local authority is deciding upon the most appropriate form for community education and is setting its own priorities.

There is, in Nottingham, no master plan for community education which identifies goals or priorities. There is, however, a County

Deprivation Study which encourages community involvement and individual schools like Sutton Centre write in community participation as a desired end.

There is a strong case for encouraging the government to produce a circular which requests local authorities to submit their plans for community education. It is possible that such a circular should not try to identify which type of community education development was most appropriate. LEAS are in a better position to judge their own district but a firm central guideline outlining possibilities may well be useful.

The other major need is for Local Education Authorities to respond to the recommendations from Community Development Projects and even the Government Commission on local government (like Seebohm and Maud) which stress community participation and a decentralization of power.

WHAT COMMUNITY SHOULD BE

Community is very rarely used in a pejorative sense. Almost always it is a 'good' word. As such, it implies a state of what should be rather than what is. In our terms, we are speaking of a geographic area where participatory democracy is a possibility. People can meet together and identify those needs and problems they face within their geographic boundary. It is of necessity small, but community is also a *product* of a community education process. People come as a result of struggle to achieve goals they have jointly identified, to identify themselves as a community even where none existed before.

We are aware of the dangers of parochialism, of an inability for such communities to see themselves as part of a larger group, but the advantages outweigh the disadvantages. Community in our sense is felt by those who sense that they can effect their own destiny or recognize that those problems are ones which require joint action with other people on a much larger scale. Midwinter's linking of 'neighbourhood' (4–5,000) with 'community' (15,000–20,000) makes sense because he identifies an involvement process in which control over your own life develops in concentric circles. You seek to control those immediate services which meet your local needs and contribute with other neighborhoods to the solution of those problems which require service provision on a wider scale.

Notes

1 Glossary, E351, Urban Education, Open University, Block 1, p. 72.
2 MIDWINTER, E. (1969) *The Philosophy of the Education Priority Area* Occasional Paper 1, Liverpool, EPA.
3 Plowden Commission Report on Primary Education, 1967.
4 HALSEY, A. (1972) *Educational Priority*, Vol. 1, HMSO.
5 MIDWINTER, E. (1974) *Patterns of Community Education*.
6 The National Community Development Project, Inter-Project Report, p. 1.
7 *Ibid.*
8 Paper submitted to the Home Office Interim Report on Community Education in Coventry, 1971.
9 Inter-Project Report, p. 3.
10 *Ibid*, p. 33.
11 Feasibility Study, Nottinghamshire Local Authority, 1971, on Sutton Centre.
12 Additional Information for Applicants, Stuart Wilson, 1973.
13 *Ibid.*
14 WILSON, S. *Report on Community and School*.
15 County Deprived Area Study, Notts County Council, 1975, p. 1.
16 *Ibid*, p. 3.
17 BELTY, C. (1973) *Job Description for Home/School Liaison Teachers*.
18 *Ibid*.
19 Plowden Commission Report, Primary Education, 1967.
20 Background Paper, Nottingham Areas Project, July 1974.
21 Management Committee Report of Project Worker, Alan Simpson, 1975.
22 Job Application Information, Sutton Centre, 1973.
23 BYRNE, D. and WILLIAMSON, W. (1972) *The Myth of the Restricted Code*, University of Durham, Department of Sociology.
24 Adult Education, Deprivation and Community – A Critique, K. Jackson and B. Ashcroft Paper to the Conference on Social Deprivation and Change in Education, University of York, April 1972.
25 THOMPSON, E. P. *The Making of the English Working Class*.
26 MARRIS, P. and REIN, M. (1972) *Dilemmas of Social Reform*.
27 BISHOP, T. Monthly Report, Balloon Woods Estate.
28 FANTINI, J. and GITTELL, M. (1973) *Decentralization – Achieving Reform*.
29 Working Party Report on Community Work in Notts, 1975.
30 Reply to Working Party Report, Paper by NAP Community Workers *et al.*

1.7 Civilized authority

Case study: Highbury Grove School, London

Rhodes Boyson

Every headmaster worth his salt has a view of life and society which is shown in his school – it is there that 'the word becomes flesh and dwells among us'. This is very much more important at a time when there is a crisis of views and authority and central guidance from local authority or government has seriously decreased.

I accept the concept of authority and the school as an instrument for the passing on of enlightened authority. No one can discover for himself the sum or even any significant part of the total sum of human knowledge and experience gathered over some 5000 years of chronicled history. The 'discovery' method is the most inefficient schooling method ever discovered! It is also built on a philosophic misconception of human life: that each child and each man and woman is not dependent, even for his freedom, on the work and discoveries of other people. No man or woman is an island, and people should grow up aware of this fact. There is only freedom within structure and young people should be taught to realise this or they will be liberated to intense agony and suffering.

My view is that man came into society for security. Outside, to quote Thomas Hobbes, life is 'solitary, poor, nasty, brutish and short'. This society, especially where it has liberal and civilized values, has to be protected. We can see what happened in Germany under Hitler when civilized society was overthrown. The civilized society is a fragile plant and no headmaster can be neutral in the battle for and against its continuance. Neither civilization, nor learning which is its flowering, is natural and spontaneous, but arises from nurture, carefully analysed respect for the past and controlled discipline. Neither civilization nor learning is something we can discover again in each generation, and once destroyed it may not be rebuilt or rediscovered.

Source: *A Question of Schooling* (1976), J. Macbeath, pp. 61–8.

I also do not believe that man is perfectible in this life. He carries, however, the primitive genes of struggle and pride and competition with him. I accept the message of Robert Ardrey's *Territorial Imperative* and Anthony Jay's *Corporation Man* that primitive genes still influence us. The educationist and the politician must realise that human nature is basically a constant and that to treat it otherwise, as if it were perfectible or transformable, in one's lifetime is to risk serious setbacks.

This does not mean that life has to be static. Learning and civilized behaviour have not only to be preserved, but must be prevented from becoming moribund. There must be a continuing process of criticism, renewal, organic growth and development which can only happen within a framework of order and rational discourse. Nor can anyone suggest improvements until he is aware of how and why present structures have arisen, and it also helps to know that happened in history whenever previous reforms were made.

Pupils and students and indeed scholars must be subject to their 'disciplines' until they have mastered them; only then will any of their criticisms have real validity. If a historian tries to write about a period before he has studied what other people have written and concluded, he will be a mere chronicler of discordant events, not a historian. He is thus only free as a historian when he has been trained in its discipline and has absorbed its knowledge.

School is a preparation for life, not life itself. Those headteachers and teachers who are either not at home in the real world outside or in revolt against it will do little good with children, most of whom are only waiting to enter the real adult world. School is a shorthand method of passing on the skills of literacy and numeracy, and a body of knowledge and any other achievements are secondary to these. Indeed the lack of the skills of literacy and numeracy is the ultimate deprivation.

I also feel that, for the health of society, social and economic mobility must be promoted. This is something which British education has always aided. Shirley Williams, MP, when Labour Minister of State at the Department of Education and Science, told the 1967 Conference of European Ministers of Education that over 26 per cent of the British University population and 35 per cent of students in all institutions of higher education in Britain were of working-class origin. This was (and is) the highest percentage in the Western world or the Soviet bloc. The figure of the percentage of university intake drawn from the working class was 14 per cent in Sweden, where 63 per cent were drawn from the upper and middle class, 10 per cent in Denmark, 8.3 per cent in France, 5.3 per cent in West Germany and 4 per cent in Switzerland. In Soviet Russia only 10 per cent of the university intake was drawn from the families of agricultural workers while 82 per cent came from the children of professional families. When in America genuine universities are separated from other institutions of higher education, the percentage intake from working-class families is lower than in British universities.

Thus a British school must continue to promote educational and economic mobility, bearing in mind the return to the mean which occurs in all genetic heredity. This is the only way to run a contented and efficient liberal capitalist or even socialist system. Nobody should be compelled to social mobility but the opportunities should be open wide.

I thus saw Highbury Grove when I opened it in 1967 as both a traditional and a meritocratic school. This was the view then held by many Labour supporters of comprehensive schools, including Harold Wilson, the Prime Minister, who said that such schools should offer 'a grammar school education to all', and that the grammar schools would be destroyed 'over his dead body'! It was the grammar schools which had been the great promoters of both traditional education and also social and educational mobility.

I believed that Highbury Grove should offer an academic education within a cheerful but a strictly disciplined framework to every one of its 1400 boys. I also believed that it was the duty of every teacher to teach and not to be an elder brother. All teachers were appointed to departments under the firm control of their heads of department, who were responsible for the syllabus, the discipline and the curriculum of the department. Every year I would analyse the external examination results of all departments and these would be available to all staff, and also to parents and boys who wished to see them. This was the discipline of external accountability, for we were dealing with the future life chances of boys in a none too prosperous area. There were departmental meetings scheduled each week where the head of department had to explain and defend his policies to his departmental staff. This meant each head of department had to remain alive and responsive to his departmental staff.

The boys were divided into three bands or streams at the age of eleven. There were three A Bands, three B bands and two C bands. The division was made purely on academic ability. All A bands in a year went to a subject at the same time; all B bands went together; and all C bands went together, so that each department could further divide pupils according to their academic ability if they so wished. I did insist, however, on a common syllabus with the same number of lessons in each subject over the whole year group. This meant that pupils could easily move bands at the termly or half-yearly examinations. The syllabus in each subject was, however, taught at different depths in each band since the A bands could move easily to a more intellectual approach. None the less some 17 per cent of pupils were moved to a different band in a typical three-year course from eleven to fourteen. There was thus considerable mobility.

As I have fully described in my book *Oversubscribed: The Story of Highbury Grove*,[1] some departments wished to non-stream or non-band their pupils. I agreed provided their external examination results at the end of the fifth year did not suffer. Half then unbanded and half remained banded. I am not convinced that non-streaming is as efficient as streaming or banding, but I believed that staff should have freedom to teach as they wished provided I could test their achievements. Unfortunately I left Highbury Grove before the first non-banded subject pupils reached their fifth year.

In the fourth and fifth years, however, the boys had all to take English and mathematics while they chose a minimum of five additional subjects. These subjects were chosen by the boys after consultation with their parents, housemasters and the careers master. It was guided choice: the choice had to make sense with regard to each pupil's ability and his future career ambitions. All boys sat examinations. Just as my remedial department, by concentrating on the basic subjects, made sure that all boys became literate and numerate, so all less able fifth-year boys sat a number of basic subjects for the Certificate of Secondary Education. Some were remarkably successful in gaining good passes and even CSE Grade 1s which are a GCE O-level equivalent. One year, sixteen less able fifth-year boys sat CSE English and twelve gained grade 1, 4 or 5 passes. The same sixteen boys received twelve grade 1, 2 and 3 passes in CSE art, including four grade 1s. Such boys did better because we did not pretend they were more able than they were, nor did we pretend they did not need special instruction. We did not expect all boys to be equally able but we had faith that every boy, even the most backward, could achieve something worthwhile. To let academically gifted boys sit examinations which are useful to their future while denying the right of less able boys to sit at least some external examinations is to play a confidence trick upon them.

Motivation is a great help to study, and up to the raising of the school-leaving age in 1973 we always let it be known that staying on at school into the fifth year was a privilege which had to be earned and that boys would be removed if they did not do their best or if they created disciplinary problems. It is of interest that the external fifth-year results in 1974 were considerably down on the previous years, because with the raising of the minimum school-leaving age there were boys who did not want to be in school who poisoned the whole atmosphere of the fifth.

We similarly made entry into the sixth form dependent upon academic merit and a good general attitude. Many sixth forms have been expanded simply to increase the salaries of heads and staff, since one sixth-former is equivalent to seven first-formers in allowances and salaries. The sixth form, like the school, should not be a waiting room for life but a place of intense study and concentration. Boys whose performance fell below this aim were removed and their absence was seen to increase the stimulus of other pupils.

The structure of the school was clear to staff and boys. I took all school assemblies three times a week. Assembly was a time for morale raising, and I tried every day to have some piece of information which would bring delight and self-congratulation to the school. I was flanked by my deputy heads; the house captains and vice-captains sat alongside; the staff stood on one side of the hall; the tutor prefects on the other; and the boys in their tutor groups were in lines. The structure was clear. Assembly was for a hymn, a prayer, a reading, uplift announcements – and then away. I also held back houses with their tutor prefects and tutor masters to inspect the boys' uniform and to make sure that all boys and staff were on their toes.

The boys were under six housemasters and a sixth-form master. Each housemaster was completely responsible for his 200-plus boys and only taught half the week so that he had time to perform his work properly. Once a week boys had assembly in houses, where they also ate daily and where all leisure and evening activities were centred.

The parents were also in houses. I saw parents three times at least before their boys entered the school. Every year there was an open evening for parents who lived in the area to inspect the school. I explained what the aims of the school were, our type of discipline and our demands on boys and parents. I warned parents not to opt for Highbury Grove unless they were prepared to work fully with us. There were then two further meetings when the housemasters and I saw parents.

I chaired all meetings of staff. Every week I met my heads of department at least once, my housemasters at least once, and I had sherry and lunch daily with the staff of the houses in turn. I ate at the high table of each house. I always visited house assemblies and I called in every classroom at least once a week. It was tiring but exciting and rewarding work.

I also attempted to attend all big parent functions in each house. There were dances, bingo sessions, cheese and wine, film shows and a host of activities in the houses. There were also clubs in the houses meeting weekly for boys. It was all very exciting, and the loyalty of the parents to the houses and the school was tremendous. We were really running a community centre and I always said that we took on families not boys. We even ran classes for parents when we changed school syllabuses. When we introduced a new maths course we ran a weekly evening class in it for parents throughout the winter and some parents even sat and passed it at O-level.

Sport also played a great part. I believe that boys are competitive creatures. We would field up to eight soccer teams on a Saturday and they knew that it was their task not just to play good football but to win. We also competed in cricket, running, swimming, life-saving, rowing, gymnastics and indeed almost every sport, and the teams and results were read out in assembly. Whenever possible I supported and cheered the teams, and parents always attended in large numbers.

Music played a great part in the school. Some 200 boys would always be learning musical instruments, and there were numerous orchestras, bands and groups. The Festival of Carols every year was a tremendous event and was followed by a Punchbowl and great celebration. Similarly the annual production of Gilbert and Sullivan was great fun. Radio telescopes, go-carts and other strange contraptions were made in the technical workshops and brought great fame to the school. The models for the new Daleks for the *Dr Who* programme were also made in the school.

Many of these achievements and events got in the local and national press, and boys, parents and even staff enjoyed reading about the school. All boys gained the reflected glory of these achievements which all helped to keep morale very high. A daily memo printed the previous evening informed all staff and boys of the daily events in the school and who were the guests being brought around by the headmaster to see the school, take sherry with the staff and to lunch in the houses.

This traditional, meritocratic, yet exciting school showed its success in its results. The school was always very oversubscribed in applicants. The area and indeed all London beat a path to its door. Attendance was high in an area with low attendance, and prizes and certificates were given for 100 per cent attendance over a year while housemasters chased up the non-attenders. Boys were always splendidly turned out. Our sporting and academic record became renowned. Staffing was always much easier than at other London schools and the heads of departments and heads of houses were very stable. Parental involvement was more intense than in any school I have ever seen or visited. All boys left for jobs or professions or higher education since the school's careers master rightly considered that this was his responsibility. Very many went on to university. There were no sixth-form revolts and indeed the sixth-formers regularly asked for more duties and more involvement in the school; nor were concessions made to them on uniform or smoking. It was a tight, cheerful ship.

Discipline was enforced by the heads of department and the house-masters. It is easier to keep discipline in a cheerful, successful school. Parents were involved in all serious cases, corporal punishment was given and about once a year a boy was suspended.

What did we give the boys? We gave them self-confidence which came from growing up in a secure structure where the rules were known and kept and yet where a boy could go for help when he needed it. They were proud of the school and its high standing and, in consequence, they were proud of themselves.

We also stretched the boys academically. We often had to put ninety of our intake each year into remedial classes under firm instruction because they could not read, write or number. Almost all could read, write and number when they left and they could thus hold down jobs in the society outside. Parents and boys were embarrassingly grateful for this basic help which is neglected in so many schools, to the suffering of pupils. We made all boys learn and they were grateful for our insistence.

Other boys passed to high academic standards who often came from so-called poor backgrounds. We gave them faith in themselves and they went out confidently.

We gave boys leisure activities: sport, music, technical pursuits, art. They came back in the evenings after they had left and one big band playing Glenn Miller music stayed together after leaving school and toured parts of Europe fulfilling musical engagements. Others continued to play football together.

We prepared boys for life as it is: competitive and cheerful and sometimes cruel. We taught boys to help and respect one another. We also taught them to respect structure and security and not to become ritualistic destroyers. We taught boys to be proud of themselves as they were without being envious of others. We taught them that all could give service to their school, their neighbourhood and their country.

We did not teach them, like some schools, that the outside world was bad, that all people were equal, that there was only liberation in personal revolt. I feel that such schools are the Pied Pipers of our time and do untold harm. I prefer cheerful, traditional education and meritocracy and so apparently do boys and their parents. It is a pity that there are not more schools like Highbury Grove. If the educational voucher was introduced or if educationists ever listened to parents, we would undoubtedly have more such schools.

The parents made clear their faith in the school not only by their desire to enter their boys but in written contact. Every report sent home had a feedback section on which parents could pass their comments back to the housemasters. There could be little wrong with a school where one Christmas 69 per cent of the 1200 feedback forms thanked staff for their work and help and 20 per cent remembered to wish the housemasters a Merry Christmas.

In 1972 the Parents Associations themselves circulated all parents to see why they had chosen Highbury Grove for their sons. The results were very clear. Less than half were even influenced by the fact that the school was the nearest to their homes, and most had ignored the recommendation of the junior school head. Instead the parents overwhelmingly had chosen Highbury Grove because, in that order, Highbury Grove had an excellent academic record, it was known for its tight discipline, there was intense sporting activity and it was a single-sex school. It is a pity that this exercise in genuine grass-roots participation was not known to the political parties when they framed their school programmes!

Note

BOYSON, R. (1974), *Oversubscribed: The Story of Highbury Grove* Ward Lock Educational

2 Curriculum issues

Introduction

What should schools teach the young? The 'Great Debates' on education that have been going on up and down the country in 1977 and the imminent Green Paper on the curriculum *may* tell us something, though the guess is that they will tell us very little.

The papers in this section are concerned entirely with the curriculum. Holly (2.10) describes and criticizes the conventional secondary school curriculum which still persists, despite the belief that there have been wholesale changes. Contrasted with this critique is the extract from the Schools Council's Working Paper on 'The Whole Curriculum' (2.1) in which the concept of an educational covenant is introduced as a way of helping schools to define their curricular aims and policies. Three papers: those by Midwinter (2.3) Newmann and Oliver (2.4) and Gumbert (2.5) look beyond the school and into the community for energizing and revitalising the school curriculum as well as education generally. Midwinter argues for the school engaging with the community and reflecting its concerns within the curriculum. For Newmann and Oliver and Gumbert, however, systematic instruction is the purpose of schools but they add that other aspects of children's learning could be more profitably pursued in the learning networks and in the broad educational resources found in all cities – streets, factories, museums, libraries etc. Partington (2.6) examines some of the consequences of community control over the curriculum for the professional educator.

Finally, four papers: those by Skilbeck (2.2) Entwistle (2.7) Bantock (2.8) and Chanan and Gilchrist (2.9) consider the cultural dimensions of the curriculum. Skilbeck discusses the concept of reconstructivism in education, with its belief that schools can promote and guide social change. Entwistle considers the relationship between education, culture and working-class education, while Bantock reaffirms his belief that a watered-down high culture for the majority of children has failed and that a recognition of difference is the only way forward. Finally, Chanan sees today no secure body of values that schools can hand on. What there is has to be consciously created, and the schools' opportunity is to rise to the occasion of both helping to create those values and to then hand them on.

2.1 Aims and the educational covenant

Schools Council

Soundly conceived and clearly formulated aims, at no matter what level or in which department, go a long way towards giving the school curiculum coherence. In the classroom the teacher will have particular lesson aims – to draw out the significance of part of a novel, to trace the contribution of a personality to an historical movement, or to show how perspective is achieved in a number of key paintings. There are also likely to be course aims of a kind to be found, for example, in the preamble to a Mode III syllabus. At another level, a department or faculty is likely to have drawn up guide-lines for its members. An English department may want to stress the development of spoken English, wide and discriminating reading or creative writing, while the science department may want the science teaching in the school to draw out the moral and social implications of science for everyday life, as well as to help pupils see how intimate is the connection between the development of technology and scientific discovery. We believe that as far as possible the aims which operate at these different levels and in different departments of the school should be made explicit so that they can be seen for what they are, discussed, evaluated and, if need be, modified.

We should remember, however, that in today's extremely busy schools teachers are already so hard pressed by the daily demands of teaching, pastoral care and administration that it is difficult for them to find the necessary time and energy to discuss curriculum aims, particularly those of the school as a whole. Moreover, because aims are notoriously difficult to formulate, it is tempting to conclude that they cannot by nature be sharply defined. Discussions of aims can also expose deep differences of view among staff which is not always possible to explore in a controlled and

Source: *The Whole Curriculum* (1975), pp. 23–32.

conscious way. For the sake of concord it may seem wiser not to lay much stress on them. We do not underestimate the difficulties of drawing up clear curriculum aims but we are heartened to find in how many schools the task is being energetically tackled.

In what sense are the aims of the school different from the collectivity of aims which are pursued by separate departments? The 1969 Scarborough Conference Report, *Choosing a Curriculum for the Young School Leaver*,[1] stated that there were no possible grounds for assuming that the sum total of the objectives of subjects in the curriculum would equal the total objectives of the whole curriculum. What is required, according to the report, is a framework of principles within which individual teachers, teams and departments can consider togther how best they might each contribute to the whole curriculum. We, too, subscribe to this view.

In seeking a framework of principles for the whole curriculum we reached the view that the school's aims should start from an acknowledgement of the legitimate expectations of various groups of people who are involved in secondary education. We saw the aims of the school as emerging from an assessment of the balance of expectations to be met and thought of them as constituting a covenant, or social compact. This covenant defines the reasonable expectations and mutual responsibilities of the pupils, for whose welfare the school exists, their parents, the teachers, and such agencies as boards of governors, local education authorities and the Department of Education and Science. Seen as a covenant, the curriculum reveals what view the school takes of its pupils, what it regards as their legitimate entitlements, and what sort of people it thinks it should help them to become. Similarly in the ways in which its relations with parents and the wider community are conducted it will show, more eloquently than in any other way, what it regards as the proper place of the school in society. Finally, in its definition of roles and responsibilities, a curriculum incorporates a concept of teacher professionalism.

The notion of a covenant has a somewhat legalistic connotation, but no purely legal ordinance can define the aims of a school's curriculum. The covenant must derive its authority from the willingness of the parties to assent to its principles and to be governed by its terms, but this they can only be expected to do if the terms are seen to be fair and reasonable. Thus the task of drawing up the covenant is essentially a process of reconciling views and interests which are often in conflict. In today's schools such a task is an extremely difficult one.

The covenant will be strengthened, however, if the principles upon which it is based are shared rather than simply reflect the beliefs and attitudes of a single group, be they teachers, pupils, parents or anyone else.

Reconciling diverse and often conflicting views will only be possible as the result of discussion and co-operation. The principles of reconciliation upon which the covenant is based should also be common in the sense that, although there is room for variation from school to school in the stress that can be laid upon them, or in the way in which they can be translated into day-to-day policies, they should nevertheless provide all schools with criteria for defining their responsibilities. What follows is a range of principles which seem to us to offer a basis of reconciliation between the various parties to the educational covenant.

The terms of the educational covenant

Pupils may reasonably expect to be treated with respect as persons. We want to stress particularly that pupils are more likely to develop as rational and reasonable people if they are treated as such and if the school attempts to realize, in its teaching, the standards of rationality, integrity and truth which are inherent in the content of education.

Pupils may reasonably expect the school, first, to do all in its power to make available to them the widest possible range of the kinds of knowledge, arts, crafts and skills which form the basis of a rich life in an advanced society. The general education which schools provide should, secondly, equip pupils to enter upon a job and, thirdly, provide them with an adequate basis for further education and training. Where unemployment is high the second of these demands cannot be fully met and morale suffers without the school being able to remedy the situation. The third of these demands implies that schools pay as much attention to the requirements and opportunities of the many courses offered in further education colleges as to those of their own sixth forms.

Pupils may reasonably expect to receive a political education appropriate to participation in the life of a democratic society. The school should not advance on its authority the standpoint of any political party or the personal views of its staff. All political opinions should be subject to impartial and critical scrutiny. Schools should help pupils understand our society as it stands and equip them to criticize social policy and to contribute to the improvement of society.

Pupils should have opportunities to gain knowledge of and to evaluate the claims of religion but the school should not advance, on its authority, the doctrines of any sect or creed. Where an understanding exists that the claims of a particular sect or creed are to be given special emphasis in the curriculum, as in voluntary schools and other schools having a religious foundation, the understanding should be an explicit one, acknowledged by teachers, pupils and parents.[1]

Pupils may reasonably expect to be treated as responsible partners in their own education, to be closely involved in the process of learning, and to have a say in the courses they are to pursue. The school's aims and purposes should be communicated to pupils and discussed with them as the need and opportunity arise. The procedures and organizational arrangements of the school should be capable of rational justification and the grounds for them should be available for pupils.

Pupils may reasonably expect the school to treat them impartially and equitably. The school should offer all its pupils open access to the knowledge, skills and talents of all its staff. It should deal with pupils as individuals rather than as types and should resist ascribing to them labels which appear to deny their worth or unfairly circumscribe their opportunities. The school should offer pupils impartial counsel on academic matters.

Pupils may reasonably expect to be treated with understanding and compassion. Pupils who live in homes or difficult environmental circumstances, or who suffer physical or mental disabilities which make it difficult for them to meet the demands which the school from time to time places on them, are entitled to special understanding and compassion from the school. Counsel with respect to personal problems should be readily available.

Parents also have claims upon the school. Parental claims arise in part from the legal duty which is laid upon them to ensure that a child of compulsory school age receives efficient full-time education 'suitable to his age, ability and aptitude, either by regular attendance at school, or otherwise' (Education Act, 1944, section 36). Because the obligation to ensure that children receive an adequate education is laid upon the parents they clearly have particularly strong entitlements with respect to their child's schooling.

Parents may reasonably expect to be informed and consulted on any decision which has a bearing upon their child's future career or educational opportunities, and particularly when decisions are made about which course options are to be taken up.

Parents may reasonably expect the school to show a degree of respect and understanding for those parental attitudes and values which relate to the upbringing of the child. This applies particularly to those problems which are linked to the education of their children. For example, parents may find a child growing away from them as a result of extended education and this can give rise to a real conflict between the values of family solidarity on the one hand and those of individual achievement on the other.

In short, parents may reasonably expect to be treated as partners in the education of their children and the school should do all in its power to explain and justify its educational policies to parents. We want to stress, however, that if the kind of pupil and parental involvement we have recommended is regarded by the school as a forced concession, it is unlikely to be profitable. For such involvement to be of real value, the teachers should see it as helping them make wiser judgments about what the school should provide, to whom, and in what form.

Society at large also has claims upon the school. If it is to provide resources sufficient to support an efficient system of education, it, in return, may reasonably expect the schools to equip their pupils to contribute to the community's economic well-being. Vocational education should not, however, be so narrow as to cast pupils in the role of mere instruments. On the contrary, the quality of their contribution to society's economic wellbeing will be improved if their initiative, rationality and discrimination are developed to the full. The problem is to find a rationale of secondary education which helps pupils make a contribution to the richness of life in our society as well as to its economic prosperity.

Society may reasonably expect that the schools will provide an education which sees today's child as tomorrow's parent and that it will offer the pupil a knowledge and understanding of what parenthood entails. The quality of the relationship which exists between the home and the school provides an important source of education for parenthood.

Society may reasonably expect that schools will help their pupils gain a general knowledge of the democratic process and a respect for the law, as well as an understanding of how to participate in political processes, to change the law and defend themselves from injustice. In pursuit of these twin objectives the school should help pupils, so far as it is within its power to do so, to realize in their individual lives the paradoxical combination of conviction and tolerance of others which is fundamental to democracy.

So far as we have spoken only of what pupils, parents and society may reasonably expect of the school. But our use of the term covenant to express the relationship between school and society implies that teachers are also partners to it and have their entitlements. These entitlements derive mainly from the responsibility which society places upon teachers to offer a worthwhile education to every child, no matter what his ability, disposition or background might be. In translating this responsibility into curriculum terms teachers in Britain have more independence than in almost any other country in the world. With this autonomy, however, goes a concept of professionalism which sees the teacher as not only having a high degree of competence in the classroom but as having responsibility for his own educational aims and methods and, increasingly, for those of the school as a whole. In discharging this responsibility a teacher has to act effectively and at the same time to acknowledge that there may be difficult conflicts of value between himself and his pupils, their parents and society at large. Moreover, the teacher is often expected to exercise judgment in matters where evidence is lacking or inconclusive, for example, over whether or not to stream pupils or how best to teach reading. However, it is in the exercise of judgment of this kind that the teacher's professionalism mainly resides.

The teacher also assumes a special role because of his continuing involvement in education. Pupils and parents come and go, and may only have a direct interest in formal education for a limited period of their lives. But the professional teacher is expected to develop a concern for the educational needs of children which survives frequent changes in clientele. If he is to meet this responsibility adequately and to develop the self-confidence which is essential to his effectiveness he is entitled to count upon the support and understanding of the other parties to the covenant.

What then are the reasonable entitlements of teachers? First, a society which demands that all children receive a worthwhile education must be prepared to will the means as well as the ends. As we contemplate the magnitude of the teachers' task, as it both exists at present and will grow in the future, we support their claims to greatly improved conditions of service, appreciable reductions in teacher-pupil ratios, more ancillary support, an increase of officially authorized time for purposes other than class-teaching, and greatly improved opportunities for in-service education. Secondly, teachers may reasonably expect that their professional training and experience will be taken into account when they offer advice to parents or pupils. Thirdly, all its teachers may reasonably expect to contribute to the development of a school's aims and policies, and to be closely involved in any decision-making which affects the content of what they teach or the methods by which it is to be taught.

The chief difficulty about the concept of the educational covenant is that the claims and obligations of its various parties are not easily reconcilable in practice and indeed may even be incompatible. There have been times when schools could count upon the support of society; they and those they served shared common educational and social ideals. Today, by contrast, only a few schools feel that their aims command ready acceptance. Indeed the concept of the covenant is, we believe, appropriate and necessary precisely because there is so little agreement in our society about what the aims of education should be. Paradoxically, conflict is often most marked among those who, in a general sense, believe that the schools should be guided by democratic principles. Egalitarians urge the schools to end all forms of discrimination based upon sex or ability and some have gone so far as to suggest that they should discriminate positively in favour of pupils who, for social or educational reasons, are prevented from realizing their full potential. Meritocrats, on the other hand, believe that pupils who are most able to derive benefit from education are the ones upon whom a proportionately larger share of educational resources should be expended. This conflict is highlighted by the issue of streaming. Manifestly pupils have dissimilar capabilities and motivation but this fact by itself does not suggest how best to classify them for the purposes of learning.

Schools are also expected to weld together in a single community pupils from widely differing cultural and social backgrounds. Differences of class, race and nationality may make for a rich cultural mix but they can also result in disruptive factionalism. How can schools respect cultural differences and at the same time avoid cultural dissonance? There is also a likelihood of conflict between the school's responsibility to provide an education which has intrinsic value and the demand of some pupils and parents for a primarily utilitarian education. The School Council's *Enquiry 1: Young School Leavers*[2] showed clearly how wide the gulf can be between the aims of teachers and the expectations of many pupils and their parents. How is the teacher to respond when his pupils ask: 'Why should we study subjects that will be of no use to us in our jobs?' or 'What's the good of education when teachers get less pay than many industrial workers?'

Attempts to bring the home and the school into closer co-operation are also surrounded by difficulties. Teachers, for example, want their pupils to attend school regularly. They want them to arrive at school punctually and to be refreshed in readiness for the day's work. Numbers of pupils, however, are not adequately cared for at home or have family responsibilities which make it difficult for them always to attend school or always to arrive on time. Some, far from having completed homework, may, as the result of too little sleep or insufficient nourishment, find it difficult even to begin the day's work. Nor is the lack always in the home. Pupils attending schools with a high staff turnover and shortened days, or working in classrooms where disorder is commonplace are unlikely to experience the continuity and stability which are essential to sustained learning.

Different conceptions of how the young should be brought up may also make it difficult for the school and the home to see eye to eye. A school which aims to bring its pupils steadily nearer independence may be expected by parents to keep them firmly under control. How is the parent whose authority is arbitrary or punitive to understand a school in which pupils are encouraged to behave rationally and responsibly? Conversely, how can a parent who treats his own children considerately persuade a school in which the views of pupils go unheeded that it should do the same?

Finally, how can teachers discharge the onerous custodial and disciplinary functions which compulsory schooling often forces upon them and at the same time encourage a respect for education as good in its own right?

Conflict, it should also be remembered, expresses itself as frequently between members of the same groups as it does between different groups. Parents seldom speak with a single voice on educational questions and the same is true of pupils and teachers. One parent will urge a teacher to give his offspring a good hiding if he steps out of line. Another will threaten with hideous retribution any teacher who so much as lays a finger upon a child of his! Some teachers will want the school to go all out for examination successes; others will see them as a defilement of all that is good in education. Every hue in the spectrum of educational ideologies can be found within the same staff room.

These and other conflicts among the parties to the educational covenant make it extremely difficult to achieve reconciliation. We believe, however, that the evidence of conflict strengthens rather than diminishes the need for the covenant. Where people share basic beliefs and standards their differences of view can be settled relatively easily. Where, by contrast, standards and beliefs are themselves in dispute the need for conciliation is the stronger.

The terms of the covenant we have outlined will not commend themselves to everyone as the right ones. But it is difficult to see how it would be possible to draw up a covenant to which all could assent unconditionally, or in every detail. British schools have for long been jealous of their independence in curricular matters. However much they may turn to outside bodies for resources, information and advice, they insist that the curriculum must be of their own making. We strongly affirm our support for this position for we believe the surest hope for the improvement of the secondary-school curriculum lies in the continuing professional growth of the teacher, which in turn implies that teachers take even greater responsibility for the development of schools' curriculum policies. Moreover, we have stressed the distinctive nature of the curriculum policies appropriate to particular schools and it would be a denial of this to attempt to prescribe the sort of policies they should adopt. When others come to consider the problem which led us to enunciate the principle of the covenant – the problem, that is, of defining the principles which should guide schools in the development of curriculum policies – they may well order and express differently the principles we have identified, but we think they are unlikely to deny their validity.

Note

1 The requirement in law that 'the school day ... shall begin with collective worship on the part of all pupils' (Education Act, 1944, 7 and 8 George VI, c. 31, s. 25 (i)) clearly raises a problem here. Much hangs upon what is made of the notion of worship and what it means to have a knowledge of religion.

References

1 *Choosing a Curriculum for the Young School Leaver* (Schools Council Working Paper 33). Evans/Methuen Educational, 1971, p26.

2 *Enquiry 1: Young School Leavers*: Report of an Enquiry carried out for the Schools Council by the Government Social Survey HMSO, 1968 (out of print).

2.2 The school and cultural development

Malcolm Skilbeck

In this paper I shall be discussing the conception of education known as reconstructionism. Many thinkers holding very different beliefs have entertained this conception, but what unites them is their acceptance that the school has a capacity to facilitate, promote and possibly guide certain forms of social change. It is more accurate to say cultural rather than social change, since the reconstructionists tend to take a comprehensive view of education, and to examine the ways in which it is influenced by and can influence those beliefs, values, attitudes, customs, skills, relationships and so forth for which the term culture is used. Throughout the paper I shall be referring mainly to cultural change, and using the term reconstructionists use to denote those thinkers and practitioners who subscribe to the view that the school can and should take an active part in assessing the worthwhileness of contemporary culture and promoting what it takes to be educationally desirable changes in that culture.

My purpose in discussing the reconstructionist conception of education is to consider how far and in what ways it makes sense to regard an educational system as a significant force for planned change in a particular society.

Periodically, in the history of western educational thought and institutions, groups of reformers have looked to the schools as principal agents of social and political change. At other times, the prevailing view has been that schools have a relatively limited role and they should concentrate their energies on performing this well. It is not necessary to illustrate the latter view as it is enshrined in the typical curriculum of our schools where the transmission of pre-established knowledge and skills is taken for granted. Examples of the former way of thinking include Plato's *Republic*, the view of education held by some of the early Christians, the plans in

Source: *The Northern Teacher*, Winter 1973.

France and America in the latter part of the eighteenth century for using schools as nation-builders, and, in the twentieth century, the widespread interest amongst the politicians and administrators of the new nations in education as a major facilitator of social development.

A closer inspection of those theories and movements in which education is conceived as one of the primary agencies of cultural development would show that they usually emerge in periods of upheaval or rapid change. The more limited view of the purpose and function of education characterises more stable situations. The culture development theories appear in countries or regions where there has been, or is impending, a political revolution, or they are systematically related by their authors to serious problems or deficiencies in the societies to which they refer. During the late nineteen-twenties and early thirties, in the USA, advocates of the movement in education which came to be known as social reconstructionism justified their radical educational policies by reference to the national economic crisis. In the developing countries the justification for using education as part of a planned policy of nation building is not dependent on crisis but rather on the supposed capacity of a certain type of educational system to develop skills and attitudes appropriate to a modernised culture.

Thus, we may find examples of the reconstructionist conception of education amongst established societies undergoing major upheaval or crisis, and amongst newly developing states. It is not the purpose of this paper to examine in detail the different forms taken by reconstructionist thinking in different social economic and political situations, but it is worth noting that these settings have been extremely diverse: reconstructionist thinking is to be found amongst democrats and totalitarians, Christians and atheists, rationalists and empiricists, conservatives and radicals. When the Napoleonic armies overran the German states, it was the idealist philosopher Fichte who, in his *Addresses to the German Nation*, proposed a far-reaching project of nation-building through a reformed education. In the Soviet Union during the nineteen-thirties, a quite different political system and philosophical approach provided the underpinning for no less determined attempts to relate education to nation-building. In the present day, practical illustrations of reconstructionism in and through education may be found in the democratic socialist republic of Tanzania, in Israel and in the modernisation programmes launched in Spain and in Portugal in 1969. Evidence of the wide variety of political systems where reconstructionist thinking is influencing education policies is provided by James Coleman in his *Education and Political Development*.

Rapid and extensive change in values, beliefs and techniques in a culture is, of course, not a new phenomenon; it is one of the declining characteristics of the western industrial state. However, rates of change vary in different societies, for example contemporary Spain and France. Rates of change also vary over what may be quite a short period of time; and there may be widely differing rates of change within particular subsections, such as the educational and the industrial systems. These differing rates of sub-sector change have given rise to the once popular theory of social lag, and to the still common criticism that schools do not adapt themselves rapidly enough to what is loosely called social change. This criticism is a peculiar one in that it is often stated in such a way as to suggest that schools are not really part of society – that society exists 'out there' and schools are over here and something different. The school is a social institution as real as any other, schooling is one social process amongst many others, and there can be no question of schools adjusting themselves to or fitting into society but only of their adjusting and otherwise relating themselves to (and being adjusted and related to) *other* social institutions.

This point is an important one since it affects both our understanding of the school's role and our response to the various demands made on schooling, such as the demand that schooling should be more 'socially relevant'. In answer to this demand we need to know to which other institution and processes schooling is supposed to be made relevant and for what purpose.

The demand for relevance helps to bring out the basic strategies which, it might be supposed, schools can adopt in relation to total cultural change. There are four of these hypothetical strategies. First, schools may swim with the tide by identifying basic trends and going with rather than resisting them. Secondly, schools may identify particular elements in the past, and seek to preserve them. Thirdly, schools may carry on their work largely ignorant of or indifferent to what is happening in other key sectors of the culture. Fourthly, schools may look forward, trying to anticipate situations in the future, assessing them for their educational significance, and influencing them through the various limited means at their disposal.

There are, of course, variations in the refinements of these four strategies and I do not want to suggest that every aspect of a school's work could be examined systematically by reference to one or other of them. Nevertheless, by considering them in turn we may be in a better position to understand many of the functions performed by the schools in our midst.

Swimming with the tide is apparently what is envisaged by the advocates of relevance and adjustment. It is a strategy that has the merit of encouraging teachers to find out more about what is happening in their society and ways in which their pupils are responding to the social situation in which they find themselves. There is clearly a sense in which teaching is futile unless its content and methodology reflect these concerns. However, a modern society is highly complex and, if it is a democracy, its values, beliefs and life patterns will be varied and conflicting. Is the school to align itself simply with what presents itself with most clamour and urgency? Even if the school were thought of as an institution whose purpose is to induct the young into the culture, irrespective of consideration of the values of that culture, the task remains of identifying and selecting those parts of the culture which a single institution – the school and a single process, education – could reasonably undertake. Clearly, criteria and objectives are needed. Granted that individual teachers may not spend a lot of time reflecting on these it is nevertheless important that there should be some in the educational system who are doing so. 'Swimming with the tide' only makes educational sense if some educationists are assessing and helping to direct the movements of the tide.

The second strategy, that of selecting elements from the past and seeking to preserve them, does at least recognise that no single social institution, such as a school, can undertake to transmit to the young all that is available for transmission in a culture. Selection and preservation imply criteria and an educative intent. Whose criteria and whose intentions are to prevail? By its nature, preservationism tends to be teacher and parent centred: the teacher decides, the parent influences. What is absent is the expressed interest of the pupils and of groups other than those professionally engaged in education, except insofar as they form themselves into educational pressure groups. Thus, the culture that is selected for transmission may be very distasteful to the young who have to be persuaded, for example by the very workings of the selective system, that it is 'good' for them. It is not surprising that the extrinsic motivations of public examinations should be so powerful in selective secondary schools.

A further point about the preservationist strategy is that it very easily lapses into an intransigence in the face of possibilities different from those which have formed the experience of the conservers. The most striking examples of this intransigence are to be found in secondary education where institutions and their curricula are sanctified because they have proved valuable in serving and sustaining the interests of particular groups. I refer, of course, to selective secondary schools whose functionality in preserving the class interest of those who exercise political and social power in this community and a certain view of the academic life which has been fostered by particular universities, is beyond dispute. The strategy of selected preservation from the past is fundamentally backward looking and uncritical. It tends to ignore emerging experience from other institutions and societies, and adopts and accepts a fixed stand towards matters which should be considered open, viz., the social purposes of education, the interests to be satisfied by educational institutions and processes, and the future which people wish to make for themselves. Of course, it does not follow from treating these issues as open that another type of institution should simply replace selective secondary schools. An experimental approach to this question is vitally important; I only wish at this juncture to draw attention to some of the consequences of adopting a preservationist strategy.

The third possibility which is open to schools in the face of a rapidly changing culture is to carry on their particular pursuits ignorant of or indifferent to these changes. This barely counts as a strategy since it is little more than a policy of inward-looking drift. It has resemblances to the first approach I discussed, namely going with the tide, but it differs in being less self-conscious and in that the designs to which it gives rise are less elaborate and sophisticated. It has resemblances also to the preservationist strategy in that the effect of drift in schooling is to make no mark on and hence to maintain unscathed those forces and interests which are uppermost in the culture.

As the American educational theorist and philosopher, John Dewey, long ago pointed out, a policy of social drift is no educational policy at all. It may emerge as a result of neglect or apathy, which unfortunately not all schools are free from. One way of overcoming the staleness and mindless conservatism that result when schools refuse to examine, reflect upon and appraise the societies in which they are functioning is to introduce a universal programme of inservice education. Apathy and narrowness are natural consequences of isolation and neglect. The teacher who is left alone to 'get on with it' can all too easily continue throughout his career to reproduce the attitudes, techniques and information with which he himself was imbued as a student. By far the most potent and exciting possibility in the James Report and the White Paper is the commitment to universal, life-long inservice education of teachers. Whether the potentiality of this measure is realised in practice depends on the nature of studies teachers undertake, hence the importance of building up strategies of inservice education which will be not only acceptable and meaningful to teachers but will also challenge their settled assumptions and provide them with new perceptions of what is educationally possible and desirable in the future.

The fourth strategy available to schools in the face of a rapidly changing culture to whose needs they are expected to respond, looks to the future. This strategy requires schools to relate their activities essentially to three things. First, schools need a set of educational criteria, possibly in the form of objectives, which have been worked through by the school staff and others who can reasonably claim to have a stake in the process. Secondly, the schools need to have formed a clear understanding of the effects of what they have done in the past. Thirdly, the schools need to look ahead, anticipating the effects of present trends in culture and relating all of their work explicitly to the assessments they are able to make.

This fourth strategy is essentially that of the reconstructionists, though it takes very different forms in different societies. For example, in totalitarian societies schools have objectives given to them and these objectives are uniform and homogeneous. In the British tradition it is open to the schools to define their own objectives – not in isolation, nor with complete freedom, but with a very wide scope for choice of direction and emphasis.

It may seem odd that one should have to offer reasons favouring a strategy of intelligent analysis, appraisal and forecasting for an educational institution. In so far as these activities of analysis, criticism, anticipation and so forth are all constituents of a rational approach to problem-solving we would expect them to be conspicuous in those institutions in society which have a fundamental and primary educative interest. The process of education is not limited to rational reflection, yet rationality, both as intention of the educator and as a basic condition of the methods and materials he uses, is what distinguishes education from all other forms of guidance, direction and influence.

Schooling and education are, however, often two rather different processes. Schools have education as one of their purposes. This is not their only purpose, nor are they always in a condition to carry out this purpose effectively: providing the conditions for an education are no less important than having a clear conception of the process. Teachers in schools are very well aware of constraints and deficiencies which limit the achievement of desirable educational results. These negative factors are not only objective so far as the teacher is concerned, that is they do not result only from the material limitations, the unsatisfactory work conditions, the reluctance of children to undertake educative activities and so forth. The teacher needs to ask himself whether his own perception of the task suffers from a cramped experience, a refusal to reflect on possibilities and a preference for easy solutions and procedures.

It must be admitted that to expect schools to undertake as complex and arduous a task as analysing the culture and projecting trends and defining educational roles in relation to those trends is unrealistic in the present situation. Apart from the negative factors I have just mentioned, schools have been designed and equipped and their work has been approved, in the light of very limited assumptions and expectations. Were schools to become the kind of nerve centres of an emerging culture that reconstructionists like H. G. Wells in England and H. Rugg and T. Brameld in America envisaged they would have to become very different and they would have to seek social acceptance as different kinds of institutions from what most of them are at present.

It might be concluded, then, from this brief review of strategies, that only the second, conservationism, and the fourth, reconstructionism, will withstand close scrutiny. Reconstructionism is open to the criticism that it makes more substantial demands on schools and teachers than they are equipped to meet. There are other objections, or at least difficulties, which it is not immediately relevant to enter into. For example, the authority of the school, as one social institution and the teachers, as one professional group, to seek to modify the directions of cultural development is by no means clear in a pluralistic society. Another point to bear in mind is the risk of indoctrination where global and holistic approaches to education are being recommended. These difficulties notwithstanding the reconstructionist strategy appears to me to be the most fruitful one can explore, in considering the relationships schools and teachers might develop with their surrounding culture.

No one is in a position to make accurate prognostications of the future main lines of cultural development. The philosopher Karl Popper has demonstrated this in a way which is important to students of cultural processes. He has argued that in modern industrialised society, one of the principal forces influencing all facets of life is knowledge itself. Fresh discoveries through research are characteristic of the growth of knowledge, thus knowledge cannot forecast its own future and as a consequence societies cannot accurately forecast their future. The importance of this argument for my purpose is that it encourages a more tentative and speculative approach to future planning, not that it rules out attempts to anticipate. Popper himself has contributed, both conceptually and empirically, to the advancement of social self knowledge. It is this kind of knowledge that a strategy of educational renewal needs. The focus of this knowledge is contemporary culture, as this is exhibited in the various cultural domains: the arts, sciences, social sciences, the polity, the economy, morals, belief systems, the principal social institutions and the forms of everyday experience.

Except for the last one mentioned, these cultural domains are sometimes treated as remote from the lives of children and their subjective experience. Hence schools, seeking a more relevant curriculum, may be inclined to focus too narrowly on those concerns which are frequently found in courses built on pupil interest, on vocational aspirations, and on local and environmental studies. These approaches may be termed the temptation of subjective experience. More traditional approaches, through the academic disciplines of knowledge, while more objective and fundamental, are by no means the best way of directing the energies of pupils and teachers towards the problems of their present world and of the future. They may be termed the temptation of academic respectability.

In the final section of this paper, I want to raise some of the issues which seem to me central in considering ways in which schools might contribute towards desirable modifications and developments of culture. There are three main aspects of schooling which it is important to consider: the curriculum, internal school organisation, and styles of teaching and learning. All three are crucial but it would unduly entend this paper if I discussed them all, so I shall consider just the first, the curriculum.

Through the curriculum, a map or chart of actual and potential experience is presented to the pupil. Typically, the experience with which he is confronted is structured according to the symbols – and the customs – of the discrete disciplines of knowledge: physical science, history, language, mathematics and so forth. These disciplines have developed and consolidated over time and they express a partial, precise and adult view of aspects of reality. The pupil, by various means, is aided and encouraged to partake of the modes of thought and the conceptual systems which these disciplines have generated and by which they maintain their vitality. The disciplines of knowledge, or indeed any item of activity which it is proposed to include in the curriculum, must be so arranged and presented as to connect with the child's experience, if he is to learn anything. Hence the disciplines are a resource, to be drawn upon, together with other resources, in the construction of school curricula.

How the disciplines and other cultural modes are drawn upon and organized for use in schools is the most fundamental question in curriculum design. Whether these intellectual resources for learning are to have certain effects on the child's perception of this social world and his attitude towards his own and others' roles in that social world depends on the purpose for which curriculum content is selected and the use made of it. For example, history, geography, politics, sociology and morality may be presented as problematic, controversial and many-sided, or as so much settled knowledge to be learnt and reproduced according to the conventions of the essay or the examination paper. A curriculum plan in a school can aim to foster critical, reflective thinking; it can stimulate and provide the opportunities for participation in practical projects by which the community betters itself; and it can encourage pupils to see themselves as the organisers of their own experiences and of their own society. Conversely, a curriculum plan very often in fact produces acquiescent, docile and socially uninvolved people.

A cynic, looking to the future, may well seek to maintain the traditional split, in education, between the creative, responsible, reflective minority, and a majority of followers. Curriculum policy makers, teachers, and all who have an interest in education and in the well-being of the community have a responsibility in actively contributing towards the formation of culture. This is not a task for schools alone, nor is it one which schools should neglect. A radical appraisal of the school curriculum is needed, to see how far in intention or actuality it is fostering the values and understandings of a just and creative society.

Of course, reappraisal of the curriculum is an ongoing task. But we need to ask whether this task is being carried on with the determination and vigour that are needed if schools are to have an effect. The countervailing forces are very powerful. Studies of attitude formation, political values, prejudice, culture participation and the distribution of economic opportunity suggest that the early formative experiences in the home and the neighbourhood, together with the socio-economic background and educational attainments of parents, have a decisive influence which the school can scarcely match. This influence is reinforced in later childhood and adolescence by the effects of television, popular journalism, the leisure industry and, in later years by the work environment.

It does not follow from these studies that schools are helpless or that it is a waste of time to seek through the curriculum to widen understanding and to develop tolerance, sympathy and other virtues of communal life. Rather, the effectiveness of extra school agencies, and the limited achievement of many of the aims earlier generations of educational reformers have held out indicates that different strategies are required. It is not surprising that political and social attitudes seem relatively unaffected by schooling when the schools have not set out resolutely and operationally to modify attitudes, nor that other forces in society exert greater influence when, in so many instances, schools have not sought to understand or to utilise these other forces: television is a notable example of this.

The study and appraisal of contemporary culture, its principal modes and manifestations, its tendencies and possibilities, is a more appropriate curriculum target for schools which wish to prepare children for future living than the snippets and fragments, mostly of a second-hand factual type, which still commonly feature especially in secondary education. This means that teachers require more sociology, social psychology, politics, economics, environmental science, contemporary history and more experience of problem-solving, critical enquiry and creative activity in their training. It may be that these are what could be most appropriately examined in inservice courses of a type where teachers are encouraged to examine their own teaching, to redesign curricula and to relate their work to the systematic analysis of contemporary cultural movements. In these courses, it will be no less important for teachers to come to view themselves as agents of change and renewal and not as transmitters of settled or slowly changing bodies of knowledge. This is a role from which some teachers may shrink, because of the demands it makes. Yet, unless teachers can learn to adopt this role and to take up the challenges that go with it the effectiveness of the school as a means of educating the community will rapidly diminish as other and more persuasive forces take over.

2.3 Teaching with the urban environment

Eric Midwinter

The child: the significance of his environment

The Malayan rubber plantation syndrome: a case history

A social environment course for teachers was once begun by asking them to inspect and then comment on a well-constructed model of a Malayan rubber plantation. They examined it very critically, lifting up the huts and looking closely at the sap cups on the trees. They admired it technically noting, presumably for future reference, tips about how this or that piece of material was utilized. Not one asked why it had been done. Not one said that this was a travesty, albeit a rhapsodic travesty, of the rubber trade, failing as it did to depict the nastiness of exploitation, colonialism, racialism or whatever. No one said that the primary child's (perhaps even the teacher's) conceptual development was inadequate to cope with the validity of the rubber plantation, hence its unconsciously dishonest reduction to a level comprehensible to the child. No one pointed out that the art and craft work was essentially third-hand, so remote was it from the experience of the child or indeed from that of anyone in contact with the child.

In short, there was a concentration on the method. Over the last score or so years, there has been a remarkable and welcome change in method, but unluckily some educationists have seen this as a fundamental revolution. It is far from being this. Indeed, the wondrous attractions of new methods have sometimes hidden the sterility of the old content on which they've been practised. What was rubbish when rote-learnt still remains rubbish when 'discovered'. If 'doing' Richard the Lionheart is a relative waste of time, no amount of ribboning, scissoring and mounting of assaults on the colour supplements will save it. Where once children copied it down from the blackboard into their books, they now copy it out of other

Source: Eric Midwinter, (1972) *Social Environment and the Urban School*, Ward Lock Educational 10–14, 16–19.

books into their books. But unless the substance is different, it is much the same exercise. Arrant nonsense on a stencilled handout remains arrant nonsense despite its transfer to a tape recorder.

College history tutors can always do a bit of magic with students preparing for school practice. 'I'm doing the manor', says the student. 'Ah', says the tutor airily, 'you have an eight-plus class' – simply because the historical eras can be neatly geared to the junior school chronology. Ancient Britons and Anglo-Saxons in the first year; monks and manors in the second; Tudors and Stuarts in the third; and other denominations in the fourth, to say nothing of another whirl around the mulberry bush in the secondary school. This cannot be right. It must make one of two cardinal errors. The topic must either be done properly and correctly, in which case the child couldn't understand; or, as usually happens, it must be done via stories at the child-level. This has produced a nation with a seven year old view of the Anglo-Saxons. An HMI once tidily completed the argument by suggesting that we did the Anglo-Saxons first because theirs was a simpler society to understand. There have been few less complex societies. It had of course been oversimplified, i.e. falsified, for his childlike delectation.

This cannot be altered by making it 'social' rather than 'political', along the lines of Egbert the swinherd's son or Tobias, the boy who knew St Paul. Nor can it be justified, as it so often is, in terms of 'interest'. 'Interest' is about method; while agreeing wholeheartedly that a child must be interested to be educated, the reverse is not true, otherwise a diet of television serials might suffice. It is equally the teacher's function, not only to opt easily for what is evidently interesting, but to make professional judgments about what is valuable, and then by shrewd deployment of methodology to make it interesting and tempting.

Unlike other areas, such as maths or reading, the teacher's traditional wisdom seems awry in the humanities, where the pupil is force-fed huge chunks of indigestible and often worthless knowledge. It is rarely developmental, as we offer our massive helpings of Masai tribesmen, Good Samaritans and Francis Drakes. It is the equivalent of starting the infant reception class reading with *Pickwick Papers* or first year juniors with quadratic equations. In social studies or humanities, as in other fields, the children need to develop awareness and sensitivity in the temporal, spatial, moral and spiritual, scientific and logico-rational aspects of their life.

A checklist of five criteria

In presenting the urban child with work in the social environment, five criteria must be satisfied as perfectly as possible.

1 Is it understandable?

Is the work too far removed in time or space or whatever other concept for children to understand, with the result that it is simplified to the point of distortion?

2 Is it useful?

Will the children benefit in knowledge or have their development nurtured by the work, or is it so distant from their experience as to be superfluous?

3 Is it interesting?

It is the teacher's task to make the work interesting, once it has been decided that the work is valuable.

4 Is it first-hand?

Even when the activity is practical and craft-like, it can still be faulted. In the classic lesson of the teacher telling the tale of the monks or the Masai tribe and the children drawing a picture or making a model, the felony is compounded. The art is just as second-hand as the history or geography.

5 Is it developmental?

Does the work sharpen the children's awareness of the social environment, as opposed to merely presenting them with chunks of indigestible information.?

Familiarity breeds response

All this is desperately important because empirically one sees (and not only in downtown areas) many people with social troubles. Many people are faced with myriad social difficulties of all kinds with only the ability to recite *Cargoes* or to catalogue the symptoms of the Black Death as their educational stock-in-trade. Thousands of our children are living in our town centres and in our municipal redevelopment estates. Some will be educated to the standard where they can legitimately and fairly expect to move to more salubrious and affluent surroundings. Some educationists seem to think that all our education should be directed to this Laramie-like policy of 'git 'em up an' move 'em out'. Unhappily, the city centres and corporation estates are not going to be depopulated. We must prepare our children not only for the life that they would like to lead but for the life that they are likely to lead. Thousands of children will continue to live in these kinds of urban conditions; soon they will be citizens and parents in these areas. Will they have been any better equipped than their parents to handle the day to day pressures of the life-issues that inevitably face them?

The teacher's task should be to acquaint these children as profoundly as possible with the context in which they live. From this they might just reach out past a resigned acceptance of their lot, or a crude, negative reaction against it, to a clear articulation of their needs and to positive responses to those needs. Eventually, a community must save itself, and education could be one of the keys to the necessary self-awareness on which reconstruction might be built. We must (to exchange an old for a new cliché) not so much move from the known to the unknown, as make the known more knowable. The emphasis is on the 'now', on bringing in the new and the external to illuminate the immediacy of the child, rather than constantly reaching out for the new and the distant which is often completely alien to the child's reality.

The urban curriculum

Three more points must be made. First, this is not (as has been complained) inward-looking, designed to nurture a ghetto mentality, or a soporific to stop the peasants from being revolting. It is an attempt to open the eyes of urban children dynamically and critically to the locality as a secure base for educational advance. It means a curriculum more social and less academic than hitherto but, by the same token, it need be no less creatively and intellectually exhilarating. Teachers talk of *widening* horizons when, by zooming off via telly, coach or book to New Zealand, the Holy Land or the countryside, they are frequently exchanging horizons and running the risk of producing social schizophrenics. Because of the ostensible drabness of the city environment, well-intentioned teachers have indulged in escapism, either be creating a culturally alien air-raid shelter in the classroom or by passionately pursuing the arcadian idyll of rurality for an hour or two – unfortunately, as many a battery hen could testify, this is now an empty dream of yesteryear. Rather should we begin by helping children to face up to their own reality competently and imaginatively, looking for the stimuli in the rich potential of the urban culture.

Second, a community-oriented or environmentally-based curriculum is more likely to engage the involvement of parents and other members of the community. So much is now known of the imbalance of home and school in socially different areas that it becomes imperative to take a step or two toward the parents. Many didn't get much out of school when they were there and now, with the added mumbo jumbo of i.t.a., modern maths and so on, it must look desperate to them. If we believe in the need for a harmony of interest between school and home, and thus a stable balance of support for the child between school and home, then it is urgently necessary to harmonize the cultural content and values between them, and these are at their most crucial in curricular terms.

Third, with a reappraised curriculum, it is sometimes argued that the slender minority who at the moment do manage to scramble out and head for the white picket fences of suburbia might take a tumble. Briefly, it is equally arguable that by rooting the work of children in what is real and immediate, traditional attainment norms like reading and writing are unlikely to decline and conceivably could rise.

These three points seem particularly firm subsidiary reasons for the emphatic inclusion and sophistication of social environmental study as the principal element in the junior school. But there is yet another more delicate issue. Much of what has been said is, in portion, accomplished by many teachers who colourfully and vitally use local pointers as guide-lines for their work. Indeed, the only major innovation suggested so far is in the scale of the enterprise which bids for a large share of the syllabus. The investigation of the urban environment requires, of course, to be tolerant and open-minded. It necessitates that very dangerous examination of varying values, standards and codes of conduct. Teachers have traditionally been seen as the guardians of the status quo, the planks of the establishment and high sounding cultural and other virtues. Occasionally there may be a teacher who in school hours fights to the death for British law and order and the virtues of saving, before speeding home at fifty through a built-up area to fill in his football pool, or who preaches Tennyson by day and watches *Coronation Street* by night. Most, none the less, would probably feel that they had certain set patterns of behaviour and beliefs which they should communicate to children for the children's own good. It is difficult to spot which of these have controversial aspects; it is difficult to replace them with the creation of an outstandingly high standard in the nobility of open-endedness. It is perhaps unfair to ask teachers, given their background of upbringing and training, to take on this function of equipping the parents and citizens of the future with well-defined powers of social criticism and action. But this is possibly the largest blank in the picture of environmental teaching at the moment. For example, teachers in urban areas who continue to teach about avuncular policemen under the heading of 'people who help us' are doing no kindness to the children, the police or themselves. It is as unfair to the policeman as anyone to dress him in this sentimental image.

This, in broad outline, is the significance of the urban environment in the education of the child. No apology is made for pitching it at a sort of philosophic level which may seem to lack those practicial tit-bits teachers adore. There must be social purpose and overall social goals in our teaching. Whatever the pseudo-realist, nursing his mug of tea in the staffroom easy chair, may say about airy-fairy (that favourite adjective) nonsense and getting your feet on the ground, there is nothing so far from down to earth, nothing so unpractical and unrealistic and unprofessional, as teaching without an aim and a vision. Some will say this is an alarming, risky prospect for the teachers. With these we sympathize; you have understood and you are correct. Others will say 'We've been doing this for years'; to these I say: 'Look out of the window; why is it still like that if you have been producing positive, radical actionists for so long?'

Eric Midwinter

The child: his concept of the social environment

Understanding the town

How much of the town or city is incomprehensibe to the urban child?

In recent years we have learned a great deal about conceptual development in the child. We know (from the work of Piaget) about the growth of understanding. But understanding of what? – speed, weight, volume, space, time, density, cause, effect, geometry, distance, velocity and number. We know that every one of these concepts is built up slowly and laboriously. Take the concept of time for example. Primitive man uses phrases like 'three more sleeps'. The egocentric child talks about playtime, bedtime, home-time. In one piece of research by Sturt and Oakden children were asked 'What day of the week is it?' Having given the right answer they were then asked 'What day of the week is it in another town?', which one-third of them were unable to answer.

But what of more difficult or less relevant concepts? What about patriotism or race or tolerance or 'your neighbour', or the unification of Italy, or the economic growth of Brazil, or the conversion of French francs into pounds and new pence? Much of our thinking about concept development has been specialized enquiry into mathematical and scientific intellectual abstractions. It is perhaps time we knew a little more about social and human concepts.

In fact we do know a little bit about some of the more human concepts which might influence the growth of the child. We know, for example, that he is slowly accumulating an image of himself. We know that he needs reassurance. Piaget has shown us that the child gains in reciprocity in a complex way. He slowly learns how many other people there are in his family. He slowly learns how to sympathize with other people. He slowly learns how to take another child's point of view. He learns how to distinguish between humans and animals. The confusion which precedes this kind of social maturity is often very great. How do children develop knowledge of rules and justice? How do they learn what proper behaviour is? Piaget has described how rules in the game of marbles developed, how the children proceed from expiation and vindictiveness – a sort of an eye for an eye philosophy – to a stage of forgiveness and understanding and a recognition of equality. How does the city child play the game? How does the city child behave when he loses? It's not always a question of not playing to win, or playing for the sake of the game, or losing graciously, or keeping a stiff upper lip, or being generous in defeat.

Let's consider some of the moral and spiritual concepts which might be developed by the child in the town or city. What does the child understand by cheating? What are the norms of the street? What is the difference between them and us? What does the child really know of the values which are placed before him by many of our colleagues? What does he understand by thrift or industry or punctuality or honesty? What does he learn about right or wrong in his home? Wrong is what is punished and when his mum says 'Shut up or I'll hit you.' We know too, particularly through the work of Basil Bernstein, that language is of crucial importance in the development of the city child. We know that words are understood precariously. They are frequently a smoke screen camouflaging ignorance and the language used by the urban child may be more restricted than it is liberating.

There are so many illustrations of how easily the teacher or other adults can mistake a child's conceptual grasp. The conventions of our society are frequently intellectual fabrications relating to the prevailing social climate. These adult notions are not so natural nor so organic that they occur spontaneously in a child. For example, many authorities are worried about vandalism. How many children in our city centres have watched hundreds of homes (possibly including their own) demolished and swept away by men well-equipped with machines? The subtle distinction between large scale legal and small scale illegal destruction is not always an easy one for a child to grasp. But perhaps the best instance is to recall how many howlers crop up in the 'social' subjects like history, geography and religious education. Children 'learn' bits and pieces of information for which they do not have a conceptual structure and they attach these to their own most approximate item of reality. Hence the difficulties over guerilla warfare, the Diet of Worms or, in the child's illustration of *Silent Night, Holy Night*, a jolly fat man in a brown jerkin sitting comfortably in the nativity stable; on questioning, the child said it was 'Round John Virgin'.

Some pointers might be mentioned as a guide to the sort of skills or faculties that need to be strengthened so that children might better understand their social environment. Children need to learn to place facts or events in time and space and to put them into context and perspective. They need to be able to work out the logic of cause and effect sequences, so that they can read in explanations and anticipations. They need to assess facts, not only in terms of accuracy, but in terms of their relationship one to the other, their relevance and their value. They need to develop their ability to express and communicate with regard to social materials. These are some of the main conceptual skills that need experience and exercise.

Anthropology at home

One of the depressing features of modern social life is the vast differences in the environment and experience of our children. Under a mantle of anthropology we find it easy to appreciate cultural relativity. We know that

Aboriginals south of Darwin are very good at rubbing sticks together and making fire. We know that Eskimos in the Arctic are extremely competent and understand the properties of snow; if they don't their houses drip on their head. We know that Bantus in Africa have highly sophisticated ways of categorizing and recording and tallying cattle. These different kinds of expertise and behaviour are different because they are determined by the needs of the environment. Aboriginals, Eskimos and Bantus are different because they adapt to different circumstances. What is less apparent is the subcultural relativity which exists in our own society. One trouble with educationists today is that they haven't studied the environment in which they work thoroughly enough. We know more about New Guinea and Samoa then we know about the East End of London. Margaret Mead has suggested that 'If fish were to explore their environment the last thing they would discover would be water.' Our society teems with dualisms and contrasts – the sheep and goats, the haves and have nots, class differences, middle versus working, regional differences, towns versus country. There are also economic differences between rich and poor, sex differences, family size differences and so on.

Our literary heritage also teems with examples, such as *Two Nations, North and South, Culture and Anarchy*. At these extremes there are two nations and two cultures. Perhaps slum and suburb would be a better contrast, since 90 per cent of our children live within built-up conurbations. In fact there will be many different environments to which urban children will be exposed. Because human development is a slow, building up process of increasing complexity, which operates in response to widely different environmental stimuli, children's concepts of the town will vary enormously. The child will relate to what is relevant to him. His growth will depend on *his* conceptual development of *his* city, street, gang, environment. He will be bombarded in school perhaps by new concepts which are foreign, remote, bizarre, irrelevant and unrealistic in terms of his background. He will reject these or distort them into some more palatable form. This is precisely the fate of masses of scholastic information, standards and ideals presented to city children in our schools.

The law of the asphalt jungle or the urban desert is adapt or die – survival of the fittest. By fittest is meant those best equipped to adapt to the environment in which *they* live, i.e. the conurbation.

2.4 A proposal for education in community

Fred M. Newmann and Donald W. Oliver

Since we believe that efforts at reform have generally failed to consider the fundamental importance of *contexts* in which education is pursued, we begin by conceptualizing alternative modes of, and environments for, learning. Imagine a hypothetical community in which learning is pursued in three quite different contexts: the 'school' context, the 'laboratory-studio-work' context, and the 'community seminar' context. Subjects or problems for study and also the relations between students and teachers would be construed quite differently in each of these contexts.

The school context

There is a clear need for systematic instruction in basic literacy skills, health and hygiene, driver education, and the like. Learning of this sort is pre-planned, programmed, and formalized. The teacher has clear objectives or 'terminal behaviours' in mind as the products of instruction. Most of the activity in schools as we now know them falls in this category. This is not to suggest that school-based learning should continue to follow traditional subject matter lines, nor that instruction be didactic and rote. On the contrary, school learning should be problem-centred and exciting and should constantly consider reorganizing basic content to make it lead toward more powerful insights and understandings; for example, coordinate and symbol systems used in graphs, charts and maps, might be combined with linguistic analysis and musical notation in teaching a course in symbolics. Technology has thrust upon us rich possibilities for more effective instruction through (a) greater opportunity for self-instruction, (b) availability of multi-media approaches, and (c) more accurate assessment of student needs and progress. Teaching within a school context may take many forms: tutorial between teacher and student, student with computer or programmed instruction, students in small groups, or large groups

Source: *Harvard Educational Review* (1967), 37 (1) pp 95–104.

watching films. The distinguishing feature of the school context is that it concerns itself only with those aspects of education involving systematic, planned instruction. It should be clear from the explanation of the following two contexts that we see this kind of learning as only *one* among three critical types.

Laboratory-studio-work context

In the laboratory context, the major objective is not formal instruction, but the completion of a significant task, the solution of problems which the learner wants to attack, regardless of educational by-products that dealing with the problem might bring. The physical location of the laboratory context might be a factory, art studio, hospital, library, science or industrial laboratory, political party headquarters, or government agency. The activity of participants would be governed, not by a skill or a product that is programmed for students to learn, but only by the developing nature of the problem-task itself. Such problems might include painting a picture, rebuilding a car, writing an essay, promoting a concert, organizing a protest demonstration, lobbying for legislation, selling insurance, programming a computer, acting in a play, nursing in a hospital, competing in a sport, participating in conservation and wildlife management, caring for children, planning and participating in a church service, broadcasting on radio and television, making a dress, printing a newspaper, making physical and chemical experiments, serving as a guide at the UN, organizing a raffle to raise money, or even creating instructional materials for use in a school context. Laboratories are contexts for learning in the midst of action; learning occurs not because it is planned, but only as an inevitable by-product of genuine participation in problem- and task-oriented activities. The laboratory is seen not primarily as apprenticeship or vocational training for breadwinning, but rather as the opportunity to satisfy broader humanistic and aesthetic goals. At present many adults are engaged in laboratory contexts – that is, their jobs – which are not recognized or supported for their educational value. Young people are deemed not 'ready' to participate until they first spend twelve to sixteen years in 'school.' We believe the laboratory offers important educational benefits at all ages; it should not be restricted to adults.

Community seminar context

The purpose of the seminar would be the reflective exploration of community issues and ultimate meanings in human experience. The seminar would provide an opportunity for the gathering of heterogeneous or homogeneous groups, for youth and/or adults, to examine and discuss issues of mutual concern. Seminars might begin by focusing on problems specific to members of the group (e.g., the meaning of productive work for people unemployed, retired, or dissatisfied with their jobs). Discussion might be stimulated by outside provocateurs who present new ways of viewing economic, ethical, or aesthetic questions. Seminars could have at their service a qualified resource staff that would gather information (readings, films, TV programmes) and make arrangements for experiences, such as field trips, to observe unfamiliar ways of life, technological innovations, social problems in action. In addition to relatively specific problems (What kinds of working conditions are we entitled to?) and general public policy questions (How should the community be zoned?), we would hope that the seminars would concern themselves with the broadest questions raised in planning for education in community. Other possible topics include: understanding various conflicts between youth and adults, the functions of the family in modern society, attitudes toward nonconformity and deviance in the community, prejudice and pluralism among ethnic groups, changing mores in sex and religion, various approaches to child-rearing, the use of increased leisure, population control, protection of the consumer, moral implications of advances in biology (e.g., selective breeding), reconstruction of the political and legal system, evaluation of current programmes sponsored by government and private agencies, creation of new professions and problems of vocational retraining. The major thrust of the seminars would be reflection and deliberation, though the questions discussed would be highly relevant to the laboratory context or the world of 'action'. Learning in the seminar would not be pre-planned, nor would there be specific tasks or problems to solve. Questions would be raised, investigated, and discussed – this process, regardless of numerous and unpredictable possible outcomes, is of high educational value. Generally both youths and adults are denied the kind of learning afforded by this context; the time of youth is monopolized by school, and that of adults by jobs or 'laboratories'.

Points of clarification

The contexts described above are intended to convey the major point that education consists of three important facets: systematic instruction, action, and reflection. The facets are not listed in order of importance, nor chronologically. All three should occur concurrently at all stages of life. A child learning how to read in a school context can participate in a laboratory project of building a model airplane (using the symbolic skills acquired in 'school'); he can also discuss with children and adults in a seminar what to do about noise control for the local airport. An adult interested in politics might study government systematically in school; he might participate in the 'laboratory' of a political campaign; and in the community seminar, he might lead discussions on political organization appropriate for the modern community. While some communities may choose to place most young children in the school context and allocate much of adult education to the seminar, we see no logical reason for this particular arrangement. Our scheme allows for various mixtures of the three components to be tailored to the needs of various stages of life or to the unique requirements of different types of communities.

Who would fill the leadership roles in such an educational scheme? If formal school comprises only one-third of the educational programme, will professional educators be put out of work? Possibly, but not necessarily. Those most qualified to carry on instruction may well be teachers and educators currently working in schools. Thus many teachers and adminstrators would stay in schools (although advances in technology suggest radical changes in their roles and jobs even if they do stay there). Since learning in school would occupy only a small portion of the student's day – perhaps three hours – one might expect school staffs to dwindle. If, however, adults also used the school for instruction, then the school's student population would increase, even though any given student spent only a small amount of time there. The demand for professional educators would remain high.

Leaders in the laboratory contexts would be experienced persons in the various laboratory areas (engineers, lawyers, mechanics, poets, politicians, athletes, secretaries) who would be given released time to take on educational responsibility for youths and adults interested in laboratory activity. It is possible that professional educationists can be converted into laboratory leaders; for example, an English teacher could take on apprentices in the writing of poetry, but in his laboratory role, he would be interested primarily in the creation and analysis of artistic works, not in teaching. The laboratory context would rely primarily upon private enterprise, government, the arts, labour, etc, to provide creative practitioners willing to assume on-the-job educational responsibility. If we are willing to recognize as teachers the vast number of talented practitioners in such fields, we shall approach a dramatic solution to the manpower problem of finding enough intelligent 'teachers.' By taking advantage of the educational value of the on-the-job activities, we may begin to break the strangle-hold by which the education profession has restricted our conception of education.

Community seminars could be run by professional educators, businessmen, politicians, parents, labourers, policemen, boy scouts, gang leaders, criminals, musicians, or journalists. The community seminar, perhaps more than the school or laboratory, raises the issue of incentive. What would induce people to participate in such activities? The success of such programmes depends upon the willingness of various organizations to provide released time for leaders and participants. Financial arrangements must insure that such activities do not economically penalize participants. On the contrary, it would be reasonable to give monetary rewards for participation in educational activities. Paying people for undergoing training is already done on a large scale (neighbourhood youth corps, Jobs Corps, scholarships and fellowships, prizes and rewards for high grades, in-training programmes of businesses, etc.), and is quite consistent with the idea of making an investment in the development of human resources. We would assume that, given the time and money, the tasks and issues explored in these contexts could be sufficiently exciting to attract wide participation.

A community concerned with implementing some of these general ideas would require coordination of several resources, including private voluntary agencies such as churches, businesses, museums, and libraries, political parties, economic and political pressure groups, and social service organizations. It would require flexibility and attention to individual differences; yet to avoid the problems of fragmentation or specialization, it would have to facilitate participation in common experiences through which members could relate across economic, racial, political, ethnic, or occupational lines.

Implementing a programme along these lines seems at first glance an administrator's nightmare, involving the coordination of disparate agencies and the cooperation of people with conflicting vested interests. Will colleges recognize the value of laboratory and seminar experience in their admissions policy? Would the education establishment be willing to relinquish much of its control over the learning of youth? Would business accept for employment people with varying, rather than standardized educational backgrounds? Who would have the power to accredit educational programmes, and what new criteria would be needed? At the moment, we have no satisfactory answers for such problems, and we recognize the difficulty of putting some of these ideas into practice. It is possible that, in implementing the three contexts, an educational bureaucracy as rigid as the present one would evolve, with tight scheduling and compartmentalization equal to, or worse than, the current system. All we can say at this point is that the implementation must be guided by serious attention to criteria for building community, else the purpose of educational change will be defeated. It thus becomes clear that when we speak of educational change, we speak of social and community change – a process for which few people have useful administrative guidelines.

Moreover, we hesitate to suggest specific plans or models, because we feel these should arise from the basic concerns of particular communities. We envisage no national model that could be replicated across the land. Instead, there should develop a plurality of structures and programs. Jencks (1966) has suggested ways in which private groups could compete with each other and with the public education establishment by offering qualitatively different types of education, sensitive to community needs. In a single community, schools, laboratories, and seminars might be run by businesses, parents' groups, teachers, and churches – each competing with each other for students. It should be possible to fund competing enterprises without allowing a single centralized bureacracy to gain total control. In some communities, literacy training may be a major problem (e.g., an urban slum); in others technical retraining (e.g. an area with a rapidly growing electronics industry); other areas may have particularly acute problems in human relations, or even in the use of leisure time.

Basing education on the needs of particular communities does not imply that students (youth and adults) are being trained for life within that community only. On the contrary, with communication and transportation breakthroughs likely to continue, all communities are becoming more dependent upon each other; their problems are therefore increasingly generalizable. The production of a TV programme to publicize the plight of migrant workers involves the same considerations as producing a programme to plead for better equipment for the local football team. Organizing tenants to protest against landlords involves processes similar to organizing real estate brokers to protest to Congress. Painting a picture of harvest time is in many ways similar to painting a scene of industrial smokestacks. A discussion of the boring process of cotton picking may be helpful in a later discussion on the meaning of work in an assembly-line. We see no reason to be alarmed that a community's education be focused on critical contemporary issues. If critical, they are, by definition, of relevance to other communities in other times.

. . . [This tri-school] proposal is not offered as a panacea; it is not intended as a model of community itself. We see the three contexts as vehicles that may broaden our search for solutions. (The existing schooling establishment generally inhibits and stifles that search.) The contexts of *action* and community *reflection* provide alternative techniques of search not ordinarily available in present schooling. Recognizing the educational value of these activities may help to nourish common commitments. The sense of community may also be improved by the dissolution of artificial barriers that tend to fragment certain experiences – barriers based on age, ethnicity, occupation, and especially the distinction between students and those who participate in 'real life.' We clearly recognize the dilemma between allowing for flexibility and diversity on the one hand, and the need to increase communication among different styles of life on the other; but the proposal argues that attacking this dilemma be acknowledged as an educational activity to be supported and encouraged; it also suggests new contexts in which this attack may be pursued. Conventional educational reforms largely ignore such problems by restricting their concept of education to formal instruction.

Assuming that one could find a community willing to alter its patterns of education along some of the general lines mentioned above, where would it turn for direction? Much of its work would move over uncharted waters. There are, however, a number of educational experiments that could be used as possible illustrations of the broader view. Such projects are not necessarily aimed at the construction of community; their efforts may focus on narrower educational matters. Nevertheless, they represent interesting approaches that could be adapted to particular community needs. The following examples have come to our attention, but we feel certain they comprise only a small portion of the total available catalogue. Additional examples should be sought and recorded.

Some examples

In connection with Harvard's Research and Development Centre, Robert Belenky, James Reed, and Jonathan J. Clark have instituted a combination preschool and school study group, which we would consider an excellent example of a laboratory activity. Four kinds of people are involved: university educationists, mothers, youths, and young children from a lower-class ghetto in Boston (consisting of two public housing projects: one white and one Negro). Under the supervision of the educationists and mothers, the youths teach young children in a basement recreation room of the Negro project. The educationists and mothers take field trips to explore a variety of the more progressive schools in the greater Boston area to provide information from which to discuss the kind of school experience they would like for their children. There is hope that these discussions will lead to constructive dialogue with the formal school establishment, and, if need be, political and social action to bring about a change in the formal schools. One member of the educationist group is from the ghetto, an artist skilled also in methods of social action and protest. Rather than viewing this project as an educational programme to improve formal education, i.e., the schools, one might view this as a continuing educational programme in its own right. Rather than construing this kind of activity as mainly temporary, compensatory, or rehabilitative (though it may in fact be the latter), why not consider this as one of a number of normal educational opportunities in which adults and youth might choose to engage?

A second example is a radio club sponsored by an electronics firm in

Concord, Massachusetts. Two days a week a group of youths comes to the main factory and works with engineers and technicians, building ham radio sets, exploring radio theory, and exchanging technical information. Presently this club is extra-curricular, piled on top of what for many high school students is an already overburdensome amount of school work. Why not include adult 'hams' as well as young people? Why not construe this as a genuine educational setting and allow the participants to account this time against the school or work responsibilities in their normal schedules?

A church-sponsored project illustrates a type of community seminar. Sponsored by the Presbytery of Detroit, the Episcopal Diocese of Michigan, and the Michigan Conference of the United Church of Christ, the Detroit Industrial Mission (DIM) sends clergymen into industrial plants to initiate contacts with men who organize small discussion groups among the workers. Topics are drawn from concerns of the workers themselves. The mission does not preach any particular point of view, but attempts to foster better communication and deeper levels of understanding among all groups in industry. The responsibility of staff members is merely to arrange opportunities for men to say to each other what they think about human and ethical issues that occur in the plant. This illustration has a number of interesting characteristics: (a) it was initiated and carried out by a private, voluntary group, without public funds or public officals; (b) its purpose was to provide neither vocational training nor an opportunity to philosophize about 'great books,' but rather to raise fundamental questions of immediate relevance and importance; (c) the 'teachers' operate from a clear ideological base but are not interested in evangelical conversion; (d) the 'students' are not seen as preparing for some distant goal, but as learning to make better decisions here and now; and (e) there are no sharp age or status distinctions – men at different points in their careers talk sincerely with one another.

Conclusion

The deliberate effort to view education in community from three vantage points and to look for contexts, outside of the formal school, where people learn is only the first step in any important effort at educational reform – but it is the hardest. After one wrenches oneself loose from the paralyzingly constricted posture that all true education must be programmed, planned, compulsory, and public, and it must all happen in schools, one's imagination trips over a host of exciting places for youth and adults to learn, by themselves, and in association with one another. Only after this first step has been taken do really important questions of educational policy arise (Thelen, 1960, pp. 13–14):

> What does the educational system have to do with the system of governement, of economics, of politics? Is is all very well to say that education is for the purpose of maintaining our nation or developing a world order, but what does that mean? Does it mean that every individual must be made literate, wise, loyal and conforming? ... Is a school a cultural island, separated from the community mainland by the same kind of things that separates fantasy from real life? Does the school lead or follow the community or both? We hear a lot about the need to 'involve' citizens in school problems. Who, how, why? Is it just to keep them quiet? or to manipulate them into contributing more money? Is school supposed to 'induct youth into the community'? What does that mean? ... Can the school do the job alone? Or is the school only one part of a community-wide educational system which exists in fact whether the school board knows it or not?

Critics of this position tend to ask for specific blueprints and definite answers to such policy questions. They ask for outlines, schedules and programmes, raising such issues as: how much time would students spend in school? Would the rest of their time be completely free or planned and supervized in some way? Who would pay for extra-curricular activities? How could adults be released from their jobs to take responsibility for community education? How would legal authority be allocated among community agencies? Would state departments of education change their requirements? Would colleges accept students with this sort of education? Would the students perform better on standard tests and attain standards of 'excellence' comparable, for example, to European education? Can we demonstrate that education organized around these ideas would have any real pay-off in later life?

To answer such questions directly at this point would be inappropriate. Until people in a community have argued about and accepted some of the premises in this paper and are vitally concerned with implementation for their particular situation, it would be foolhardy for armchair professors to prescribe programmes. Providing blueprints in the abstract, not tied to a specific situation, would be inconsistent with our premise that education should arise from real needs and issues within community, not from the drawing boards of distant national planners.

We are chastised for evading the issue of practicality, as critics throw up their hands in despair with our 'unrealistic', 'unfeasible' ideas. This basic criticism and questions like the above reflect a commitment by critics to the present system, a reluctance to search for fundamental deficiencies in the status quo. The major issue from our point of view is not our inability to give blueprints and specific answers to such questions; financial, logistic, and adminstrative problems of plural educational contexts are relatively minor difficulties. Instead, the major issue is whether or not we can find people willing to begin serious discussion on premises and ideas rather than only on blueprints and programs. The next step lies not in a more concrete plan, but in a *search for a group of people*, some 'missing community', with the courage and energy to re-examine how education, most broadly conceived as the interaction between reflection and action, can invigorate the lives of all its citizens.

References

JENCKS, C. (1966) Is the public school obsolete? *Public Interest* (winter issue) 18–27

THELEN, H.A. (1960) *Education and the Human Quest*, New York: Harper & Row

2.5 The city as educator: how to be radical without even trying

Edgar B. Gumbert

It is the contention in this paper that a simple but effective change which could save the schools for the benefit of future generations would be for them to renounce their alleged power to do social good beyond themselves. They should be purged of their service and non-educational functions – e.g., custodial care and manpower supply and should withdraw from any specific social initiatives – from trying to shape social change. Schools on the whole are powerless to produce social development or to influence either its amount or its speed.

To claim otherwise involves both schooling and education in a double danger. In the first place, there is the possibility that public opinion will swing from expecting too much from the schools to denying their ability to provide any useful instruction. Thus disillusioned, the public might withdraw value from all school activities, some of which continue to be of worth. Indeed, the schools will grow in stature and esteem as intellectual institutions as their attempts to affect social issues in the world decline. That is to say, the less effective the school is as a social power, the more effective it will be as a pedagogical power. The school's power lies in its ability to help us engage in a variety of intellectual exploratory activities, at different levels of sophistication and inclusiveness, under the direction of educational leaders. The function of the reformed school should be to make a contribution to our powers of understanding and control over ourselves and our environment which could not be made as elegantly by any other institution. The school should help initiate us (see Peters, 1963; 1966, pp. 46–62) into the specialized discourses of the structures of knowledge – expressed in a variety of 'languages' – that are necessary for an understanding of the full meaning of human development.

Their physical resources, the willingness of many excellent teachers to

Source: *Education and Urban Society* (1971), 4 (1), 8–17.

work in them, and some of their traditions favour retaining schools as one kind of educational agency. Taken together, these resources, teachers and traditions enable the schools to contribute to the improvement of our intellectual and creative powers. These powers are developed in our attempt to master materials. In the dynamic transactions between men and materials, both are shaped and defined. This 'struggle' gives form and meaning to our feelings and concepts. Discipline develops from our work with materials, as does our humanity. Freedom and dignity rest upon our access to materials and to tools – physical and symbolic – with which to fashion them. The schools can contribute to our development by providing materials, tools, leaders, and a setting, *when and how we need them.*

The second danger attached to making exaggerated claims about the power of schools to effect broad social reform is that, if social energies were focused on school reform alone, our attention would be distracted from changes that are urgently needed in virtually all other social institutions. Problems which seem to be school problems frequently are social or economic problems – problems of housing, of town planning, of transportation, for example.

There is a limit to what we can expect from tinkering with the school system. The massive federal investment in schooling in the sixties brought about few of the consequences so ardently desired by its supporters. A feverish search for even more funds to solve the problems would be tragically misplaced. Instead of patching up the traditional school system with the help of enormous funds, we should radically change the schools by giving them limited and clearly defined functions. This new radical school would be austere, modest, simple, direct, trusting, at once reverent and irreverent towards the mysteries of knowledge and of ignorance. It would not be part of a system in the sense that the school is today; consequently it would not need the administrator-ridden, inflated bureaucratic machinery that we have currently. Instead of patching up the old conveyance or of making it even more luxurious, which would limit the roads on which we can travel and the places to which we can go, we should now park it, get out, and honorably walk. This makes more experience possible. We might need assistance from time to time to get us to where we want to go; therefore we might need a pilot or driver. But his influence over us would be temporary and according to our needs; we would be travelling on our schedule, not on one drawn up by some other person for his profit or for his bookkeeping convenience. If applied to schooling, this analogy presents a picture quite different from what now exists.

Educational reform: the networks in cities

Obviously our efforts must not be solely to improve schools and schooling;

they must also be to change the conditions under which and the agencies through which education takes place. The specialized function of intellectual instruction in the schools can develop only on the basis of widely diffused general education. One radical reform calls for another. In this case, the radical departure consists of unlocking and using rather than wasting the enormous and powerful educational resources we already have. Many of the functions of schools as they now are constituted – e.g., skill learnings and peer activities – could be redistributed among other institutions which now exist, particularly in cities.

Within the city there are what Ivan Illich (1970b: 7/1–7/38) calls 'educational networks' of fantastic richness and variety waiting to be unlocked and utilized. Illich's four networks are: (1) educational objects – e.g., botanical gardens, libraries, museums, shops, and factories; (2) skill models – e.g., persons who can teach a foreign language or play a musical instrument; (3) peer matches – persons who are interested at a given time in a selected problem or topic; and (4) educational leaders who can assist in exploratory activities, already referred to.

Public funds for education which now go almost entirely to schools could be distributed in such a way that they would better 'exploit' for educational purposes these other already existing community resources. For example, annual educational expenditures, in amounts publicly and officially agreed upon, could be distributed directly to individual learners in the form of educational vouchers, which could be exchanged for the educational goods and services the learners desire. Moreover, tax advantages could be given to jewellers, rare book collectors, seamstresses, oriental rug merchants, or to other specialists who undertook to devote time to instruction in their fields. Some individuals, organizations, and businesses, no doubt, would provide educational materials and services free.

Virtually everybody in the community could take on educational responsibilities. Instead of infrequent field trips from schools, learners would return to schools for varying lengths of time. Mini-buses which would individualize point-to-point transportation to educational resources could easily be made available. Precincts for walking, cycling, or even for animal carts could be created.

Given these new experiences with authority and with community, it is possible that the schools in the city would be reawakened and their intellectual tasks strengthened. Both education and schooling in this case could contribute to an 'awareness of new levels of human potential and the use of one's creative powers to foster human life' (Illich, 1970a, p. 166).

The first three networks exist largely or entirely outside schools and their control. Most time would be spent, and probably most learning would occur, in them. The fourth network exists both within and without the schools as they are discussed above. Although less time might be spent in exploratory activities, they are more powerful, because it is primarily through them that we are rendered able to unlock and to use with more awareness and adroitness the resources of the other three.

The educational power and potential of the city

The city itself can be seen as an educational object. It provides for its inhabitants, young and old, an education of both the intellect and the emotions which is far more immediate and dramatic in its effects than an education provided by formal schooling. It would be difficult to argue that any other single area of land offers as wide a scope for learning and for shaping the lives of men as do cities. Schools can be ascetic, as suggested in this paper, because cities are opulent.

Cities contain many of the best – and the worst – elements of our cultural heritage; they are centres for the fusion of the past, present, and future, the old and the new. The constant interplay of contrasting elements can enhance and help expand our intellectual activities. Many enlivening experiences are available. Untold pleasures, adventures – and escapes – suggest themselves. Different life styles conflict and compete with each other for credibility and acceptance. Social class, race, and ethnicity, for example, are complex social forces with which it is edifying to deal. The character and quality of these forces are subjects of considerable importance, for they play a prominent role in the formation of our personalities and intellects. The personality must find 'new moorings' in the city (Illich, 1970a, p. 146). 'Urbanization for the individual,' Illich points out (ibid), 'means the search for new coordinates to his most intimate feelings and drives.' In effect, cities can afford us new insights into social actualities and social possibilities. These new perspectives in turn make it possible for us to increase our comprehension of and our control over our own lives.

The architecture of a city exerts a constant and significant influence on the life styles of its inhabitants. Buildings are valuable items in a network of educational objects; at the same time, they provide the infrastructure for other educational networks. That is to say, urban architecture and design are educative as both content and form.

As educational objects, city buildings are documents linking us to our past. They can be thought of as palimpsests – records of time and change. Like public records, they should be available to all without privilege or prejudice. Everybody can learn to 'read' them. Anything which denies us this connection with our past is, in part, an attack on our person and our property – on our psychological health and our cultural heritage.

As infrastructure architecture provides the 'permanent setting of a culture against which its social drama can be played out with the fullest help to the actors' (Mumford, 1952, p. 111). Le Corbusier (1964, p. 25) claimed that 'civic spirit can be born of living architecture.' Lewis Mumford (Howe, 1971, p. 68) has suggested that 'perhaps the best definition of the city in its higher aspects is that it is a place designed to offer the widest facilities for significant conversation.' Urban structure – architectural forms, their uses, and the spatial relationships among them – obviously can either help or hinder movement and meeting, contact, and communication. If it fosters conversation, then it is, in the broadest and best sense educative. For by meeting and by talking we continuously create and recreate social life and reality. Urban structure, thus, is one of the single most important influences on the quality and scope of the four educational networks discussed above and on the ease and frequency with which they are used. As these networks, when taken together, have unrivalled educational power, urban structure is an indispensable component of the foundations of education.

The density of a city – an outgrowth of structure – also is an important ingredient in its educational value. It clearly has important social consequences. The quality of human relations changes in a dense city society. Individual expression and eccentricity, rather than conformity and homogeneity, can develop. Deviant and diverse subcultures, such as bohemian and student groups, are more likely to emerge; movement among and mingling within them is made easier. Human mix stimulates awareness and increases our ability to communicate with each other. Richard Sennett (1970, p. 68) holds that:

> In the dense, diverse communities the process of making multiple contacts would burst the boundaries of thinking couched in homogeneous small group terms. Since urban space would be free for all manner of incursion, the neat categories of spatial experience in cities – such as home, school, work, shopping, parks and playgrounds – could not be maintained. Men would find community problems and community experiences, as well as community conflicts, not limited to the sphere of their own small jobs, just as the region where a man lived would not be immune to a diverse circle of influences and modes of life.

In dense societies, city streets are important educational objects. The streets of Paris or Florence or Vienna, for example, invite people to stroll about, with or without aim or purpose, to take in rather than to reject impressions, to think, to feel, to enjoy, to mix, to see, and be seen – in short, to celebrate existence. As Bernard Rudofsky (1969) has pointed out, classrooms cannot compete with streets for many important kinds of learning experiences. The ancients knew this. The great teachers of Greece preferred to talk and to instruct while walking in the streets. The Stoics took their name from stoa, the protected walkways on which they liked to teach. The Romans, too, used porticos as educational centres. The visual pleasures of walking, the opportunities for coming into contact with other people, the awareness of community when on the streets – all can enhance our humanity.

In addition to being educational objects in their own right, streets are vital networks taking us to other important educational objects – to parks and squares, to markets, to libraries and museums, to shops, cinemas, and theatres, to restaurants, pubs, and cafes, to schools and universities.

It seems, then, that radical changes in education should begin with a reform of schooling along the lines indicated above and with changes in the texture and density of our cities. They should take into account the way our streets and other educational objects are made available to us. That is to say, radical changes in education involve nothing more nor less than rearranging our cities so as to release their educational powers. We should try to create again, in principle although obviously not in all details, urban communities where people can have the kinds of experiences that Parr describes, communities where children and adults can live, work, play, and learn together.

The task obviously will not be easy. Ideological and material forces have fused to create formidable barriers to developing and using the educational potential of cities.

References

HOWE, I. (1971) 'The city in literature', *Commentary* 51 (May), pp. 61–8

ILLICH, I. D. (1970a) *Celebration of Awareness: A Call for Institutional Revolution*, New York, Doubleday

ILLICH, I. D. (1970b) Ciclo Lectures, summer. Mexico, Centro Intercultural de Documentacion (CIDOC cuaderno 1007)

ILLICH, I. D. (1971) 'Education without school: how it can be done', *New York Review of Books* 12 (7 January, pp. 25–31)

LE CORBUSIER (1964) *The Radiant City* New York Orion

MUMFORD, L. (1952) *Art and Technics* Colombia University Press

PETERS, R. S. (1963) *Education as Initiation* London, Evans

PETERS, R. S. (1966) *Ethics and Education* London Allen & Unwin

RUDOFSKY, B. (1969) *Streets for People: A Primer for Americans* New York: Doubleday

SENNETT, R. (1970) 'Urban peace through disorder or the uses of anarchy', *Psychology Today* 6 (November), pp. 66–9

2.6 Community school and curriculum

Geoffrey Partington

The main conscious pressure for community schools in England in recent years has been in areas where traditional neighbourhood loyalties have been eroded and a sense of community has disappeared or where no strong community feeling ever existed. Examples of the first come from run-down inner-city districts which have experienced major population changes: the Sidney Stringer Community School in Coventry, the Abraham Moss Centre in Manchester and the Liverpool EPA schools associated with Eric Midwinter. The second may be found in large, impersonal post-war housing estates, such as Bristol's Lawrence Weston School which was developed successfully by Cyril Poster. There is a need to provide common interests and sympathies between disparate ethnic and cultural groups in the inner-city areas and between uprooted and rootless tower-dwellers in new estates, and it is not surprising that schools should be turned to for a major contribution.

Comprehensive reorganisation makes it more likely that all schools will be more representative of their neighbourhoods, although the extent will be influenced by the extent of denominational schooling available. It must be admitted that conceptually community or neighbourhood schools are incompatible with a wide exercise of parental choice of school, or with policies designed to provide schools with intakes balanced for ethnic or academic composition. Most LEAS which have pioneered comprehensive education, have sought to create neighbourhood schools; these neighbourhoods may be wide though relatively homogeneous as in Suffolk, or quite small and socially or ethnically distinct urban areas such as Waltham Forest or Brent.

The interpretation of a community school as one which uses its neighbourhood as a major or, in some cases, a central curricular resource and a major stimulus to teaching must be distinguished from the alternative

Source: *Forum*, Summer 1976, Vol 18 No. 3.

concept of a school which is itself used extensively by community groups other than children and teachers.

Educational advocacy of the interpenetration of school and the immediate outside world often coalesce with financial arguments to bring about multiple use of school facilities. Dual and triple use of school premises is by no means new. I never attended or taught in a secondary school which did not have other users. But I cannot recall outstandingly constructive results in the realm of mutual understanding. My recollections are rather of institutionalised hostility between day school and night school teachers. It seems doubtful whether the provision of Sports Halls and Swimming Pools in our Secondary Schools will in themselves have the wide effects anticipated by some.

The influence of the outside world on the life of schools may well become powerful when resources are shared *during* school time. For instance, at Countesthorpe and some other Community Colleges in Leicestershire the mixing of Sixth Formers and adults in 'A' level classes may lead to pedagogic changes; there may also be a creche so that mothers can engage in cultural activities on the premises. Lawrence Weston in Bristol has a public library within its buildings. Harry Ree, among others, considers the shared use of facilities the most radical aspect of a community school.

Interaction potential

Willard Waller described schools as 'despotisms in a state of parlous equilibrium' which may easily be overwhelmed by parental interventions. Other schools are laissez-faire or semi-anarchial regimes whose equilibrium is as parlous as that of more authoritarian structures and these too, will be susceptible to parental and community pressures. Community use of schools during school hours will reduce the insulation of teachers and weaken the frame of the school in Basil Bernstein's sense of control 'over the selection, organisation and pacing of the knowledge transmitted and received in the pedagogic relationship'. The presence of numerous adults whose livelihood lies outside the school system is likely to modify many aspects of pupil-teacher relationships and may have some implications for the control of education.

Community involvement may also threaten the traditional role of the school as 'a museum of virtue' (another of Waller's phrases) preaching ideals which are little practised in the outside world. Facilities may be demanded which are not deemed worthwhile by educationists: Bingo, Birth Control Clinics and All-in Wrestling may be community needs which the school is asked to meet.

Curricular implications

A related point on which I want to concentrate is what the community school should imply in terms of curriculum: the extent to which it should reflect 'community needs', the criteria for determining what those needs are, and the degree to which the curriculum ought to be influenced by the specific characteristics of the neighbourhood or community. These are issues on which opinions are deeply divided and about which very various views have been advanced which it is worth summarising and examining.

National culture?

At one extreme stands Dr Rhodes Boyson who argues for a return to the 'understood' national curriculum which apparently existed in Britain until 15 years ago to well nigh universal satisfaction. Dr Boyson makes no explicit separate provision for Wales and Scotland.

All primary children would study, for example, in history 'evolution and the dinosaurs, the legends of Greece and Rome and great events in British history, approached largely through "great lives" '. All secondary pupils would attain in geography 'a thorough grasp of British geography and an in depth look at Europe ... linked with a basic knowledge of the continents and the major countries'; projects are regarded with deep suspicion 'since they can be one of the great wasters of time and money'. Dr Boyson sees such a compulsory national curriculum as a major contribution to the creation, or resurrection, of a common culture without which 'the country would fall apart'. This approach could, perhaps, be regarded as a form of community education with Britain as the community unit, but it is antithetical to a high degree of neighbourhood responsiveness in the curriculum. A former London Head and MP for the London Borough of Brent, which has considerable ethnic heterogeneity, Dr Boyson eschews any non-British influences on literature, history or other aspects of curriculum; but paradoxically, he favours the 'opening of Voluntary and Controlled schools by the various religious and ethnic groups' because he believes that a 'joint religious belief is a great help in cultural identification'. While there is no reason why Moslems or Sikhs should not establish confessional schools, it seems bizarre to advocate this in conjunction with calls for a common culture.

Local criteria?

The opposite position on curriculum and community is exemplified by Joan Leighton's description of a scheme she helped to plan at Levenshulme School in that city. The scheme is entitled 'The Manchester Child', its basis local history from pre-Roman times to the present, to which geography, RI, music, drama, dance and art are geared. The aim 'is to show that Manchester is more than a Victorian City, and that it has been at the centre of national and international affairs since pre-Roman times'. Specific parts of the scheme include 'Manchester's part in drawing up of Magna Carta, its contribution to Renaissance education, its reflection of the religious strife of the sixteenth century'. Religious education includes a study of 'religious developments from pre-Roman and Romano-British cults through the Anglo-Saxon conversion, the Reformation, Anglicanism, Puritanism, Non-Conformity, Judaism, Islam and Humanism in Manchester'. (*Forum,* Autumn, 1972).

This sort of scheme seems more of a strait-jacket than a springboard. It is one thing to increase children's awareness of their immediate environment or wider community, by exploiting its local history, buildings, customs, arts and industries; it is another matter to use the mere chance of local examples as a determining criterion of content. Whether or how we study Renaissance education should not depend primarily on the presence of an Elizabethan or a Jacobean grammar school foundation. The amount of theological nicety with which we regale twelve year olds cannot be rationally decided by the extent to which the locality was involved in doctrinal dispute.

It is worrying, too, that the Levenshulme Curriculum Project was 'intended for first and second year pupils in an urban comprehensive school of predominantly working class children with a considerable number of immigrant pupils'. Are we to assume that a quite different project would be more suitable for a secondary school with a different ethnic or social composition – Sir Robert Peel in and the Battle of Peterloo out so to speak? This problem is raised especially sharply by the arguments for 'Black Studies' and the like. It is certainly true that the curriculum of many schools fails to develop appropriate self-images for black children, but lack of suitable models may handicap indigenous children too. It is by no means certain that separate community curricula are appropriate solutions. It is more likely that these would be increasingly divisive.

On the other hand, an 'understood national curriculum' will fail to win the loyalty of ethnic minorities if it includes insufficient of their experiences and cultures. Indeed, Eric Midwinter and other critics have argued that the standard secondary curriculm never had much positive influence on the average pupil and that 'the man on the Clapham omnibus' gained little or nothing from lessons on the Black Death, the customs of the Masai and the exports of Latin America. Even these favourite Midwinter examples of irrelevance may have more interest and significance for children than some local and environmental studies, such as the '97 Bus' Project suggested in the Schools' Council Working Paper *Society and the Young School Leaver* and subsequently savaged by John White. It is important that the many children who change school or even region during their school lives should have some curricular continuity based on criteria of significance in content and suitability of method; it is equally important that scope for initiative and innovation be not stifled and that rootlessness and anomie be combated. Community and local studies can and must be so structured as to enable intrinsic interest and relevance to contribute to systematic conceptual development of a universal character.

Radical intent?

One conclusion seems clear. The greater the influence of neighbourhood and community on the curriculum, the weaker the frame and insulation of the school. This may be particularly the case when teachers wish not merely to reflect their communities but to change them.

Christopher Searle, for instance, wishes to sharpen the political consciousness of working class children so that they can speed the demise of an unjust social system. In the short-term he would mobilise East London schools to defend the jobs of dockers and the continued use of local hospitals claimed by the Regional Hospital Board to be antiquated and redundant. Projects on the problems of Dockland can help children to understand changing patterns of trade, industry and population settlement, problems of job demarcation within the docks and between dockers and other transport work, and the difficulties involved in establishing social priorities; such studies of community problems and possibilities ought to be part of every child's secondary education. But teachers should not be surprised or resentful when there is interest in and sometimes criticism of their schemes.

Battles for control

Once the curriculum penetrates the community there will be a dialectical play of forces. It would be ingenuous for teachers to assume that they will be regarded as the sole authorities, or somehow above all battles, once the realities of outside life are seriously studied in schools.

Radicals may rightly object that political and religious indoctrination of children to accept the existing social order has always pervaded schools, and that powerful influences are still exerted by religious festivals and by at least implicit assumptions about the rightness of British institutions. Almost by definition, traditional forms of ideology arouse less attention because so much has already been internalised; but rapid flux in mores and beliefs and the development of a pluralistic society in which authority is weaker and more widely diffused may have put educational radicals and conservatives on level ground.

An extension of community studies in schools must sharpen controversies about the control of the curriculum. There is likely to be a wider tolerance of various interpretations of the Gracchi, the Norman Conquest, the French and Russian Revolutions or even the General Strike than of other than the blandest approaches to the study of contemporary conflict. Most teachers will continue to believe that curricular decisions should be made by themselves as the professionals. A greater emphasis on community or neighbourhood in curriculum may strengthen the hands of the 'locals' as against the 'cosmopolitans' or broader groupings of national professional or subject associations or the Schools' Council.

However, from Robert Lowe and long before to Sir Arnold Weinstock and doubtless long after, stretches the alternative view which distrusts the power of the vested interest of teachers. Evidence to the Taylor Committee suggests there is no more concensus among the foes than among the friends of teacher control of the curriculum, but it is likely that the more general and national the curriculum the greater will be the influence of national bodies such as the DES or HMI. On the other hand, the greater the interpenetration of school and community, the greater the likelihood of local control, however, exercised.

Curricular control by the local community will at least be based on knowledge of local conditions and direct concern for the success or failure of policies. On the other hand there are dangers of narrow parochialism, increased nepotism and severe restrictions on the social as well as the professional life of teachers.

The most likely immediate and important implication of neighbourhood schools is a reduction of the wide discretion in decision-making in curriculum and organisation enjoyed by teachers. The degree to which this freedom has existed may have been exaggerated or may have depended for its formal continuance on its very limited exercise. Dr Boyson is right that there was a great deal of 'agreed national curricula', different though these were in Grammar and Modern Schools, until some twenty years ago. Consensus has since become more limited, the range of idiosyncratic or ideological differences wider, while local educational innovation has increased.

Professional accountability

Readers of *Where?* can study the rival merits of varying schools and fee-paying parents can pay their money and take their choice. For the overwhelming majority of parents choice of school, apart from between a county and a voluntary school, has always been very restricted, especially in rural areas. Comprehensive reorganisation, especially in the form of neighbourhood secondary schools, further restricts choice even though some urban LEAS can consider parental requests for alternatives if more than one school is actually accessible. In such situations, even more than in any other home-school relationship, the school must win the confidence of the decisive majority of parents if major conflicts are to be avoided. If William Tyndale had been the *only* primary school and/or Highbury Grove the *only* secondary school available to a large number of parents, London's County Hall might have followed the Bastille or the Winter Palace into history. Leicestershire's educational hierarchy might have been under seige, too, if those parents who were most convinced that Countesthorpe was a centre of subversion and permissiveness had not been able to send their children to another school.

The greater the effective degree of compulsion to send children to a particular school, the more strongly will parents demand that curriculum and organisation correspond to their own educational ideas. This increase in public accountability may not be a loss for teachers. No innovations in curricular content, teaching methods or pupil-teacher relationships can strike deep or permanent roots unless parents and public are convinced of their value. If their professionalism is of substance, teachers will find ways of justifying their policies and of winning support and more active community cooperation in the future than in the past.

2.7 Working class education and the notion of cultural inadequacy

Harold Entwistle

Old fashioned socialists, as well as old style sociologists of education, have recently been perplexed by the thesis that cultural deprivation is a myth. In a now familiar essay,[1] Keddie argues that it is not clear of what culture lower class families can be deprived 'since no group can be deprived of its own culture'. The logic here is impeccable. Culture is not like property or wealth, of which one might be deprived by the bailiff, a burglar, or the collapse of the stock market. A person's culture is much more like his education, his knowledge and his skill, which he possesses existentially. Except by techniques of brainwashing, it is clearly impossible to deprive a person of what he has learned, of the mental or emotional dispositions which he has acquired: as easy to deprive a man of his height without amputating his limbs, as to deprive him of his culture, his knowledge and skill, his education. These attributes define what one is as a person: a man's culture *is* what he is. Hence it is part of the meaning of culture, when used in this personal sense, that one cannot be deprived of it. But this logical truth is a trivial truth and its social and educational implications unclear. For it is ludicrous to imagine that the statement, 'That child is culturally deprived', means 'I have deprived him of his culture'. What is probably intended is something like, 'That child's culture is an inadequate basis for the good life and he ought, in his own interest, to be put in a position where his culture can be enriched'.

The impeccable logic (in the sense just examined) of Keddie's 'no group can be deprived of its own culture' in no way entails her further conclusion that 'so-called minority group cultures may be seen as ... adequate in their own right', or that any culture is 'a way of life that has its own validity'. The qualification 'in their own right' is puzzling. It is odd

Source: This article is taken from the paper which Professor Entwistle read to the Cambridge Branch of the Philosophy of Education Society of Great Britain, Easter Term 1976. *Cambridge Journal of Education* (1976) Vol. 6. Issue 3.

that the word 'adequate' is assumed sufficient without one of the prepositions 'to' or 'for' which always, if tacitly, accompanies normal usage. Without a prepositional phrase to give it context, the word 'adequate' is vacuous. Nothing is simply adequate. Adequacy must have reference to some standard of performance or some criterion of value by which a person or thing may be defined adequate. Having 'its own validity' also suggests that no further questions should be asked with reference to the quality of life of a group: the group is self-sufficient and ought to be left to carry on undisturbed. Neither individuals, nor the group in community, need look critically at the the given way of life with a view to its improvement. Presumably, so far as the culture may exhibit manifestations of injustice, exploitation, alienation, these are phenomena about which no one need be concerned – most of all, people from outside the group itself.

Nevertheless, paternalistic or not, political radicals have subscribed to the notion of cultural deprivation, sometimes tacitly, often explicitly. It is difficult to see how any advocacy of radical social change could be legitimised except by reference to the fact of cultural deprivation, or the inadequacy of a particular way of life when assessed against some conception of the good life or the good society. Indeed, one of the founding fathers of Marxism gave an account of the conditions of working class life in England in the middle of the nineteenth century which could only be described as culturally deprived. Throughout his account of *The Conditions of the Working Classes in England in 1844*, Engels emphasised the demoralisation of the workers he observed. The worker was 'deprived of his humanity', having become 'a soulless factor of production', a mere machine.[2] In a different metaphor he was described as degraded 'to the level of animals'.[3] The detailed descriptions of brutalising factory discipline, insanitary housing in streets which were open sewers (one recent biographer of Engels concludes that he painted a picture of 'millions of English men, women and children ... virtually living in shit'),[4] loss of domestic skills (the ability to cook, for example) and the affections of family life, leisure largely spent in drunkenness, these are too familiar to relate in detail. Sufficient to record a comment on the condition of child labour which itself became an objective of half a century of agitation for reform:

> Mr Horne, an official of the Children's Employment Commission, stated that in Willenhall the workers lack all moral sense, and he gives ample evidence to support this assertion. In general he found that children had no affection for their parents and recognised no obligation towards them. These children were so brutish and so

> stupid that they did not realise what they were saying. It was by no means unusual for them to assert that they were well treated and perfectly happy, although in fact they worked for twelve to fourteen hours, were dressed in rags, were not given enough to eat and were beaten so hard that they felt the effect for several days afterwards. They simply had no experience of any other way of life than to slave away from morn till night until they were given permission to stop. They had never before been asked whether they were tired and did not know the meaning of the question.[5]

The conventional, 'enlightened' response to this kind of evidence has been approval of a succession of legislative acts restricting the inroads of the working life into childhood and extending opportunities for education, although the recent advocacy of de-schooling society associated with Illich and Reimer also entails a process of 'de-childing' society by reversing the intrusion of compulsory schooling into periods of life formerly and elsewhere (in the Third World, for example) available for gainful employment. But it now appears that his enlightened, reforming response can be faulted. The fact that the exploited have no 'experience of any other world' gives no warrant for anyone's acting on their behalf, since they cannot be regarded as culturally deprived and enjoy an adequate and valid way of life.

The relevance of Engels' account of working class life for current discussion of cultural deprivation and its educational implications is not vitiated by the historical distance which separates Engels' England from the modern world: evidence of the cultural deprivation of any group in any place at any time must falsify Keddie's assumption that no group can be deprived of its own culture. However, Engels' account of working class life a century ago recalls Oscar Lewis's descriptions of the 'culture of poverty' in the present day.[6] The culture of poverty is characterized by the cognitive poverty of its 'members' who do not seek access to power through membership of political parties or labour unions, and make little use of even those welfare agencies which exist for amelioration of poverty. Lewis concludes that 'most primitive peoples have achieved a higher level of socio-cultural organisation than our modern urban slum dwellers'. This assumption is interesting since those who deny the possibility of cultural deprivation amongst modern lower class groups appear to arrive at that conclusion by reference to anthropological evidence of rich and complex cultures in primitive societies.

But, as Lewis notes, though the culture of poverty has its compensations and adaptive mechanisms, it has little to commend it in terms of historic notions of the good life within Western society. This was also Engels' conclusion: 'Even if I had not given so many examples as I have done to illustrate the condition of the working classes in England, it would still be self-evident that the proletariat can hardly feel happy at the present situation. It will surely be granted that the state of affairs I have described is not one in which either an individual or a social class can think, feel and live in a civilised manner'.[7] This statement is at the beginning of his chapter on 'Working Class Movements'. For Engels there was no explanation of these Movements apart from the facts of cultural deprivation. The two are dialectically related as he had hinted in his introduction: 'The Industrial Revolution ... turned the workers completely into mere machines and deprived them of the last remnants of independent activity. Yet it was this change that forced the workers to think for themselves and to demand a fuller life in human society'.[8] For Engels the fact of cultural deprivation and the notion of 'a fuller life', a nobler conception of man, were the antithetical components of the dialectic from which revolutionary action could be forged. Clearly, deprivation is built into the notions of exploitation and alienation. Only the conclusion that the working classes were culturally deprived can make sense of Marxism, and justify the disturbance of existing ways of life which is implicit in even modest social democratic proposals for reform.

To argue the reality of cultural deprivation in this way, however, focuses one of the many ambiguities in the notion of culture. Characterisation of the condition of the poor as cultural deprivation could evoke the response that what Engels and others [9] describe is essentially economic, not cultural, deprivation. However, for a Marxist this separation of economic base from cultural super-structure would make no sense. Any such separation would require a very restricted conception of culture. For one thing, it should be remembered that at the time of Engels' observations, the English working class was almost totally disenfranchised and, hence, chronically deprived with reference to the political culture: without an assumption of political deprivation it would be difficult to explain Chartism, however much its origins were economic in character. As we have already seen, Engels was also convinced that economic deprivation was a cause of deprivation with respect to other cultural institutions – especially family life and the use of leisure – prompting his conclusion that in the economic conditions he observed no one could feel and live in 'a civilised manner'. In any event, it is apparent that Keddie's conception of cultural adequacy can only be sustained in terms of the anthropological sense of the word as a total way of life. Although Keddie says as little in elaboration of 'culture' as she does with reference to 'adequacy' or 'validity', her characterisation of so-called deprived children as 'experienced participants in *a way of life* that has its own validity' suggests the anthropological culture concept.

But for an educationist the essential limitation of the anthropological concept of culture lies precisely in its failure to discriminate normatively amongst items in this cultural aggregate. Culture conceived as the total way of life, unexamined, unrefined, unselective, cannot be an adequate conceptual tool for anyone concerned with intellectual, aesthetic or moral development. As I have argued elsewhere,[10] in its anthropological, descriptive sense, a culture must include strands which are technologically and economically dysfunctional, others which aggravate social injustice, and yet others which offend aesthetic and moral values: anthropologically, the criminal sub-culture is a part of culture as are the drug culture and alcoholism. The political culture, for example, is a totality which must include Watergate and 'the unacceptable face of capitalism', as well as the Declaration of Independence, the Bill of Rights, Civil Rights legislation and the Welfare State. As E. P. Thompson suggests, in criticism of what he calls Eliot's 'sloppy and amateurish' version of the anthropological culture concept (and Raymond Williams' 'bland' extension of Eliot's list), any characteristic list from the totality of cultural activities and artefacts must include items which reveal areas of power and conflict: 'strikes, Gallipoli, the bombing of Hiroshima, corrupt trade union elections ... the massive distortion of news and Aldermaston marches', for example.[11]

Just as it is difficult to see any justification for advocacy of social reform or revolution apart from conditions of cultural deprivation, it is also difficult to imagine how some notion of cultural inadequacy or deprivation can be separated from the concept of education itself. Even the voluntary pursuit of one's own education seems to require a perception of personal deficiency or inadequacy with reference to some aspect of the culture. Given that a person believed his skill or knowledge to be adequate it is difficult to see why he would take steps to further his own education. And this is true for anyone, irrespective of social class.

Perhaps this is exactly the point of the new sociology's rejection of the notion of cultural deprivation. Its concern seems to stem, in part, from application of the notion exclusively to the working class: one has the impression that its polemic is in the spirit of *épater la bourgeoisie*, evoked by the impertinence of the middle class kettle calling the working class pot black. To the extent that new sociologists want to separate the concept of a valid way of life (and definition of an appropriate curriculum) from middle class norms and values one has little quarrel with their intention. Indeed, in this we are in step with Engels who found the middle class, in its own fashion, no less deprived and demoralised than the working class; also with Arnold who thought it philistine. It is interesting that Arnold could not conceive of culture in relation to social class. Each of his class labels –

Barbarian (upper), Philistine (middle) and Populace (working) – carries pejorative overtones.

Whatever the totality which confronts the educationist – whether working class, middle class, national or Western culture – it will be a cultural curate's egg. Hence, in pursuit of an educationally useful, normative concept of culture, he is confronted with three related tasks. First, there is the articulation of criteria in terms of which one is justified in speaking of 'the best' culture or, at least, in terms of culturally better or worse. This involves reference to intellectual, aesthetic and moral standards and values. Secondly, there is need to examine particular cultures – regional, ethnic, social class, for example – for the way in which they exemplify, concretely, those cultural abstractions which serve as our normative criteria and, hence, are available as the concrete data of the curriculum through which we cash, on the classroom floor, those concepts and principles which define the subjects, disciplines or forms of knowledge and skill through which we choose to widen the student's cultural horizons. Thirdly, there is the matter of the way in which particular sub-cultures do or do not interpenetrate each other and the cultural mainstream, such that activities and artefacts from different cultures ought to be universalised through transmission in a common curriculum. It is the conventional wisdom that it is only middle class culture and values which the school attempts to universalize in this way. To the extent that this assumption is valid, curriculum innovation should take account of working class contributions to the cultural mainstream. This is not to make a claim for the inclusion of bingo, pigeon-fancying, or brass band music in the curriculum. Arguably, the distinctive working class culture lies in the institutions created by the Labour Movement. With increasing proletarianisation of the middle class (as evidenced, for example, by increasing militancy of professional associations and their affiliation to the TUC), the case for attention to the social history of the Labour Movement is strong (to the extent that it has not always been a component of the history syllabus).

The criteria which define 'the best culture' are the subject of continuing debate in democratic societies and it is a commonly accepted educational purpose that alternative criteria should receive appropriate consideration. But, historically, a tradition of humanism has developed criteria of interpersonal and social behaviour which rules out exploitation and has found certain forms of human life (whether suffered or chosen) degrading. In turn, these norms have been extended to cover categories of person not formerly regarded as having claims to recognition as 'fully human' and denied respect as persons – slaves, subject peoples, women, children. And it is to this humanistic tradition which Engels appealed (however vacuously, as it might now strike us) in seeking to liberate those working class groups whom he saw deprived of humanity and degraded to resemble machines or animals. His appeal was to 'MEN, members of the great and universal family of Mankind, who know their interest and that of all the human race to the same ... members of this family of "one and indivisible" Mankind ... Human Beings in the most emphatical meaning of the word ... '[12]

In much the same way, the philosopher of education typically speaks of *the* concept of education, *the* aims or objectives of schooling, without reference to limiting categories like class nationality, race or religion. Sociologists of education are apt to presume them naive for ignoring social and economic 'determinants' of educability, or the differentially motivating effects of varied social environments. But, philosophers are right in implying that education, like Engels' MAN, is one and indivisible. And there is little evidence that the working class has ever conceived of its own education exclusively or even substantially in relation to working class cultural artefacts and forms of knowledge and skill. Working class autodidacts and working class groups in adult schools have usually focused their attention upon the seminal works of Western culture in the mainstreams of literature, music, philosophy, history and science, and it is not clear how any learning which can be dignified as 'educational' could do otherwise. In taking the mainstream culture as its educational point of reference, the working class has been partly in pursuit of distinctively working class aims – knowledge of those institutions which were the instruments of its exploitation, and knowledge and skill appropriate to the creation of counter-institutions for its own economic amelioration and political liberation. This knowledge was usually sought in the disciplines of history, philosophy, ethics, political economy and literature. But part of its aim was also the pursuit of personal culture and the enrichment of leisure. Thus, for example, working men and women were found giving their own distinctive expression to 'the high culture of Salzburg and Esterhazy.'[13] As Thomas Burt, the first Labour MP, insisted: 'We say educate a man not simply because he has got political power, and simply to make him a good workman; but educate him because he is a man.'[14]

It is apparent that any characterization of working class culture must include what is sometimes called 'the high culture'. And, paradoxically, to define the scope of a sub-culture in this way is to de-classify it.

Notes

1 KEDDIE, N., ed. *Tinker, Tailor ... the Myth of Cultural Deprivation*, Editor's Introduction.

2 ENGELS, F. *Conditions of the Working Class in England*, translated and edited by W. O. Henderson and W. H. Chaloner, Ch. VI.

3 ENGELS, *op. cit.* p. 241.

4 MARCUS, S. *Engels, Manchester and the Working Class*, p. 184.

5 ENGELS, *op. cit.* p. 229.

6 LEWIS, O. 'The Culture of Poverty' in *Anthropological Essays*.

7 ENGELS, *op. cit.* p. 241.

8 ENGELS, *op. cit.* p. 12.

9 See, for example, KUCZYNSKI, J. *The Rise of the Working Class*, especially his Appendix on 'Historiography of the origins of the Working Class'.

10 ENTWISTLE, H. *Child-centred Education*, pp. 131–6.

11 THOMPSON, E. P. reviewing *The Long Revolution*, *New Left Review*, No. 9, 1961.

12 ENGELS, *op. cit.* p. 8.

13 MARTIN, D. 'The Road from Rochdale to Rome', *Times Higher Educational Supplement*, February 21st, 1975.

14 Quoted by SIMON, B. *Studies in the History of Education 1780–1870*, p. 367.

2.8 A question of quality

G. H. Bantock

As our social life has become increasingly egalitarian, the crisis in the educational system has become, in one important respect at least, a crisis of quality. If the quality of schooling and of the educational experiences provided appear to be deteriorating it is because, caught between the contrary demands for quality and equality in our country, we have opted for the latter.

The present situation cannot be understood without an appreciation of the historical forces that have given it shape. We must, in the first place, grasp the importance of the two cultures – the one based on the written word, historically the culture of the upper classes, the élite, the aristocracy; the other an oral culture coming down in an unbroken succession through the ages, broadly speaking a culture of the ordinary people. This was the situation at the end of the eighteenth century and the beginning of the nineteenth on which early industrialization impinged.

Even earlier the invention of the alphabet, confined to a limited number of symbols – merely twenty-six letters – taken with the coming of the printing press, offered opportunities in the long run for total literacy. There are certain types of script (Chinese, for example) which will never become democratic or demotic because they take so long to learn. Our alphabet and the invention of movable type represent two forces having a major effect on the development of modern European culture and the attempts at total literacy which are one of its most characteristic features.

First of all they facilitated technological development. Without books, the printed page, diagrams, and so on, there could be no modern industrial society. With the beginnings of technical development, in which this country took the lead in the eighteenth century, children were no longer necessary for primary production – the production of food, for example – and might be released for schooling. In a pre-industrial or agricultural society, unless they belonged to rich families, many children were needed

Source: *A Question of Schooling* (1976), pp. 23–32.

for food production. Furthermore, technological advancement assisted urbanization: the land could be made more fertile, and fewer workers were needed on the land, thus enabling people to cluster together in large conglomerations. The communications system enabled food to be brought to all.

At the same time, technological development brought about an end to the traditional culture of the folk. The nature of work became fundamentally different – and work was always a prime factor in the cultural creativity of the people. Their songs, their crafts, their folk tales and legends, often had a close relationship to the work they did. A factory system of production may induce a national plenty undreamed of by the cottagers of a domestic economy – but it inevitably trivialises the nature of the work done. In the nineteenth and early twentieth centuries, industrial folksongs of inferior quality may have replaced the traditional songs, but even these have now disappeared largely as a result of the mass communication of 'pop'.

Accompanying such industrialization is the growth of an increasingly mobile society which a factory system requires. There is also a tendency for religion to be replaced by politics, because, of course, technology is an expression of man's will. Once man feels that he can order the natural environment – and such is one of the implications of an advanced state of technology – God comes to take a less and less important place. God's will tends to be replaced by man's will, and one of the major expressions of this is political action, enabling him to order his society as he thinks he wants it.

As politics becomes more important, formal education provided by the state also becomes more important, because there is a sense in which education has always been one of the tools of politics. As man's technological advance brings him to see that he can to some extent change his own destiny, so education becomes important, in part at least, as an instrument of state control. For education comes to seem one means by which man can exercise his will – as exemplified by Helvetius's eighteenth-century pronouncement that 'L'éducation peut tout' – education can do everything. 'Through education', thought John Dewey, 'society can formulate its own purposes, can organize its own means and resources, and thus shape itself with definiteness and economy in the direction in which it wishes to move'; and Dewey's fundamental aim was essentially a sociopolitical one – the production of the egalitarian democratic society.

So man comes to think that through education and politics there can be the realization of the dream of equality. Equality is clearly one of the key words of the nineteenth century. 'Liberté, égalité, fraternité' – *egalité* was one of the key concepts of the French Revolution, and it is a key word

F

today. Man has come to believe that it is circumstances that create hierarchies and that such circumstances can be altered. Furthermore, he has also come to believe that having, through the development of his capacities, learned to control nature, he has also the capacity to control society.

Clearly, the comprehensive school is one manifestation of this concern, in education, for equality. But in the arguments for comprehensivization there is an ambiguity. The drive for equal access to a uniform kind of secondary school might be described as the desire for a fairer opportunity for more people to become unequal. This implies a greater *initial* equality provided in the single institution. But another argument in favour of comprehensive education can be seen to carry different implications. In this argument opportunity is interpreted as giving people a fairer chance to achieve a kind of terminal equality – equality of *outcome*. Here what is sought is homogenization in terms of culture, achievement, experience. Again in Dewey we find an expression of this latter purpose; he seeks a democracy of shared meanings in which people are to be brought to similar states of consciousness so that they are able equally to understand and handle the relevant concepts: 'To have the same ideas about things which others have, to be like-minded with them, and thus to be really members of a social group, is to attach the same meanings to things and to acts which others attach', as he put it in *Democracy in Education*.[1] And Dewey portened the 'democratic' social argument in favour of comprehensivization. There is implied a shift from arguments concerning access to educational institutions to arguments concerned with 'access to forms of knowledge, modes of perception, ways of thinking – in short, to varieties of reality'.[2]

Now these two manifestations of the egalitarian will, which constitute the major impulses behind the move towards comprehensivization – equality of *opportunity* and equality of *outcome* sought within the same institution, necessarily imply a conflict of aims. The resulting dilemma can be seen in the way in which comprehensivization has fostered two very different conceptions of the role of the school, both of which can be identified as the polarities within which the developing argument over comprehensive schooling is increasingly being discussed in this country. Recently, for instance, there has been considerable controversy over the replacement of Dr Rhodes Boyson as headmaster of Highbury Grove School. Dr Boyson, who has become Member of Parliament for Brent, was, before his election, the headmaster of a highly academically oriented comprehensive school in North London. While care was taken to foster good social relations in the school, the prime aim was academic, in line with Dr Boyson's belief that the purpose of schooling is learning.

Discipline was good, and achievement excellent. The controversy has arisen because of the fears of some of the governors of the school that the replacements for Dr Boyson shortlisted for interview were not of the calibre necessary to maintain the school's high academic reputation. Dr Boyson in fact stressed the instrumental role of the school.

Move to Leicestershire, the first fully comprehensive area in the country, and a different controversy has arisen over the reputation of Countesthorpe College, an upper school on the outskirts of the city. A careful sociological study of the school in its early days by G. Bernbaum pinpoints the concern that many parents in the area feel over the academic viability of the school – for it is worry over results expressed in academic terms which has, in the main, caused the controversy, one which has exercised the local press for many weeks.[3] Mr Bernbaum refers to:

> a large number of staff, whose attitudes towards the academic work of the school is ambiguous ... when teachers were given a list of 12 items by means of which the influence of the school would make itself felt ... the two items which received the highest number of 'Highly Important' rulings were:
>
> 1 visible improvements in pupils' social adjustment
> 2 visible improvements in the community's involvement in the school.
>
> ... Significantly, also, visible improvement in pupils' academic achievement was placed eleventh out of twelve in the 'Highly Important' column.[4]

The emphasis here, then, is on the expressive role of the school. Again, the graduates on the staff do stress academic achievement; but the non-graduates and junior members are much more concerned about social attitudes. They tend to see the school as a sort of glorified youth club.

Yet this is not to say that the schools are not in a genuine dilemma – and the polarization which is occurring, both as between and as within schools, is a manifestation of this dilemma. The post-war euphoria over education implied that it was the nature of institutions which contributed most to the lack of achievement among 'The Young School Leavers',[5] Once the *system* was changed and the sense of inferiority and failure felt by the secondary modern school population removed, the vast reserves of talent thought to exist among, specifically, the working-class population would be revealed and the equalizing process would be under way. Alas, it has not worked out like this. Reorganization does not necessarily alter the attitudes of pupils or teachers; and the polarization which has taken place among staffs and which has been briefly noted above, is in fact a response to a situation which raises much profounder issues than any that can be settled by fiddling around with organization; for organization has at best an enabling function.

Yet the disillusionment is dangerous – for it suggests that, in the desperate attempt to find something which will hold the 'young school leavers', the traditional standards which were upheld by the grammar schools are of diminishing importance. Egalitarianism – concern for equality of *outcome* – demands sameness or similarity of exposure to curriculum; the obvious inability of many to benefit has led to the extension of progressive methods, with their ambivalence over content[6] and their emphasis on what is vaguely termed 'socialization' as opposed to serious academic study in the secondary range : methods, it can be added which may have a limited part to play in the education of young children but whose value where older children are concerned is much more ambiguous unless carefully controlled by a keen sense of relevance in specific contexts. It is highly significant that the following passage from an article by Michael Irwin, entitled 'The Left in Education', should appear in the left wing *New Statesman* (4 May 1973), a strongly pro-comprehensive journal and normally much more addicted to the lucubrations of Mr Christopher Price:

> The problem of reconciling egalitarianism with the maintenance of traditional standards has remained not only unresolved but largely unexamined. Yet for many teachers, students and parents this is a fundamental problem. If a grammar school is to be absorbed into a comprehensive, the parent seeking reassurance about academic standards will find in the progressive educational literature, two answers and the shadow of a third. One answer, illustrated by statistics, is that standards might even rise, and occasionally in comprehensive schools this has happened. The second is that any loss will be outweighed by social and other gains. The half answer is that the old academic values are elitist, outmoded and best dispensed with. Whatever the future of the school concerned the progressive theorist can't lose. The parent isn't necessarily so lucky. About university expansion there is a similar disingenuousness. The bold type claims academic standards will not be impaired by increased student numbers, the small print adds that if they are, no matter.

Yet this developing indifference of the radical Left to the question of standards – the acceptance of the amorphousness over content of progressivism, attempts at positive discrimination in favour of the low achievers – encounters two stubborn, irreducible elements in the educational situation which will necessarily frustrate (though not before much damage may have been done) their egalitarian aspirations for equality of outcome.

There is first the demands of the industrial-bureaucratic society; these necessitate for their very functioning a hierarchy – one different from the heirarchy of aristocracy or church, but a heirarchy nevertheless. Such a society needs managers and technologists, technicians and clerks, all manifesting different kinds and levels of skill. Without such skills the machines slow down and eventually stop – and the people starve. It is as simple as that. And such skills, especially at the top end, are demonstrably in short supply.

This, of course, is to stress the instrumental function of education. In its liberal guise – the fostering of talent for personal individual satisfaction – education is inescapably divisive. Man is the product of both genetics and history. For whatever reason – original endowment or social upbringing in the family – the ability to grasp meaning varies ineluctably from child to child in a way that no social engineering, other than the most frightening totalitarian imposition of arbitrary meaning at the will of the Party in the manner of *1984* (so that 'War' becomes 'Peace'), can erode. This produces those social and cultural divisions which so offend the egalitarian.

When we speak of meaning, of course, we come to the heart of the problem which was briefly adumbrated earlier on. For sets of meanings, whether transmitted through words, musical notation, in two- or three-dimensional forms, are what constitute a culture, in the selective, evaluative sense relevant to an educational system. What the system of universal education imposed over the last hundred years has attempted is to impose much the same culture – one based on literacy and the book, and the developed scientific and literary disciplines that the invention of movable type has helped to foster – on a total population. I have drawn attention, earlier, to the fact that, for many people in our society – and especially for those families whose children go to make up the bulk of the 'young school leavers' – historically their culture has existed in different terms – oral, imagistic and affective. ('For the mass of people', wrote D. H. Lawrence, 'knowledge *must* be symbolical, mythical, dynamic', and, in the education of children he urged, 'The voice of dynamic sound, not the words of understanding'.) Only the purveyors of 'pop' have learned to exploit this situation – and 'pop' is inimical in ethos to what the school is trying to do.

Something of this has recently penetrated even the minds of our egalitarians; and during the last few years there has been a significant shift in the way in which equality of outcome as a result of the school system is being sought. The older type (who is still with us) anticipated such equality, as I have pointed out, as a result of equal exposure to the same culture. The newer type, forced to admit to cultural differences broadly manifest in different class and social groups, is prepared to face differentiation of exposure on the assumption of difference but equality of *culture*. The working classes (by and large), it is admitted, *have* a different culture; but it is as 'valid' (a favourite word) and as worthy as that of the middle class (often there is a suggestion that, in fact, it is superior).

The latest twist to the egalitarian argument can be traced to some extent to the attempt to cope with the somewhat unpalatable empirical findings of Professor Bernstein. Professor Bernstein's theories concerning class speech are much more complicated than they are often given credit for; furthermore they have undergone considerable refinement and modification over a lengthy period of time. Nevertheless the over-simplified but not totally erroneous notion that he has claimed that the working class speak a 'restricted' code and the middle class an 'elaborated' one has become part of the conventional wisdom of our times; and, of course, the pejorative implications of 'restricted', despite protests from the author, have stuck and given grave offence in certain quarters. The realization that the culture of the school demands, at secondary level at least, a certain sophistication of concept usage would at least seem to provide one possible explanation of the persistent lack of achievement on the part of certain sections of the community. Bernstein himself has protested at the conclusions drawn from his work concerning the attributed inferiority of the restricted-code users both on the grounds of their potentiality for elaborated-code awareness and on the validity, for alternative cultural purposes, of the restricted code in itself. Thus he has protested against the notion that 'restricted code' should be equated with linguistic deprivation, and floated the alternative need for the school culture to come to terms with the symbolic world of the working-class child.[7]

Thus the way has been prepared for the move from equality of outcome as the aim of the school through the deprivation debate to the alternative culture resolution. On the way the whole problem of linguistic and cultural *control* has been adumbrated; and the radicals have followed up the Bernstein hints with a full-blooded attack on the putative restrictive power of the middle-class cultural ethos on the working classes. The current power structure of society is sustained not only through institutional control and access but through the symbolic knowledge systems which help not only to maintain middle-class hegemony but, to quote the *Times Educational Supplement*, 'to keep the poor in their place'. As a defensive move, it is necessary to insist on the viability of an alternative culture equally 'valid' and worthwhile. (It is symptomatic that they see knowledge exclusively as a means of control – which in part, of course, it is – and not as a means of release, or of an extension of powers.)

The trick, of course, is to juggle with two uses of the word 'culture' – one a general anthropological term implying the total pattern of a society's life, and the other the restricted one relevant to an educational debate; for education in the formal sense implies the selection of important areas of understanding and feeling for the purpose of transmission. In the first sense the working classes clearly have a culture and one which differs significantly from that of the middle classes – the theory of *embourgeoisement* has recently taken some significant knocks. But there is no evidence that they possess a qualitative culture sufficiently differentiated from that of the middle classes to require a special system of education for transmission.

The cultural bankruptcy of the working classes is indeed manifest in the frantic efforts working-class apologists make to produce viable areas of concern. Colin MacInnes has recently[8] produced a profile of working-class culture which includes horse and dog racing, boxing, brass bands and choirs, variety and pop, betting shop and bingo sessions. Only gardening and 'hobbies' supply anything with the slightest potential for transmission through a formal educational system. Brian Jackson has a similar enthusiasm for brass bands, and adds pigeon fancying. His more recent attempt, indicated in the article reprinted in this volume,[9] is to find educational potential in such manifestations as chalking on walls, pulling a motor bike to pieces or 'dolling up each other's hair' – a strange ragbag which oddly enough indicates a covert contempt for the potential of those he wishes to assist.

And indeed, in all the analysis of working-class culture there is a strange mixture of romanticism and contempt. There is the romanticism which stresses the 'validity' of a non-existent culture (in the restricted sense). One can diagnose this as a twentieth-century version of pastoral – that convention which throughout the centuries has found a superior way of life in the simpler life of peasants, shepherds and shepherdesses. Though this type of regressiveness is endemic in the human situation, the stress laid on it today betrays the same kind of bankruptcy as the play-acting of the French court in the late eighteenth century as the preamble of breakdown and revolution. There is contempt because the haphazard indulgences of 'children's chalking competitions' are allowed to replace any serious attempt to work out a viable curriculum genuinely related to the *potential* of the folk.

The consolation that can be found is that at long last we have at least realised that the crisis *is* a cultural one – a matter on which I have been trying to insist these last fifteen years in the face of the naïve optimism of the comprehensivists. What is needed is a curriculum which will build on the historical consciousness of the folk as manifest in the clues given by their pre-industrial culture, supplemented by such evidence, linguistic and psychological, as we can glean about the *levels* of abstraction at which they can work, and their characteristic folk behaviour. I have attempted such a curriculum and published it elsewhere.[10] It is intended to be both specific and liberalising, structured and yet in line with potential, neither condescending nor unrealistic.

For what is important is that quality shall be maintained at all levels. The old, watered-down high culture failed with many; but attempts at homegenisation only weaken the demands made on the able without really satisfying the low achievers. A frank recognition of the demands of quality within differentiation is the only proper way forward.

Notes

1 DEWEY, J. (1947) *Democracy in Education* Macmillan

2 LAWTON, D. (1973) *Social Change, Educational Theory and Curriculum Planning* Hodder and Stoughton

3 About a school similar in ethos to that of Countesthorpe, the *Leicester Mercury* on 28 June 1973 revealed a similar disquiet among parents, mainly middle class in origin. An action group of protest had been set up consisting of an architect, a businessman, an accountant and a Conservative representative on the new council. The sort of disquiet manifested is defined in terms of lack of 'self-discipline among staff and pupils', 'faction in homes where what the school is teaching is completely opposed to parental standards', 'lack of concentration on the 3 Rs', 'insufficient emphasis on examinations and any form of competition', 'insufficient provision of out-of-school work'

4 BERNBAUM, G. (1973) 'Countesthorpe College', in *Case Studies in Educational Innovation*, Vol. 3 OECD

5 The title of an investigation by the Schools Council, published in 1968. The aim was to discover why many children were so discontented with school that they left at the first possible moment

6 *Cf.* my essay in *Black Paper*, 4

7 *Cf.* 'Education Cannot Compensate for Society', *New Society*, 26 February 1970, pp. 344–7

8 *Times Educational Supplement*, 5 October 1973. See RAYNOR J. and

HARRIS E., (1977) *Urban Education I: The City Experience*, Ward Lock Educational, pp. 262–6

9 Paper 1, 'A Question of Equality' (ii), pp. 18–19

10 'Towards a Theory of Popular Education', *Times Educational Supplement*, 12 and 19 March 1971; reprinted in HOOPER R. (ed.), (1971) *The Curriculum* Oliver & Boyd, pp. 251–64.

2.9 Cultural revaluation

Gabriel Chanan and Linda Gilchrist

Cultural revaluation does not mean merely new interpretations of art and literature. If traditional culture fails to carry conviction with many of today's teachers and pupils it is because it seems to have been relegated to a department of its own, highly revered in theory, sometimes invoked as an ultimate reference point for *personal* behaviour and experience, virtually ignored as a source of values for policies and practices in society as a whole.

Our emerging culture will distinguish itself from all former dominant cultures by not being tailored to the interests or glorification of a ruling class nor being an instrument at the disposal of priestly castes or academic experts. It will need to be able to inspire values relevant to questions like: how can members of hitherto exploited classes or nations become self-determining? How can classes or societies which hitherto saw themselves as 'humanity', and the alien as expendable, exploitable or barbarian, learn to take nourishment from diversity? What forms should personal fulfilment take when liberated from the notion that pleasure and achievement consist in being better, happier, richer or more powerful than others? What forms should communal fulfilment take when liberated from the notion that social good consists in the creation of ever more sophisticated material needs and a permanently escalating exploitation of natural resources?

There can be no illusion that culture alone (like education alone) could *solve* questions like how to end exploitation, how to prevent the depletion of world resources, how to reconcile hostile factions, and so forth. Culture has more to do with activating values and modes of perception *favourable* to the solutions of the problems than with the prescription of specific solutions. But the role of culture in making solutions firstly conceivable and secondly acceptable is clearly immense; and its role in deepening the way we experience those problems is paramount. Culture cannot be adequately

Source: *What School is For* (1974), pp. 120–30.

explained as a 'superstructure' on an 'economic base' (the Marxist formula). Despite the inevitable ideological element in culture, the fact that the strength of this element varies, and often in inverse proportion to the quality of the work of art (or whatever) shows that the phenomenon of culture as such cannot be wholly accounted for or evaluated by ideological or economic determinants.

In order to be able to illuminate such questions the new culture will have to be built on respect for the autonomy of all human beings. That educationalists are still far off from appreciating this need is shown by its conspicuous neglect in most discussions of educational aims:

> The attention of children should be directed towards their duties and rights as citizens, towards the responsibilities involved in marriage and bringing up a family, and towards opportunities for service to the neighbourhood and to a wider society. It is also necessary to prepare them for responsible adult personal relationships by way of personal manners, poise and courtesy and by developing their capacity for personal relationships and sympathetic response to persons of the same and of different traditions and cultures ... Pupils should be prepared in order to cope with the circumstances of work in a modern industrial society. This would involve particular regard for: (a) the speed of technological change and the accompanying shifts in the balance of work and leisure, (b) the need to accustom them gradually to the requirements of the world of work, (c) training in the practical complexities of adult life, e.g. money management, hire purchase, housing.[1]

Of course, everyone would agree with many of these prescriptions. But what is so unsatisfactory about formulations of this kind is not simply the manifest wish that pupils should fit in with society as it is, disturbing it as little as possible, but the apparent bland belief that society *can* be fitted in with – that it is in itself coherent and fair; that reality is negotiable by simply attaining a maturity in the prescribed terms. One would get no inkling from this statement that personal relationships or working situations are continual areas of conflict, both of interests and values. There is no attention to the fact that conflict, in oneself and between self and others, is one of the most fundamental human experiences – the very one, indeed, that makes values necessary. There is no hint of the fact that 'the speed of technological change' is itself a cause for alarm; or that its benefits, including 'shifts in the balance of work and leisure', are not automatically and equitably passed on but have to be fought for. There is no felt need to warn young people that 'the requirements of the world of work' are frequently dehumanizing and would need to be resisted by any self-respecting human being; or to alert them to the fact that society coheres as much by resistance to conventional norms as by conformity to them. And there is no apparent attachment of importance to the existential problems of autonomy which underlie all values in society – how to structure time, how to attribute relative values to different experiences, how to cultivate extended personal memory, how to cope with grief, how to enjoy.

Yet it must not be thought that 'progressive' educational reasoning generally gives, by contrast, proper recognition to the element of people's autonomy in shaping their future. Man the chooser is often lost in the image of inexorable social change and impersonal progress. 'Reality' is given a sparkling new brand image, but we're still being told that it's impervious to our influence and we just have to fit in with it:

> In the decades to come we shall have to reckon with an accelerated process of change in many fields, triggered off by innovations in electronics and computer technology ... This growth will be accompanied by a rise in individual standards of living. But a problem arising from this kind of change is the 'culture lag', found not only in institutions, e.g. the education system, but also in personal attitudes and values, which derive from a state of society where the external determinants of technology, economics and institutions were different.... The new technology will require many people ... to undergo total retraining.[2]

The dynamism of this vision distracts attention from its bleakness. Culture, values and attitudes – the entire mind of man – are seen as mere reflections of particular technological conditions. There is no room for values to be what they really are – people's judgements of whatever affects them by their effect on themselves as human beings. If social progress is to have any real meaning technology must be judged by its effect on us, not we by our attitude to technology!

Correspondingly, the easy promise of higher living standards is made without any concrete thought about, firstly, what people have to do in order to obtain these higher standards, and secondly just what makes a living standard 'higher'. When we detach standard of living from autonomy we end up with a criterion which is external to man. To see social change as something that happens to man irrespective of his wish or decision (rather than as a process which affects his wishes and decisions in frequently unforeseen ways which he must then judge afresh) is to encourage resignation to the uncontrollable – which may then indeed become uncontrollable.

Our values are permeated by an abstract idea of change or progress, instead of a progressively refined image of the condition we want to progress to. In the deification of the idea of progress man is distracted from his capacity for fulfilment in this world just as much as he was in the middle ages by the idea of the hereafter. It deflects him in the first place from the relatively short-term motivations which are the real springs of *chosen* social change, and in the second place from the existential problem of living one's own life in one's own lifetime. Fixation on too abstract a concept of progress may deflect attention from both life and death. It is one way of avoiding the consciousness of death (since our lives are seen as primarily contributing to some ideal state to be enjoyed by future generations, without our seeing that those generations are going to live through essentially the same suspended consciousness that we do now) and hence of cheating ourselves of the necessary framework for the full valuing of life.

The attack on human autonomy, representing perhaps a fear of freedom, has a wardrobe which can make it respectable in any political company. Where the conservative sees society statically, as if values culled from the past could be applied to our own times without reinterpretation, and the progressive sees a future of endless change, evolutionary and impersonal, the radical is tempted to seek not endless but 'total' change – to believe that at the orgasmic moment of revolution, changes will occur which so alter our idea of what is possible that there is no point in trying to make any provision for them now. A simplified dialectical model permits the assertion that pure opposition is all that is needed to create the future synthesis out of the present. Yet there is, of course, no such thing as a total qualitative break in history, even in a revolution – and if there were it would become meaningless to those who experienced it, since it implies a break in their consciousness as absolute as that in social organization. In those who insist on the need for *total* change we must assume either that there are unexamined mental reservations, or a concealed attraction to oblivion.

Respect for autonomy means, in education, recognition for the fact that pupils, like all of us, are already actively engaged in the refashioning of a culture. Real sources of original thought are impossible to ascertain. The conventional image of the original thinker is of someone who adds a new bit on top of existing thought, a bit which may or may not eventually result in the reinterpretation of existing thought. But new forms of thought do not necessarily manifest themselves first as additions to an existing store of knowledge which has already been mastered. They may very well manifest themselves first as disagreements with some aspect or other of the existing store of knowledge, and when they are incipient they are not likely to be fully articulate and cogent. When pupils show their rejection of some aspect of received knowledge (mediated, we must always remember, by a single, fallible teacher) they are almost invariably interpreted as incapable of mastery of it. Yet their rejection may be an incipient form of rational disagreement.

Subjectively, autonomous thought does not experience itself as an attempt at originality but as an attempt to understand given reality, including the reality of received knowledge. It only discovers its degree of autonomy by gradually coming to understand why it *cannot* understand received thought, why the received thought fails to satisfy, fails to illuminate reality. We cannot wholly understand what seems to us untrue because 'understanding', in normal usage, means precisely seeing that the thing *is* true. Only later, with the maturation of the autonomous thought, will the thinker after all come to 'understand' the received thought in the sense of grasping its origins and its function for the person who thinks it is true. Only at this stage could he, if he chose to, demonstrate conventional mastery of the conventional thought. Only now could he 'assume temporarily complete agreement with the statement', as 'objective' testers would have required of him at the start.

Admittedly, when pupils appear to reject 'high' culture – that is, a particular teacher's particular representation of 'high' culture – impatience, prejudice, insecure attachment to crude cultural norms are all possible explanations. Yet it is also possible that the pupil has an incipient disagreement with values or notions attributed to that culture; but this explanation is almost universally ignored.

The emerging culture to which schools should be host and midwife will be a culture of universal humanitarianism. Critics use the term 'humanism' to designate the post-religious culture of the Renaissance and onwards – the culture that includes the beginnings of modern literature, philosophy, science and all that schools are said to hold most dear. But whether this humanism includes or implies universal humanitarianism remains ambivalent. Conservative critics are still not wholly rid of attachment to the class-biased, chauvinist, racist, anti-feminist attitudes that can be found embodied in traditional culture alongside the more enduring humanistic elements. The response of twentieth-century criticism towards the embarrassment of reactionary values in traditional art and literature is essentially a retreat into formalism, a devaluation of subject matter in general. In the past this has been a source of confusion to humanities teachers, who have found themselves trying to argue pupils into appreciating the sonnet form or the construction of metaphors, when these things can have no interest except in relation to the direct representational preoccupations of the poet about love or death; or, on the outing to the art gallery, trying to make out that the fact that it's a naked woman or a dying soldier who is vividly depicted is somehow unimportant compared with the use of perspective or the handling of brushstrokes.[3]

The school of criticism which still provides the basic perspective for the academic valuation of high culture – the school of T.S. Eliot and F.R. Leavis – is one whose humanism is of a passionately abstract-idealist temper. The prevailing notion, the framework for evaluation, is T.S. Eliot's 'ideal order of art'[4] – art as a sublime competitive hierarchy. Ultimately only the degree of greatness of a work of art is of importance, as if all art were trying to do the same thing for the same people, and in a historically static landscape. At the same time, marks of greatness are awarded on values of psychological insight and moral depth. While many of the individual critical insights developed with these criteria are immensely valuable, and do represent substantial contributions to an emerging culture of universal humanitarianism, fixation on the notion of the authority and ideal nature of cultural standards gives rise to the blinkered rigidity of the Black Papers (whose editors edited a 'high culture' literary journal for some time before branching out into educational politics).

The explanation offered by 'high culture' critics for the survival of some works of art while others have perished is their profounder insight into and compassion for the human condition. Yet the original patronage of 'great' art was the patronage of a ruling class which was anything but compassionate in its actual social relations to the mass of people in its own time. Thus the artists we now call great did a job that went much deeper than their patrons had paid for. Starting with the brief of embellishing the life of the court or reflecting the glory of the rich, they not only gradually introduced elements of satire and criticism but depicted their patrons (who were also their subjects) in such a way that everyone could identify with their pleasures and weaknesses, and therefore everyone could come to realize his basic human equality with them. As both artists and patrons became more aware of this process, artists came to be regarded, and to regard themselves, as somewhat abnormal, unconforming people. This contributed to the Romantic image of the artist, which reflects the basic tension not between the artist and *society*, as if society were a unified body of 'normal' people with 'normal' attitudes, but between the artist and his *patronage*. Romanticism was the artist's way of insisting on the importance of this tension, but it was neutralized by the academic solution. The power of art could not be denied, but it could be isolated by accepting its nonconformity and making it into a freak called 'genius', to be idolized but at the same time attributed to individual peculiarities and denied significance as contemporary social criticism. Kicked upstairs, art became Art, something of a substitute for religion, but said to be appreciable by ordinary mortals only a generation or two after its appearance, when its actual context had passed and its 'eternal' qualities began to appear.

The conservative critics are right about the fundamental humanism of great art, but while they can deal safely with its implications for an age now gone they do not see its implications for our own age. They fail to see also that many of those artists who, under the influence of academic criticism, aspire to the mantle of 'high culture' have become, over the past half century, more and more emotionally constipated, self-absorbed and trivial, while much of the vigour and humanism of great art has passed or is passing over into popular culture.

Neither the abdication of judgement glamourized by some progressives nor the secure academic authority assumed by conservatives will really answer the cultural challenge with which we find ourselves faced. The problems posed in our school by the presence of immigrant children are merely the most visible part of this challenge. It is as feeble to speak of the need for immigrants to 'fit in with our way of life' as it is to talk of the need of pupils in general to 'fit in with society'. For we have not *got* a 'way of life' which we can prescribe in that manner, other than the democratic idea itself, which changes its forms and meaning as new social forces seek expression through it. Democratic principles must certainly provide the structure for our arguments, but cannot themselves settle those arguments. We have the problem of developing a culture adequate to an unprecedented social and global situation; and our cultural history, including our increasing awareness of cultures developed in other societies, forms a store of resources on which we may draw in the fashioning of our values, not a body of ready made values.

Meanwhile what holds us together is a sort of federation of subcultures in various states of tolerance and tension, 'high' culture itself being one of these subcultures rather than *the* culture of our society. Certainly this pluralistic condition will continue, and there will be cross-fertilization. After experiencing the rich cultural diversity of our time it would be torture to arrive after all only at some new monolithic cultural state. But culture is not merely private lifestyle or sublime entertainment. The major social and political problems of our time demand from us continual complex collective value judgements and hence some degree of reconcilability in our values. We might more reasonably, then, speak of the need for immigrants to accommodate to the way of life which is now in the process of creation – a process in which their influence is as valid as ours, and our effort of reaccommodation as necessary as theirs.

That such new syntheses are psychologically possible, and indeed liberating, is shown by hippies who, in contrast to the passive tolerance which is the most that most of us can manage when faced with the unfamiliar, take positive delight in cultural diversity. It would be instructive to study how, in psychological terms, it is possible to transcend one's cultural limitations, or one's hollow attachment to cultural forms which do not actually inspire one's beliefs or behaviour. Clearly some kind of inner confidence is required, which perhaps comes from exercising the sense of creativity, so that one is less dependent on familiar external forms to 'guarantee' reality – and more able to distinguish when they genuinely make reality more manageable.

The values by which we must live in the last quarter of the twentieth century do not exist, then, as a secure body of doctrine which schools can simply hand on, nor will they arrive automatically through some evolutionary adaptation to conditions created by our own technology. They must be consciously created, and are now in the process of creation throughout society; a process in which, if they can rise to it, schools have a vital part to play.

Notes

1 From the 'Joint statement of objectives' for comprehensive schools produced by a committee of leading educationalists and reproduced as Appendix A in Ross, J.M. *et al* (1972) *A Critical Appraisal of Comprehensive Education* Slough, NFER.

2 Husen, Torsten (1972), 'The "learning society" and tomorrow's schools', *London Educational Review*, 1 (2).

3 In his television series entitled 'Ways of seeing', John Berger restored the necessary emphasis to subject matter in painting. See Berger, J., (1972) *Ways of Seeing*, London, BBC and Harmondsworth, Penguin.

4 See Eliot, T.S. (1919), 'Tradition and the individual talent' and 'The use of poetry and the use of criticism' (1933) in *Selected Prose*, ed. John Hayward (1953) Harmondsworth, Penguin.

2.10 Conventional secondary school practice

D. Holly

Changes in secondary education are happening in the context of a conventional situation which defines the norm of teaching and learning for the age group. This situation can be termed 'traditional' in the sense that it has changed very little over time – thirty or forty years for some schools, a century or more for a large number. Secondary education has become identified with specialist teaching, separate periods for separate subjects, whole-class instruction even in practical lessons, relatively formal relationships between teacher and pupil, a proportion of work required to be done out of school as preparation or homework, emphasis on testing and examinations with class positions and regular reports, and an overt system of rewards and punishments connected with academic performance and general conduct. So familiar is this to many people that they will be surprised that anyone should bother to describe it. Even the upheaval of comprehensive reorganization has left the pattern largely unchanged – predictably, since it is one which became common to both grammar and modern schools.

Here the conventional pattern will be assumed as background for limited and specific curricular and methodological changes. It is only the most recent and most radical which have involved wider reappraisal of what constitutes a secondary school education.

There is another sense in which the standard secondary school is traditional. Secondary education carries with it a strong element of concern for what is often termed the pastoral role of the school, a formalized system of values and relationships related to the 'moral well-being' of pupils. Over and above the performance of academic tasks and conformity to rules related to work, secondary schools usually claim to promote general social and ethical attitudes. These attitudes and the teachers' functions connected with them owe a great deal to the nineteenth century and to the ideals of men like Thomas Arnold and the other public school reformers. This

Source: *Beyond Curriculum* (1973).

'pastoral care' tradition is something which distinguishes British secondary education from that of most other countries. Whether effective or otherwise it has aroused enthusiasm in some, hostility in others. Recently sociologists have related it, often in rather an indefinite way, to the value system of the middle class. Although not central to the question of actual curriculum – except in the specific area of religion and morality – it forms an important dimension of the total situation in the standard secondary school.

These traditional elements in secondary schools merit fairly close attention since they represent common practice and define what it is that is being changed. While they are all closely inter-dependent it will be easier to consider them as separable into matters of organization, content of learning, methodology and general values.

The central organizational unit of the conventional secondary school is the *form*, the teaching unit. This is based on age but is also generally differentiated by some criterion of ability, usually attainment in what are considered the basic subjects of English and mathematics. Such 'streamed' forms are to be found in selective, modern and comprehensive schools alike and the number of streamed forms in a year-group of pupils depends on the number of teachers available, together with the size of teaching group aimed at. Thus selective schools have commonly had about twenty-five to thirty pupils in a form, while modern schools have often had from thirty-five to forty. This gives about three or four forms per year in most schools. Comprehensive schools, catering for the whole age range of a locality, tend to have seven or eight, though, exceptionally, large urban schools may have twelve or even fourteen.

Streaming is a practice which has grown with the expansion of secondary education. At one time selective grammar schools were too small to admit more than one form per year, and this covered the ability range of the school, while the elementary schools had 'standards' related to age as well as attainment, a practice only recently disappearing in other countries. The least able pupils were kept down in a class until they grew too big to remain with the rest of their standard. Similarly the most able were put up to a standard above their age peers. This system has been known in America as 'repeating a grade' or 'skipping a grade'. In the traditional grammar school, too, it was not uncommon for a form to contain a wide age range, with able pupils missing one or even two forms. Scholarship examinations for transfer from the elementary to (selective) secondary systems allowed pupils to start at a variety of ages from nine to twelve and the old School Certificate examination was similarly elastic with regard to the age at which pupils could be entered. All this meant that form groups of homogeneous ability could in some circumstances be achieved by means of a wider age range. The standardization after 1944 of transfer to secondary schools at eleven-plus and of public examinations at sixteen has led to the adoption by both primary and secondary schools of promotion by age and division by ability in an attempt to achieve homogeneous forms. For twenty years this – which was recommended in the Hadow Report of 1932 as a reform – has been accepted as the natural dispensation. Variations from it have been self-conscious experiments, as when many grammar schools adopt parallel mixed-ability forms in the first year as a diagnostic measure to enable them to make more precise allocation to streams thereafter.

By and large, then, the secondary form has been a teaching unit of thirty to forty pupils with as narrow an ability range as possible. A refinement of this has been the practice of *setting* for individual subjects, most commonly English, mathematics and science. Here the attempt has been to achieve as narrow an ability range as possible *with regard to a given subject*, recognizing that ability in one subject is not necessarily matched by ability in another. Such setting has normally been done across two to five streamed forms in a year group, the constraining factor usually being the availability of staff and specialist rooms for more than one teaching group to be following the same subject at the same point on the timetable.

In some comprehensive schools a further complexity of organization has been the system of *banding*. This has been operated in one of two ways. In the first way it has allowed setting to take place across defined groups of forms in a given year. A large school with fourteen streamed forms in any one year group could have an 'A' stream (or band) of five forms, setted for subjects which could offer five specialist rooms and teachers at any one time, five 'B' stream forms similarly setted, and four 'C' stream forms. Thus 'prismatic streaming' could be further refined for individual subjects with the possibility that the ablest pupil in English, for example, would find himself in Form 3A1, Set 1, and the slowest in Form 3C4, Set 4. In a school where I once taught, the least able pupils were afforded the added distinction of being labelled the 'X' group.

Mindful of the aims of comprehensive education, other schools have used the band system in a different way – to relax the pressures of streaming. Thus a school with seven forms in a year group will have two parallel forms for more able pupils, three parallel forms for average pupils and two further parallel remedial forms for the least able. Within these bands, however, setting is still possible and often demanded by, say, mathematics or French teachers who argue that their subjects require especially homogeneous teaching groups. We will see shortly that the nature of the teaching approach is intimately connected with the organization of forms.

So much for the traditional ways of organizing the *grouping* of pupils. What about their *accommodation* in terms of space? A form has to have somewhere to work. In conventional secondary schools there have been two main approaches to this, related to the prevalence or otherwise of setting. The first approach, adopted where the personnel of teaching groups tends to change for different subject sets, may be termed the 'pupil-nomadic' approach. Under this system groups of pupils move about the school from one lesson to the next, forming and re-forming according to the subject set in which they find themselves. In a large, glass-walled, multi-storey comprehensive school this periodic migration can take on awe-inspiring dimensions with myriads of uniformly-attired ants moving purposefully and apparently instinctually at the buzzing of a bell. The problems of traffic-flow by this system have kept many a senior master busy for considerable spaces of time. At lunch-times and breaks the ordered purposefulness of the ants' progress tends to be replaced by frenetic activity with consequent calls on the staff and prefecture for policing duties. A student of animal behaviour would no doubt be intrigued by this variation in pace and orderliness as between school time and pupils' time. Teachers and pupils in conventional schools of this type are less mystified.

The second approach to the accommodation of teaching groups is older and typifies schools where the form, however narrowly or broadly streamed, is taught together for all academic subjects. This may be termed the 'staff-nomadic' approach. The pupils remain in their own form room and await, more or less patiently, the arrival of the subject specialist. The only movement of pupils is for subjects that absolutely require specialist rooms, like science and physical education, or during free times. Such a system seems to typify the more ancient and traditional foundations and no doubt reflects the assumed sedateness of such institutions. The reality is perhaps rather less serene, with pupil sentries posted to 'keep cavey' and warn of the approach of staff.

In either case the typical classroom of a conventional secondary school is essentially an arid environment with little of the visual stimulus to be found in primary classrooms. Even where the pupil-nomadic system operates and the teacher has his or her 'own' specialist room the constant procession of different classes through it gives it the air of a public space, common to a wide variety of pupils, with little motivation for widespread and frequently-changing display of pupils' work. In the circumstances of relatively concentrated occupation, at most for forty minutes a day, what opportunity is there for the pupils of any one form to inspect each other's work in this way or for the teacher to communicate much that is new in visual terms? Typically a geography room will have a few dusty models, some yellowing maps and some ink-stained posters, an English room may have some equally ageing fair-copies of poems and a maths room nothing at all.

In the one-form-room dispensation the environment is likely to be even more spartan in its functionality. When a procession of teachers takes the place of a procession of forms, the irrelevance of any one set of visual stimuli to the rest of the activity discourages the use of wall spaces and the deployment of models. Quite apart from the natural modesty of the teachers, considerations of access to the room during free times limit the contribution of any one subject specialist to the display of work – unless he or she happens to be also the form teacher.

The same undynamic quality affects the arrangements of furniture. Even with lighter-weight desks and chairs than once were common, the effort of changing and rearranging the room for either different groups of pupils or different subject activities is daunting. Under these circumstances the usual appearance of a conventional secondary classroom in grammar, modern or comprehensive school is archetypal: serried rows of desks face the teacher's table which, in really venerable institutions, is on a higher plane with a supporting diäs. Behind the teacher is the blackboard on which information directly confronts the pupils. Spatially the arrangement neatly symbolizes the conventional relationship of pupils and teacher to education: education in this perspective is a unilinear process in which knowledge is communicated to pupils via the mediation of the teacher. Many readers may never have considered any alternative view of learning – as it affects secondary schools, anyway.

The final aspect of organization relates to *time*. In the conventional secondary school, time is divided between different activities in a comparitively intensive way. The school day commonly starts with either Assembly or Registration. The very fragmentation of learning activities makes these institutions important. In a primary school the class teacher registers the presence or absence of his pupils continuously: only bureaucracy may require the completion of a formal register at a set time. In a primary school too the basic similarity of the pupils' experience in different classes gives them a functional sense of unity, so that Assembly is specifically devoted to general or 'moral' purposes. In the traditional secondary school, Assembly, though legally a 'moral' occurrence, is essentially an opportunity for inspiring a sense of unity among diversity and, on a mundane level, for *communicating* with the whole body of pupils. It is a functional use of time – especially where there is no loudspeaker system.

Teaching time is even more specific, and jealously guarded by each subject department. It is carefully parcelled out for each form according to a notional balanced diet of subject intake during the working week – which may be six or seven days in some timetables. Thus English may be ingested once a day, French every other day, geography once a week and so on. One of the most significant activities for the newly arrived secondary pupil at the beginning of each academic year is 'filling in the timetable'. Those virgin blank forms with their ordered rows and columns somehow symbolize the ordered and fragmented existence of the secondary pupil in a conventional school. Indeed the ritual nature of standard secondary school activities is aptly represented in visual terms by the master timetable grid in the Head's office and in auditory terms by the automated buzzing of bells between each period. The whole thing is powerfully reminiscent of an elaborate game, with buzzers and periods having very much the same significance as they do in ice-hockey. Human relationships, too, tend to be governed by games-like considerations arising out of a fundamental alienation of the whole educational process. There are strong ritualistic elements in the most seemingly utilitarian happenings in conventional secondary education and these are most obviously seen in the time division of the school day. The thirty-five- or forty-minute period is the most distinctive aspect of the traditional secondary school, placing important constraints alike on the flow of time and, as we shall see shortly, on the very *nature* of the learning activities.

So much for the actual organization of schools in terms of pupil-deployment, use of space and use of time. What of the educational assumptions that can be inferred from the organization?

Consider first the question of the homogeneous pupil groups which are fairly universally aimed at in conventional organization. In terms of teaching method, to be examined below, these clearly assume the primacy of *exposition*: pupils are to be told things – facts, interpretations, principles. Education is obviously visualized as a unilinear process – as noted already – with knowledge and feeling being mediated to the pupil by the teacher. Where the approach is thus expository, common sense dictates that maximum effectiveness demands an audience whose receptivity is as alike as possible. This indicates pupils as far as possible on a level with regard to attainment at least and, if possible, emotional maturity. Age grading and intellectual streaming seem the ideal combination for a pupil group: hence the conventional streamed form and subject set. It is important that the teacher should be able to reach all the pupils in the teaching situation and this is hardly possible if age and intellectual range is too wide.

The implied conception of *educability* is also reasonably clear. It is assumed that (a) attainment is a fairly close correlate of capacity and that (b) capacity is relatively fixed and not open to basic improvement. These related propositions must underlie the practice of allocating pupils to groups on the evidence of performance in school subjects, otherwise the educational needs of pupils would be sacrificed to the convenience of teachers. For if capacity is not in large measure constrained by genetically determined characteristics, then it is open to the influence of the educational process itself and 'grouping by ability' is simply a prescription for doing nothing. Jack is likely to stay a dull boy if you treat him as one. Now, as a matter of fact, the 'genetically determined' thesis is at least open to question at the theoretical level. Empirically there have been indications that treating pupils optimistically does indeed produce encouraging results: the hypothesized self-fulfilling prophecy by which young people labelled 'bright' or 'dull' conform to expectations irrespective of measured ability has received some degree of experimental support.[1] But even if one had no reason to doubt the given nature of some kind of general intelligence of the sort, until recently so confidently described in terms of Intelligence Quotients, one would still have to believe that developed ability in various school subjects is closely related to it. Otherwise one would not be streaming by ability at all but by attainment – which is a demonstrably negative procedure: 'thus they are performing and thus we will be content for them to perform'.

The persistence of streamed forms as teaching units therefore needs some explanation. A naïve acceptance of genetical determinism could explain *mixed-attainment* groups based on similarity of measured intelligence: it is insufficient to account for the prevalence of groups based on *similar attainment*. Such groups illustrate the conviction of working teachers in conventional secondary schools that the job is not remedial – unless they happen to be teachers of the least able pupils. Remedial teaching is seen as a specialism and applicable only to the problem children at the bottom end of the ability scale. On the whole secondary teachers accept pupils as they find them – 'bright', 'average' or 'slow'. They see their job as catering for a range of ability almost fully developed by eleven. Thereafter it is a question of developing maturity and cultivating skills. The secondary teacher in the conventional school is almost wholly subject-orientated. For him the job is to do with teaching his *subject* to pupils whose receptivity is given. He does not really see it as his business to foster the development of the young: this he leaves to the primary teacher. Consequently streaming by ability is seen as the most efficient arrangement of pupil groups.

The notion of 'the subject' thus lies at the very heart of conventional secondary school philosophy. It is linked with the whole question of the content of learning – the curriculum in its strictest sense – with the methodology of teaching and with the general values of the system. Just as most secondary teachers take their pupils as they find them, so they take for granted what it is they are supposed to be teaching. What they are teaching, if vague ideals like 'cultivation ' and 'liberal knowledge' are set aside, is a body of subject-matter related to their college or university specialism. Sometimes, this knowledge is seen as simply utilitarian and directly vocational, sometimes, as a training of the mind or even as an opportunity for self-awareness. On the whole, though, such thinking, where it takes place at all, is a way of rationalizing the already existing state of affairs by which subject specialists are recruited to teach predefined areas of knowledge in a way that is not really open to discussion. It is a rationalization rather than a rationale. A true rationale is only possible in an open situation where the decisions have not already been made. In the conventional secondary school all the real curricular decisions have been made.

Who makes these decisions? Technically, in most schools under the British system, it is the headmaster. In practice the decisions are made by convention and by the institutionalized demands of higher education and the labour market. Convention dictates the list of subjects which are recognized by secondary schools: history is included, archaeology usually is not; geography is taught universally, but not sociology; classics is still relatively common, philosophy or logic almost unknown; French is widely studied, German relatively rarely – and so on. Some of this – as in the case of sociology – is due to the belief that a subject is not suitable for the secondary age range. But sociology also illustrates another factor: the recency of a subject's development. On the whole, the most well-established secondary school subjects are those which were developed at universities during the nineteenth century, the time when the secondary curriculum was last basically reformed from the classical tradition of the Renaissance – hence English, history, geography, arithmetic of the stocks-and-shares variety, Euclidian geometry, algebra, Newtonian physics, inorganic chemistry, 'governess' French, muscular-Christian games, classifactory biology, plus a residue of Latin. With the addition of religion and 'vocational' and 'fringe' subjects, this still forms the curriculum of the majority of ordinary secondary schools as well as of the academic ones. To say that such a curriculum in the last quarter of the twentieth century is rationally derived would be to fly in the face of reason. Demonstrably, it is the result of a historical process.

Examined logically, 'English', for instance, is a strange phenomenon. It replaced the study of classics as the major humanistic subject, yet it has none of the impressive universality claimed for classical learning. By contrast it is curiously chauvinist, even parochial, especially in that until fairly recently it did not include American literature even at university level. Its arrival as an academic study coincided, in fact, with the peak of imperial self-confidence: English was seen as the fitting heir to Latin and Greek, the new language of world civilization, and the study of Shakespeare and Milton the natural replacement for the study of Homer and Virgil.

Once established, this curriculum became accepted and was accorded the status of received wisdom just as the preceding classical one had been, but in a very much shorter space of time. It still defines the nature of learning in all but a few secondary schools. Though various reforms have begun to challenge some of the assumptions implicit in it, on the whole 'learning' in our conventional secondary schools is seen in terms of the activities which characterize physics, English, algebra and the rest. Like so much else dealt with in this chapter the fact may seem hardly worth comment because it is so universal and so apparently unexceptionable. Yet an alternative view of learning is possible and the conventional view is being challenged in some schools. For the moment it is sufficient to notice that school learning is a matter of well-defined categories whose early stages are usually narrower than their later ones. The younger and less able the pupil, the narrower the possibilities of the syllabus: any form of liberation usually has to wait at least until the fifth form and, more usually, until O levels are over.

Much of the conventional secondary school learning is at an informational level, the aim being the acquisition by pupils of a body of knowledge. In history and geography there is the idea of a framework of facts which ought to be completed in five years. In English, great emphasis is placed on conventions of spelling, punctuation and 'standard' grammar, together with some knowledge of the works of major writers – as defined from time to time by examining boards. In science, emphasis is placed on the knowledge of formulae and standard experimental procedures of laws and classifications. In mathematics, again, there is emphasis on knowledge of standard procedures for solving problems, formulae and computational drills. In modern languages, pupils are expected to have by heart a basic vocabulary and know the rules of syntax, often in a very standardized form such as paradigms of inflexion: knowledge of the rules may be said to take precedence over ability to manipulate the language, just as it did with the classical languages whose only surviving form is written and which accordingly have to be dealt with like a code – by the application of rules for deciphering.

It is usually only at sixth-form level that an attempt is made to place the main emphasis on comprehension rather than the acquisition of ideas. Before this, even formal English exercises in comprehension are really aimed at discovering pupils' levels of *interpretation* of given facts and concepts – a much humbler mental activity than genuine comprehension. The essential characteristic of learning in conventional schools is the acquisition and manipulation of other people's ideas, basically a passive activity requiring a minimum of commitment from the learner. In an important sense school learning is external to the learner, alienated from him. To make learning truly your own, really to 'comprehend' facts and relationships between them, you have to enter into the learning process actively, to be involved. In one sense this has to do with what the psychologists call 'intrinsic motivation', an urge springing from the intrinsic interest of ideas or skills being internalized. But in a more important and pervasive sense it has to do with genuine learning being a development of the human potential within the learner, a realization of humanity, in fact. There is virtually nothing of this in the activity we call education in our standard secondary schools. Even at sixth-form level, ideas are presented to the young for their admiration or rejection and for formal analysis and 'evaluation'. Very seldom are they invited to apply the intellectual skills they acquire in anything but scholastic exercises. Very seldom is it suggested to them that, young as they are, they might have something valid to contribute themselves. This, not libertarianism, is the root of unrest and rebelliousness. Recently, a general climate of political awareness and social criticism among the post-adolescent generation in secondary schools, colleges and universities has caused them to turn with resentment upon the alienated drudgery of their school experience. Because they are still only half emancipated their criticism has been directed against the organization rather than the content of education. They have tended to look only at the status of the pupil and have not yet considered what it is that schools require pupils to *do* – presumably because as yet they lack any alternative perspective. This is true even in the universities where the criticism of curriculum, when it has occurred, has been largely preoccupied with content in the more superficial sense – this particular piece of knowledge rather than that. But the content of learning in secondary schools, as elsewhere, is basically not a question of competing syllabi. It is rather a question of aims and intentions. Whether I study the career of Napoleon or the General Strike is really less an issue than *how* and *why* I study them. This leads directly into the intimately connected questions of methodology and general values.

The methodology of education, or what elsewhere than in England is called the science of pedagogy, has been consistently neglected both by practising teachers and, more culpably, by theoreticians of education. It is significant that in our colleges and departments of education the basics of educational theory have come to be identified as psychology, philosophy, history and sociology – all disciplines borrowed from elsewhere and none springing from the study of education itself. Method, where it is dealt with systematically at all, has been relegated to a sub-theoretical status.

In part this is a function of the new-found respectability of 'education' as an academic study: a theoretical basis had to be found and that most readily available was a composite construction using such pre-existing disciplines as might obviously be applied to educational questions. These have proved uneasy bedfellows. To them have been added descriptive exercises such as 'comparative education' and 'curriculum studies'. Curriculum development, like methodology, has been viewed with suspicion as not quite academic.

But another reason for the low status of methodology in Britain is simply a failure to identify questions of method as theoretically problematic. Teaching method has been thought of on the level of tricks for teachers – often quite sophisticated tricks, but nevertheless tricks. This feeling has been shared by most practitioners. Criticism from serving teachers about college and university courses has generally concentrated on the inadequacy of practical training, a feeling that 'method' should be less rather than more theoretical. Such criticism is understandable given the generally superficial approach to theory of education which most teachers have experienced. It is nevertheless perverse. The theory of classroom practice is vital: without it practice is not merely blind, it is mindless. But such theory does not arise from the preoccupations of philosophers, sociologists and the rest. It arises from the definitive activity of the classroom, which is not the refined articulation of human thought, nor the interplay of social forces, nor the unfolding of historical processes, but the *planned learning of young human beings*. It is important, of course, that intending teachers like anyone else should critically examine the basic assumptions upon which practice is founded, but there are interesting theoretical questions which arise out of the learning situation of the nature: 'given that our intentions for the pupils are so-and-so, *how* does this happen, how can we *make* it happen?' This requires a notion of 'learning method' and 'teaching theory', both conspicuously absent at the moment. In terms of our conventional secondary schools, certain things might be observed about current practice but most of them usually go unexamined, as has been noted already.

The conventional secondary classroom affords a relatively narrow range of activities. Much of the time it is a matter of the teacher talking and the class listening more or less attentively according to the histrionic skill of the teacher and the intrinsic interest of what is being said. Sometimes a teacher asks questions designed to discover the degree of attention. When these questions are asked in general of the whole class they elicit the highest degree of attention maintained by any single member of the class – or at least the highest degree of attention attained by those motivated to answer. When the teacher is more subtle, questioning elicits roughly the range of attention as between the least or most attentive, depending on his knowledge of the probabilities in that class. Occasionally questions are carefully phrased so as to elicit the degree and range of comprehension, as opposed to simple attention. Even more rarely a teacher will engage in a dialogue with members of the class to discover and direct the pupils' ability to relate what he has been saying to other parts of their knowledge and experience. Very rarely indeed will a teacher, dealing with a whole class, be able to lead pupils to weigh evidence and form judgements: the degree of involvement required for this is just not possible in a one-in-thirty situation. From abortive efforts in this direction most teachers in standard secondary schools probably think that this activity is unattainable by any but the most gifted few.

Indeed the general tendency in secondary schools, as in the more formal primaries, is to act in terms of 'giftedness', 'slowness' and 'backwardness' as measured and attested by pupils' response to teachers' attempts to 'get them to think'. This is an important factor in streaming. Those pupils who are most alert are put in the top streams and the less alert are put in the lower streams. This is the function of written attainment tests, too, which merely interpose the extra screens of reading ability and co-ordination in writing to reinforce the teachers' perception of 'brightness' and 'dimness'. These colloquial terms of the staffroom – and the classroom – are significant in showing how teachers and learners perceive the activity of learning at school.

The other major activity of the conventional classroom, more or less silent reading and writing, is simply an extension of the activities mentioned above. When a pupil is working through examples or reading a text or answering 'comprehension' questions he is actually involved in an internal dialogue with a teacher-surrogate, the author of the book: and this dialogue is of course even more inflexible since the writer cannot know to whom he is speaking.

Learning in the average secondary classroom is seen as response to the expository efforts of the teacher or the textbook writer. Even in literature lessons – where these take place – the 'learning' is a matter of acquiring a store of highly regarded words and thoughts plus a few standardized accepted responses to them as passed on by the teacher. Pupils' own individual writing is usually in the form of essays, which allow them to respond in an accepted format to the equally limited demands of the teacher. Attainment in all areas is a measure of the success of the pupil in retaining and effectively regurgitating the ideas which the teachers and textbook writers have expounded. Given these prevailing conditions, a critical faculty is difficult to encourage since it would be tantamount to asking the pupil to challenge the teacher's *authority* in both senses. As remarked earlier, genuine 'comprehension' is equally difficult to achieve, since at no stage have the pupils been required to make these ideas their own, to internalize them in any genuine sense of articulating them with previous understanding. A person can go through the whole process of formal education without really understanding a single idea or integrating it with his pre-existing experiences. This commonly happens to those whose native culture is not that of the educated and dominant classes; they may acquire great sophistication in the manipulation of other people's ideas: their own remain quite simple. In this way a man may become a capable scientist and yet remain socially and politically more naïve than the man who mends the fuses on his computer. To this extent 'education' as it is understood in our society can be termed alienated: it remains basically outside the experience of the mass of the people, unrelated to their personal and human development. It is not necessarily a vehicle for the realization of full humanity. Sometimes it can be quite the reverse, a burden of confusion and the means of subjection.

Which leads us directly to the question of the general values promoted by conventional secondary schools.

Since the whole system of the school is one which represents learning as unilinear and teaching as simple exposition, the bravest attempts to form a 'critical intelligence' by means of it are unlikely to succeed. Here we are faced with the opposition between the overt and latent value-systems of conventional secondary schools. The proclaimed values of our schools, particularly of the more high-status and academic ones, are the values of a liberal democracy: fearless integrity, questing scepticism, social and personal responsibility, wide-ranging sensitivities. The operative values are rather different.

What is asked of the successful pupil? First and foremost, cheerful acceptance of authority in the sense of the presumed better knowledge and judgment of teachers and those who write books. This academic authority is buttressed by a more general moral authority covering questions of relationships and behaviour. This is what is meant by 'discipline' and 'order' and it assumes considerable importance in most secondary schools, more particularly where it is challenged.

The prevalence of concern about 'discipline' in secondary schools is often explained by the incipient anarchy of adolescence. The developmental psychologists obligingly explain that the adolescent's psyche is disorientated and chaotic: he is confused by the gap between his growing physical maturity, the promptings of his instincts and the demands of social responsibility. The implication is that what he needs is externally imposed restraint. Hence the importance of 'order'. One might as reasonably suggest that the young are confused by the conflict between their natural vitality and the paternalism of the schools. It is an interesting possibility that adolescence as a problem phenomenon is itself a social product. Little was heard of it before the commercial cult of the teenager emerged in economically advanced nations. The very economic development of advanced societies is giving the young more importance and therefore relatively more power. The contrast between this and the expectations of conventional secondary schools is extreme and was first apparent in the secondary moderns. It is now a factor even among those sections of the secondary population identified as most 'able' and therefore having most to gain from the system.[2]

Certainly the operative value-system of the schools is at odds with that of the youth culture. As regards music, for instance, the assumption of the schools – where music is admitted to the curriculum at all – is that only 'serious' music is worthy of commitment. The attachment of pupils in their after-school hours to jazz-derived forms is considered as hysterical, a typical adolescent disturbance. The proclaimed value of catholicity and wide-ranging sensitivity is denied by the operative value of received judgment and safely conventional criteria.

The ethical pretention of schools is scarcely less hollow. While headmasters moralize daily about honesty and fair play, senior pupils are encouraged by their teachers to become involved in the game of tricking the examiners. Cheating in school exams, when indulged in furtively by schoolboy amateurs, is condemned and punished. Cheating on a grand scale in public exams by practised professionals is accepted. Somehow the consulting of a hidden 'crib' under the desk in more heinous than an open conspiracy to defraud the examining bodies by perfecting model answers, concentrating on certain sections of the syllabus at the expense of omitting others altogether, and perverting the whole intention of the examination. It is little wonder that so many involved in the formal education system seem unable to take learning seriously. After all, their teachers appear to think so little of it that they are prepared to turn it into a rather mean sort of sport. Indeed to talk of 'learning' at all in the context of the conventional secondary school and the traditional examination system is considered a shade pretentious.

What then *are* the values promoted by the operation of the conventional school? Apart from acceptance, already mentioned, the most important seems to be *instrumentalism*, the elevation of otherwise meaningless activities into worthwhile goals because of the rewards which successful performance brings. In many schools, for instance, great emphasis is placed on 'marks'. No one asks the worth of the tasks which are performed or whether they are educative: what matters is whether they can earn points. For this purpose, knowing how to spell Othello is of greater moment than understanding what is at stake in Shakespeare's play, since the orthographical knowledge though humble is easy to score while conceptual awareness is a complex matter and difficult to assess. Pupils are therefore led to amass minute items of knowledge rather than seek for the sort of understanding which teachers theoretically rate higher. To object to any given system of marking, though, is to miss the point. It is the idea of marking itself which is in question. Pupils working for marks are working for something external, not only to themselves but to the very subject-matter they are dealing with.

The concept of learning and curriculum prevalent in conventional schools is thus very tightly bound up with the related values of acceptance and instrumentalism. Learning is seen as a matter of ingesting pre-packaged ideas and information which demand an acceptance of both the moral and intellectual authority of teachers, headmasters and examining boards. The curriculum is seen as, literally, 'a course to be run', a process to be got through as smoothly and efficiently as possible without reference to what the race itself may mean or why the track is marked out in one way rather than another: it is the finishing tape which matters, the mark, the examination pass, the entry to a career or further education. This is essentially instrumental thinking. It is also essentially alienated, separating the meaning of the activity from the activity itself. Not surprisingly there has been a growing revolt against it among thinking academics, teachers and – latterly – pupils themselves.

Notes

1 ROSENTHAL, R. and JACOBSON, L. (1968) *Pygmalion in the Classroom*, Holt, Reinhart & Winston.

2 LACEY, C. (1970), *Hightown Grammar: The School as a Social System*, Manchester University Press.

2.11 No alternatives to truancy

Val Hennessy

Tolerant Teacher: Now look Andy, old man, I know *all* about you bunking off and where you go. I don't really want to tell the Head and I'm sure you don't want me to tell your Social Worker do you?

Andy: I don't give a fuck who knows to tell the truth ...

Andy is a 'problem pupil' who has decided for himself that the school curriculum is totally inappropriate and meaningless for him and along with thousands more pupils from urban secondary schools he is voting with his feet by walking out of school. 'Bunker-offers' like Andy aren't really so much of a problem because at least they keep themselves out of the teachers' hair but kids like Ted: 'I ain't gonna sit there readin' bleedin' *Cider with Rosie* all morning – I told him he can stuff his poxy old lesson and socked him one on the gob' – are much more difficult to deal with, particularly when they are so desperately insecure that they dare not truant but prefer to hang around school wrecking the lessons, threatening teachers and generally demanding total attention. Faced with the increasing numbers of 'Teds' in our schools, kids who refuse to accept the old authoritarian standards, the local education authorities are having a little panic and suddenly building trendy 'Retreat Units' all over the place. The philosophy behind these 'Retreat Units' is that you round up all the worst troublemakers, stick them in 'Sin-Bins' where they can get rid of their aggression on some liberal teacher-in-charge whom they call 'Mick' instead of 'Sir'.

While we should welcome the fact that LEAS are beginning to acknowledge that there *is* a problem, this plan to build such facilities for disruptive pupils is an extremely unacceptable solution to the problems of violence and adult rejection in schools for it is ignoring the very real social and economic causes of child maladjustment.

Source: *Peace News* (August 1975).

My local education authority is planning to set up four 'Retreat Units' and when the teacher-in-charge job was recently advertised I was interviewed. There was a great deal of confusion about what precisely the job might entail and indeed in one school the teacher-in-charge of the 'Retreat Unit' was not even allotted a room but was expected to work 'in close liaison' with form tutors. I imagined myself prowling along the corridors all day rounding up the recalcitrant kids and having the odd chat to a tutor through a smashed form-room window. At a second school no one seemed to know anything at all about the proposed 'Retreat Unit', one teacher said: 'We all think it's a bloody stupid idea to pander to the little bastards, they all want a good kick up the arse'. At school number three a special little hut, well away from the main school among the woods, was being converted and I grew quite keen at the thought of planting potatoes and lettuces with the 'disruptive pupils' and even keeping a goat or two, but as soon as I mentioned these ideas at a teachers' meeting the general opinion was: 'Look, if you tell all the soppy bastards that they can get out of your maths lesson and bloody well go over to some 'Retreat Unit' and listen to records and grow tomatoes – well, it's not going to take the keen hard-working ones long to catch on to the fact that they're missing out on it. They'll all be clamouring to get into the 'Retreat Unit' won't they?'

And here, of course, is the curious contradiction about this kind of concessionary provision for the 'disruptive pupils' – if the LEAS are at last prepared to admit that much of what goes on in schools is tedious, trivial and totally irrelevant to many pupils and if they are prepared to build units to stimulate and attract the kids who have demonstrated their absolute rejection of conventional schooling, then they have a huge future problem on their hands when the 'good kids' realise what they're missing! It's obvious isn't it? We should be building thousands of these neighbourhood 'Retreat Units' for all kids, they are a model of what education should be all about, and it implies, of course, a greater expenditure on educational resources, higher staff pupil ratios and more attention to individual kids – all impossible if you 'mass produce' kids as under the present system.

At my interview, when I began to discuss my ideas of cultivating the land and keeping goats and going to films and doing video, the panel freaked out and one of them said: 'But what about the punitive aspect of these Units – you make them sound like holiday camps'. Another interviewer (it was an all-male panel and I found myself humbly apologizing for actually taking a few years out of the profession to bear two babies) said in one of those appalling plummy voices Tory councillors must work at for years: 'Really, my dear, do you have *any* idea of the kind of violence one may encounter in secondary schools?' For someone who only that week had narrowly avoided being concussed by a flying toilet seat hurled at me across the playground while I was on duty I felt I probably had a considerably clearer idea than he was ever likely to. 'We mustn't treat these chaps and lasses like heroes you know – the teacher-in-charge must be a person to show them the error of their ways ... '

The job I was after went to an ex-warden of a remand home for wayward girls. It seems a clear indication to me of the way things are going....

3 Children and race

Introduction

The four papers in this section consider the educational experience of black children in our schools. Quality education for children is the demand of all parents, but how to achieve this with different ethnic or black groups is a puzzle for the professional educator. Though there have been many earnest efforts and much concern within our schools, it is fair to say that no education authority has yet produced a coherent strategy to meet this demand.

The arrival and settlement in this country of members from the New Commonwealth, continues to pose one of the more intractable problems faced by educationalists. Broadly, the educational response to this has moved through three overlapping phases. The first was based on concepts of assimilation; the second on integration and more recently on a belief in the concept of pluralism. Assimilation has come to appear less and less viable as it is increasingly rejected by black groups themselves as well as groups within the indigenous culture. Genuine cultural integration has foundered against the fact of massive under-achievement of black children in British schools. At this time, cultural pluralism, with its increased awareness of the effects of racism in the classroom, may indicate a way forward, although it has great implications for the organization and curricula of schools.

Milner's paper (3.1) reviews the educational experience of black children which, though drawing on American situations and research, speaks directly to the British experience. Proctor (3.2) looks at the overt and covert racism present in educational textbooks. Coad (3.3) presents a case that the British school system serves to denigrate black children and deny their cultural roots, making them resentful, bitter and demotivated. Low self-image and low self-expectations go hand in hand for the black child. Little (3.4) concludes by examining the educational performance of children from different ethnic backgrounds.

3.1 Education and black children

David Milner

The American education system has attempted two remedies for the black child's underachievement in school: *de-segregation* and *compensatory education*. School de-segregation follows from the 1954 Supreme Court ruling that there should be equality of educational opportunity for Negroes and whites alike. Negroes should be allowed to benefit from the superior educational experience provided by white schools. The process is far from complete nearly twenty years after the ruling. It has been deliberately speeded up at one time and slowed down at another by various incumbents of the White House, and pockets of resistance in the South have successfully held out against its implementation there. De-segregation has been achieved by 'bussing' black children into surrounding white neighbourhoods, closing majority-Negro schools and dispersing their populations, and 'pairing' schools and exchanging proportions of each to achieve inter-racial balance.

'Compensatory education' is an umbrella term designating any number of different attempts to improve the quality of education for disadvantaged children. The US Commission on Civil Rights describes it like this:

> One approach – remedial instruction – is to give more intensive attention to students in academic difficulty. Remedial techniques usually include reduction of number of students per teacher, provision of extra help to students during and after school, counselling, and use of special teaching materials designed to improve basic skills. Another approach – cultural enrichment – ... attempt[s] to broaden the horizons of poor children by giving them access to activities which ordinarily might be beyond their reach such as field trips and visits to museums, concerts, other schools, and colleges ... A third element ... involves efforts to overcome attitudes which inhibit learning ... to improve self-esteem and to raise confidence by providing successful academic experiences and

Source: *Children and Race* (1975), pp. 168–210.

> recognition. A fourth approach ... pre-school education ... seeks to provide disadvantaged children with training in verbal skills and cultural enrichment activities before they enter the primary grades.[1]

Stated in this way the objectives and techniques of compensatory education seem wholly worth while, and certain to improve the lot of the minority child. However, the consensus of opinion seems to be that, with certain notable exceptions, compensatory educational programmes have not delivered the goods. In fact they seem to have had *less* success in boosting achievement than de-segregation programmes. Evaluations of compensatory education projects suggest that the children involved have not reached significantly higher achievement levels than non-participants, and have been surpassed by those who have been integrated into majority-white schools.[2] Both the Coleman Report[3] on 'Equality of Educational Opportunity' and the report of the US Commission on Civil Rights compared the relative performance of black children in racially isolated and de-segregated schools, and provide a lot of evidence of greater gains in achievement for black children in majority-white schools. More recent reviews of compensatory education programmes, while drawing attention to the methodological inadequacies of the studies that have evaluated them, have nevertheless come to essentially the same conclusions (e.g. Passow, 1970,[4] Wilkinson, 1970).[5]

The assertion of the superiority of de-segregation has to be looked at rather carefully because an emotive issue is involved, further complicated by all manner of political considerations. Residential, educational and employment integration have been political articles of faith for liberally minded people for some time. Thus the value-judgement that de-segregation is desirable had been made long before these alternative educational policies were compared for effectiveness, and could conceivably cloud objectivity. There is a little evidence of this in the selection of evidence presented on these issues; some of the *negative, harmful* effects of de-segregation on black children have been rather glossed over. Thus in Weinberg's detailed appraisal of research into the effects of de-segregation he writes: 'De-segregation has most often benefitted the Negro child's self-esteem and virtually never harmed it.'[6] Yet Irwin Katz maintains that:

> low expectation of success is an important detrimental factor in the performance of minority children attending integrated schools. The evidence is strong that Negro students have feelings of inferiority which arise from an awareness of actual differences in racial achievement, or from irrational acceptance of the white group's stereotype of Negroes.[7]

So bi-racial situations are by no means automatically beneficial; in Katz's[8] experiments, Negroes were found to 'display marked social inhibition and subordination to white partners' in group tasks. In cooperative problem-solving tasks they 'made fewer proposals than did whites and tended to accept the latter's contributions uncritically'. When actually displaying equal ability on tasks, Negroes still rated whites higher. Again, Negroes 'tended to accept passively the suggestions of their white companions' even when these were actually wrong answers to problems. Katz concluded that these dispositions were primarily the result of social threat.

In another experiment, although Negro students performed an 'eye-hand coordination task' better when tested by a white adult than by a Negro adult, when the same task was described as a test of IQ, their performance with the white tester was depressed markedly and elevated slightly with the Negro tester. Eye-hand coordination, says Katz, is not an ability which Negroes are stereotyped as lacking. On intellectual tasks, however, it is possible that 'the Negro subject saw very little chance of meeting the white experimenter's standard of excellence ... As an additional source of impairment in this situation, low expectancy of success could have aroused fear of incurring the white testers' disapproval (failure threat).'

Katz maintains that there is *not* yet enough evidence to draw firm conclusions about Negro performance in inter-racial situations, pointing to both the positive and negative effects. He catalogues the potentially harmful elements for the black child – social rejection and isolation, accompanied by emotional stress, fear of competition with whites, and unrealistic inferiority feelings – which detract from the benefits of integration. All of these involve stress for the child, and as he emphasizes: 'Research on psychological stress generally supports the assumption that social threat and failure threat are detrimental to complex learning.'

So we have a situation in which de-segregation of schools appears to boost black children's performance more than compensatory education, *in spite of* a number of influences which tend to depress that performance. Katz's experiments might be thought of as looking at the strictly *inter-racial* aspects of the situation, lifting them out of the school context. They demonstrate a number of potentially harmful influences, so that it seems unlikely that *integration per se* – the simple fact of mixing black and white children – is responsible for boosting performance. A review of the evidence for the superiority of de-segregation points in rather the same direction. St John[9] points out that no studies have provided unequivocal evidence that racial mixing alone boosts performance; that *social class* integration and quality of schools may account for quite as much of this superiority as racial integration, for these have not been adequately controlled; and that lack of controls in these studies may have exaggerated the differences between segregated and de-segregated schools, through factors like self-selection (via ambitious parents) of children to be 'bussed', and 'Hawthorne effects' on children studied in this way.

In other words, the superiority of black children's performance in de-segregated schools may have been inflated by biased sampling. Secondly, social class integration may be more important than simple radical integration. That is, at the same time as being racially integrated, black children are also being transported into a higher social class environment in the white schools. On the whole this factor is discussed in terms of the social class background of the black child's white classmates, and the social influences towards achievement exerted on the minority. In situations where whites are in the majority this is said to lead to higher achievement levels for black children. The Coleman Report, for example, found that the 'social class climate' of the school correlated highly with achievement.

Now while the social class background of the pupils may be very important, there are other factors which contribute to the 'social class climate' of the school, and which have been neglected. There is the immediate environment of the school, its fabric and upkeep, the quantity, quality and type of its teachers and teaching materials, its reputation, and so on. We know with absolute certainty that most white schools are better equipped in each of these respects than most black ghetto schools. (For example, we know that there is a strong correlation between the social class of the school and the quality of its teachers, the most proficient teachers being attracted to the most academic schools with the best working conditions.) Yet these crucial factors which largely determine the *quality of the school* have seldom been controlled in comparisons of segregated and de-segregated schools; which leads us to hypothesize an obvious and plausible explanation for the superior performance of 'de-segregated' black children (despite the hazards of inter-racial situations described earlier): namely, that the white schools which black children are integrated with are simply *far superior* schools. Hardly an earth-shattering discovery, but one which, incredibly, appears to have been largely overlooked.

The shortcomings of compensatory education

Or we can approach the problem from the other end. Why is it that, despite enormous expenditure, compensatory education programmes have manifestly failed to improve black children's educational experience to the level enjoyed by white children? First of all, it is difficult to generalize about programmes as they have varied so much from one project to another, so that the term 'compensatory education' covers (it seems) a multitude of sins. Although the overall objectives, listed earlier, are admirable, the content of the programmes themselves could never realize these objectives. Many of the language programmes (e.g. the Peabody Kits) were based on an outdated stimulus-response view of language acquisition, quite apart from the erroneous view of the children's 'language deficits' for which they were designed to compensate. Similarly, the classical music inputs and museum trips of the 'cultural enrichment' programmes could not conceivably attain their objectives, even assuming that the children's culture needed enriching.

Secondly, it emerges rather clearly from evaluations of compensatory education programmes that many have remained almost 'outside' the normal school activities. That is pre-school programmes have tried to improve the child's readiness for school and extra-curricular activities have added 'enrichment' out of school hours, but relatively less attention has been paid to changing and improving the normal daytime educational experience of the child. Thus, O'Reilly writes:[2] 'Typically, compensatory programmes are supplementary to the regular school programme or may comprise a few short weeks of concentrated effort'. In a similar vein Gordon[10] believes that:

> it is significant that so much of the current work in the education of the disadvantaged has been directed either at pre-school children or at youngsters who have dropped out of high school. So little attention has been given to investigating the over-all appropriateness of contemporary educational processes. If school people were not such a decent lot, one would think that these two emphases have been so widely accepted simply because they require the least change in the school itself. It often is easier to add extensions than to change the basic structure of institutions.

There are serious criticisms here. Clearly it is ludicrous to expect a vacation-long pre-school programme to compensate for several years' experience of disadvantagement and a group history of oppression and inferior status. Adam (1969)[11] puts this in perspective when he describes 'a Head start centre [as] not so much a nursery as a crash-course in western infancy which aims to bring the disadvantaged child level with the Spock-raised one between now and next Autumn'. It would be surprising, then, if the evaluation[12] of the Head Start summer programmes had come up with any finding other than that the participants did not achieve lasting gains in cognitive and affective development over non-participants. Significant gains were only achieved in those programmes which lasted for a year before the children started school, but the gains were still not very great, underlining the futility of single summer projects. (Of significance for the de-segregation debate was the finding that programmes based on all-black centres were the most effective.)

It seems that if these deficits are to be made up, programmes should be organized long before children enter school. Gordon[10] makes the point that intervention should begin after birth if we wish to alter this situation; more logically, this should extend to improving the environment of the child even before birth. Short of that, it is important that pre-school programmes should begin as early as possible, *but that they should not be a substitute* for improvements in school itself. They should also be based on an objective analysis of what the child's 'defects' *are*, an issue we will return to.

Some writers complain that even when school curricula are changed, it is in the direction of intensification, that is, 'more of the same thing', be it teachers, materials or whatever. There seems to have been comparatively little *innovative* change in teaching methods. Nevertheless, this may be adequate for certain areas of learning; an evaluation of one of the few programmes which has produced significant gains in achievement, known as Title I, concluded that 'one effective approach may be nothing more complicated than systematic teaching'.[2] However, in view of the number of unsuccessful projects which have tried just this, two conclusions may be reached: the intensification of existing teaching methods is not great enough to make up the children's deficits, and/or there are other factors connected with achievement which are not being catered to by this method. The US Commission on Civil Rights gives some clue to this in stating the assumptions which lie behind most programmes:

> Compensatory education programmes instituted in predominantly Negro schools attended mostly by disadvantaged students rest upon the assumption that the major cause of academic disadvantage is the poverty of the average Negro child and the environment in which he is raised.[1]

No mention here of that complex of factors which retard black achievement deriving from race and caste, independently of poverty. It does seem that more attention has been paid to achievement per se and rather less to boosting self-esteem, group pride and identity; certainly when one reads evaluations of the programmes it is by the yardstick of educational achievement that their success is usually measured. It is also true, of course, that greater achievement is likely to boost self-esteem which would justify this emphasis. However, we have a situation where achievement is not being substantially boosted, so that self-esteem is not growing from that source. In which case we should ask whether it is lack of attention to race and caste factors which is hindering compensatory education, and whether they (operating in the ways described earlier in this chapter) are among the most important factors in under-achievement in the first place. After all, anxiety and self-devaluation, two of the consequences of these factors, have been shown to depress school achievement. Now although 'improving self-esteem and group pride' do figure among the objectives of these programmes, they suffer in translation. They are global and abstract objectives which are difficult to realize in concrete activities. Sometimes the organizers may not understand or be in sympathy with them in the first place:

> Such concepts as self-esteem, language development, and academic motivation are frequently little understood by programme directors and teachers alike. The resultant lack of definition leads to a plethora of nonstandardized and varied activities having varied degress of relationship to the programme objectives, assuming that even the objectives are clear.[2]

Some, however, have met with more success. A programme in San Francisco includes a creative arts centre, while in Philadelphia devices like displays emphasizing the contribution of Negroes to American life and displays of student art work are used to 'raise aspiration levels beyond those held by the child's immediate social environment'. These objectives can be pursued in all-black or majority-black schools. The US Civil Rights Commission heard testimony that this sort of homogeneity assisted curriculum planning and the development of special techniques for overcoming language deficits, for example. To this must be added the finding that Head Start programmes in all-Negro centres were among the most effective, and Stalling's[13] finding that Negro pupils made the greatest gains in achievement *when they remained with Negro teachers and remained in segregated classes* after de-segregation into white schools (that is, a situation of racial homogeneity but vastly improved facilities).

People have raised objections to the idea of all-black schools on the grounds that this is segregation, and that experience has shown the black schools taking part in compensatory education programmes are somehow further stigmatized. The first objection demonstrates the value-judgment to which we drew attention earlier; segregation contravenes the democratic ideal of inter-racial integration. But there is nothing intrinsically wrong with all-black schools, *only with the educational experience that they have, in the past, provided.* Which brings us to the second objection: there need be no stigma attaching to schools involved in compensatory education programmes if these schools are seen to be successful. If the school can become a showpiece, as good as any white school, rather than a patched-up imitation, there will be no question of stigma.

There are a number of lessons here. If we pour resources into all-black or majority-black schools on a massive scale so that they are at least as good as white schools, we create the conditions in which black children's educational deficits can be made up *and* their self-esteem and identity developed. None of the previous attempts at compensatory education appear to have done this even half-successfully, either through an inadequate scale of aid, or a neglect of race and caste factors, or both. Educational achievement and self-esteem go hand in hand, and any attempt to boost either in isolation is doomed to failure. The black child requires both before he can integrate with white people on an equal footing, and to precipitate that integration before both are achieved may bring some successes but also many casualties.

These criticisms and recommendations can be accommodated within the framework of compensatory education as it is currently conceived. However, there is a far more fundamental critique which contests the basic premises of compensatory education; it argues that action programmes cannot help but fail because the analysis of black disadvantagement on which they are based is simply *wrong*.

First of all the authors[14] question the universal assumption of Head Start and similar programmes that black children *do* have linguistic and cognitive deficits. Baratz and Baratz maintain that current linguistic data do not support this assumption; rather that 'Many lower-class Negro children speak a well-ordered, highly structured, but different, dialect from that of Standard English.' While linguistic competence is equated with the latter, linguistic differences are interpreted as deficits. On this argument the black child's speech collides with the Standard English of the school (which is the medium of instruction, expression and complex conceptualization) in much the same way as a West Indian child's *patois* in an English school. Forbes (1971)[15] cites a recent study of language in Pittsburgh which revealed that 'slum children there used 3,200 words, including idioms, not recognized by their teachers or by educational tests'. Add to this the mis-match between his own culture and values, and those of the school and we are some way towards explaining his difficulties and 'under-achievement'. Ginsburg (1972),[16] too, has offered explanations of racial and social class differences in not only language development but also cognitive skills and IQ, which contradict the notion of the 'deprived' and 'inadequate' lower-class child. He concludes that, 'While poverty is not a desirable state and while it may not ennoble those who live in it, it also does not produce serious retardation of their thought-processes.'

These cultural differences are not given due importance because of a more fundamental error on the part of educationists and social policy-makers: an ethnocentric belief that Negroes do not have a separate culture.

Cultural differences are recognized, surely, but they are not accorded the respect that anthropologists accord to alien cultures abroad. Rather urban Negro life is seen as a 'deprived', 'disorganized' version of white culture. This has been termed the 'culture of poverty' (or more properly, the 'subculture of poverty'). It is based in a long tradition of viewing Negro existence as an unstable, chaotic, amoral disintegration of 'normal' social life, a picture which emerges from the statistics of illegitimacy, father-absence, crime and drug addiction. It centres around the self-perpetuating and self-inflicted inadequate 'life-style of the Negro poor, which disables future generations through its ignorant and ineffective socialization practices.

Valentine[17] has presented a devastating critique of this model which had been the dominant perspective for years. He shows, for example, how theorists have been so concerned with *dis*organization and chaos in Negro life that they resent the opposite when it does appear. He quotes Frazier, the sociologist:

> The behaviour of Negro deserters, who are *likely* to return to their families even after several years of absence, often *taxes the patience* of social workers whose *plans for their families are constantly disrupted.*[18] (Italics added.)

And because of the 'culture of poverty' concept, Valentine argues, poverty is seen as a disabling way of life rather than an involuntary adaptation to an inequitable income distribution. This has the effect of locating the causes of deprivation somehow 'in' the minority and its 'chosen' way of life not in the economic forces which oppress them. Consequently, with the failure of compensatory education programmes in the school it has been necessary to reach further back into the child's life-history to deal with the 'inefficacious' child-rearing practices of mothers and the lack of stimulation in the home. The logical extension of this is the suggestion that specialists should be introduced 'into the home who would not only provide the missing stimulation to the child, but also teach the mother how to raise her children properly'![14]

This model has also been called the 'social pathology' model because it depicts Negro life not as a different culture but as a deficient pathological one. Compensatory education programmes based on this model (as they invariably are) therefore put emphasis on developing the child's competence, thereby improving life-chances; in other words, enabling the poor and black to pull themselves out of poverty by their own bootlaces. Not only is this philosophy ethnocentric and misguided, it actually obstructs progress by distracting attention from the need for structural change, which is the only way the mass of black people can improve their lot. So compensatory education and other programmes speak only to the symptoms of a much deeper malaise, ignoring and even obscuring the causes of these deprivations and 'deficits'. It is rather like ministering to the casualties of a battle, while assuming that they appeared on the battlefield by chance and that their wounds were self-inflicted.

The logic of this analysis leads to the conclusion that there can only be superficial improvements in the educational sphere until the fundamental causes of poverty and racism are dealt with. The wider critique related here conveys the real context in which initiatives like compensatory education are taking place. They are solitary attempts to deal with the outward manifestations of only one aspect of a larger socio-economic condition. To the extent to which governments fail to alter that total picture, so will efforts at compensatory education be circumscribed.

However, this holistic approach and conclusion does not invalidate the previous discussion of smaller issues within compensatory education. While accepting the validity of the analysis, we cannot afford to wait for the revolutionary social change required to implement it. For, realistically, we can see that no government, here or in the US, is going to undertake the radical social action involved in eradicating poverty and racialism, unless compelled to do so. In this regard governments are assisted by social scientists like Daniel Moynihan (one of the foremost proponents of the culture-of-poverty view) who states his belief in the need for active *resistance* to social change quite unequivocally:

> Liberals [should] see more clearly their essential interest in the stability of the social order, and that given the present threats to that stability, it is necessary to seek out and make more effective alliances with political conservatives who share that concern.[19]

So there is still a case for lower-order reforms like compensatory education bringing immediate benefits. But these must be undertaken with the eyes open, and not seen as panaceas that will bring justice and equality of opportunity, but simply as a means of equipping some black children to confront their predicament more effectively. But the name 'compensatory education' itself connotes inferiority. Rather we should be pursuing *bi-cultural education*, free of the value-judgments which create 'deficits' from cultural differences. Labelling accepted sub-cultural patterns as pathological or (in the case of children at school) 'wrong' only adds to the devaluation of the minority by the majority. Baratz and Baratz summarize it this way:

> Education for culturally different children should not attempt to destroy functionally viable processes of the sub-culture, but rather

> should use these processes to teach additional cultural forms. The goal of such education should be to produce a bi-cultural child who is capable of functioning both in his subculture and the mainstream.[14]

They give as an example of more appropriate teaching methods the use of Negro dialect in the teaching of reading. It is important to define the sort of educational milieu in which this philosophy could be enacted, that is, in racially separate or racially integrated schools. Obviously to give this radically different style of education to black children would be easier in all respects in all-black schools; within integrated schools it might tend to reinforce racial division. And we have seen evidence that the former is the case, and evidence of the greater success of all-black centres in the Head Start programme. Against this we have to weigh the higher achievements of 'de-segregated' black children, and against *that*, the caution that these claims may be artificially inflated and more related to the class and quality of the school. In short, if we could improve the quality of black schools to that of white by *positive* discrimination, by massive injections of resources to improve their structures, working conditions, and staff-pupil ratios, we would cater to most of those objections.

One important objection remains: the fact that achievement is only a part of the picture. Equally or more important is the question of racial attitudes, and the evidence points in the direction of less polarized attitudes in inter-racial schools. However, a pre-condition of this inter-racial friendship has been shown to be an atmosphere of acceptance between the races in the school. In so many schools this is manifestly not the case, particularly now that 'bussing' has become such a divisive political issue in the US.

It may be that some combination of the alternatives will be the best solution. Black elementary schools could provide a long period of bi-cultural education that would both accustom the child to mainstream cultural patterns and methods of school achievement *and* develop within him self-esteem and a sense of group identity, based in his own cultural heritage. To integrate children on entry to the secondary level would coincide with the normal breaking down and re-forming of friendship groups. The benefits of inter-racial contact would then be built on an equality that does not exist in current efforts at integration. It is precisely this sort of contact – in equal-status situations – which has been shown to break down stereotypes and prejudice. Given that sort of racial atmosphere the negative effects of inter-racial situations on black performance could also be mitigated.

Education and black British children

In the previous pages the research material comes entirely from work with black Americans. Very little of it, however, is specifically 'American' in the sense that it could only have originated there. Through the emphasis on 'caste' influences and deprived material conditions the bulk of the material could be translated into many cultural settings, given certain conditions: namely, the existence of a deprived ethnic or racial minority subject to prejudice and discrimination. And so the findings have an immediate relevance in a number of other inter-racial contexts, not least the situation of 'coloured' immigrants in Britain.

Some of the difficulties encountered by the principal immigrant groups in British schools are essentially cultural, although less a question of cultural *deprivation* than of the mis-match between the culture of the sending societies and that of the host community. To some extent these difficulties are being catered for. They have received recognition from the very beginning, probably because they present themselves in an immediate way through language difficulties customs and dress. In response, some special provisions have been made in the education system, for the Asian groups in particular, in the form of orientation and language classes. (Less obvious cultural differences, however, have received scant attention. For a long time West Indian children's *patois* was regarded simply as poor English when in fact it virtually qualifies as a foreign language in its relation to Standard English. Many children who actually needed to learn English almost as a second language only received help to 'improve' their 'bad English' which was not an adequate foundation for complex language skills.) As Townsend[20] has described:

> In class [the West Indian child] finds his teacher partly intelligible, he is frequently corrected for speaking bad English although this is the way he and his parents have always spoken their language, and he receives little in the way of special help, although the Asians in his class disappear every day for extra English lessons.

However, the operation of caste distinctions and the ways they enter into the child's educational experience are much less tangible. As yet these influences have received no attention whatsoever in the British education system. Now it is obviously wrong to equate the British and American situations in a simple way and assume that our black children face exactly the same problems; but given the evidence of prejudiced attitudes and their effects on immigrant children, presented earlier, it does seem plausible that some of the processes described may also operate in our schools.

Bhatnagar's[21] recent study of secondary-school children in London showed some of these processes at work. He found immigrant children to be considerably less well-adjusted than English children:

> The adjustment level appeared to be strongly related to the status given by the community to the group to which the child belonged. English children were found to be the most adjusted group followed by white immigrants (the Cypriots) with the black immigrants (the West Indians) coming a poor third.

Bhatnagar measured four aspects of adjustment – social acceptability, personal satisfaction, freedom from anxiety and objectivity of social concept – and calculated a mean adjustment score. The West Indian children were found to be the least socially acceptable in the eyes of the other children, the most anxious, and to have the least objective self-concepts. In 'personal satisfaction' the Cypriots and West Indians were not statistically distinguishable, but both scored very much lower than the English group. In the other tests the Cypriots (who qualify as immigrants, and culturally different, but not 'coloured') fell between the English and the West Indians. Nor were levels of adjustment related to the immigrants length of stay in this country, in fact 'a longer stay is just as likely to result in deterioration as in improvement in adjustment.

There also emerged a positive correlation between adjustment and academic achievement: that is, the less well-adjusted immigrant groups did less well on a variety of measures of attainment, IQ, and so on. While the vocational aspirations of the three groups were similar, the expectations of the immigrants were much lower than those of the English children.

Many important influences are illustrated in these findings; most important of all is the combination of low social status, low social acceptability, and personal satisfaction, high anxiety, coupled with low school attainment and low expectations, a syndrome with a familiar ring to it. In this country we might have expected cultural factors to be more influential than caste factors, whereas in America they appear to be more evenly balanced. Here we are dealing with the importation of alien culture patterns, rather than the culture of an indigenous minority. Bhatnagar's study, then, should alert attention to the effects of caste-status in British education, appearing in a context thought to be less severely stratified than America.

However, these influences are not entirely separable; they tend to interact and to reinforce one another. Hence in a *caste*-tinted atmosphere, the *culturally* 'different' may be perceived as inferior. This is harmful enough when applied to dress or customs, but has a more serious dimension when it extends to educational assessment. We have seen the effect of teachers' and others' expectations on the child's performance.

Caste not only creates expectations of inferiority but colours the interpretation of actual performance. In this context it is easy for the unusual productions of a child from a different culture to be regarded as inferior (or the absence of production through lack of familiarity to be seen as deficiency). This sort of process may well lie behind the problem of West Indian language mentioned earlier. For in a climate of caste, of alien behaviour, discipline problems and learning difficulties, West Indian *patois* was all too easily seen as 'bad English' – that is, as *retarded* language symptomatic of backward children, rather than as normal children's *different* language. This was the result of several factors: (1) the superficial similarities of West Indian dialect and Standard English, (2) the notion of the children as 'culturally deprived' and therefore probably 'linguistically deprived', reinforced by (3) the relative lack of production of language *in the school situation* by West Indian children, particularly the younger ones, who were often withdrawn and silent. It is easy to see how, in the context of the overall picture of West Indian children as members of a lowly and deprived group, these mistakes were made.

But if we acknowledge that the first language of West Indian children is substantially different from Standard English – that it has a different lexis, phonology and syntax – we get a more realistic picture. The situation of a French child coming to an English school illustrates the point: he too would be silent and withdrawn initially, and his difficulties would also continue if he were given no specific instruction which took account of his first language and eased his transfer to the second. There are two points of difference with the West Indian child's situation: one is that the French child in this situation would not be seen as *backward* because of his linguistic difficulties; the second is that in the efforts of the West Indian child to acquire Standard English he suffers from *interference* between the first and second languages because of their surface similarities. In other words, he soon learns that some aspects are 'right' in both languages, and some are not, so that this is an additional source of confusion not suffered by our hypothetical French child, whose two languages are quite dissimilar. (An additional confusion comes from the influence of the local dialects of the child's white peers, which also differ from Standard English.)

It is more difficult to understand why it took us so long to wake up to these facts, when a few minutes' listening to West Indian children talking among themselves out of school makes it clear that they are equally articulate, that their language is very different from Standard English, but is equally complex, rich and descriptive and communicationally efficient. But the problem is not simply one of teaching children who speak 'West Indian dialect' to use Standard English. Apart from differences between different islands, there are also differences in dialect within islands. For example, there is a continuum of dialects within Jamaica, from the most rural dialects at one extreme to the Jamaican 'Standard English' of the education system at the other (which is still different from 'English Standard English'). Different children will have learnt different dialects, depending on their parents' position on that continuum, *their* accommodation to English speech patterns, the length of their stay here, and so on. And at this end of the problem we have to recognize that there is a similar continuum of dialects in Britain which includes Geordie, Scouse, Brum and Cockney, all of which are far removed from Standard English. But Standard English is held to be the *correct* form. So as well as the individual issue with each West Indian child of where on the (say) Jamaican continuum the child is located, we have the wider issue of where, on our implicit continuum of 'correct' English, we wish to 'take' the child.

The general answer to the latter issue is that we should attempt to provide the child with the kinds of spoken, and, particularly, written language which will enable him to deal with all the situations that will confront him. In other words, as a form of Standard English is the medium of instruction and assessment in the education system and the passport to higher-paid employment, we are handicapping the child if we cannot give him this facility. But the crucial issue is how this can be done without explicitly or implicitly devaluing his own language. We have to explicate the language situation: to teach about the *differences* in language, not that one is 'right' and one is 'wrong', but that all are equally valid. In other words, we have to depict the learning of different forms of English *to the child* as a simple instrumental process of acquiring the tools to do particular jobs, *not* as a process of acquiring virtue.

With this perspective we can avoid the misunderstandings (both on our part and the children's) that have surrounded the issue for so long, and in particular the way connotations of inferiority and 'language difficulties' have reinforced each other. 'Caste influences' and 'language', separately and in interaction, are the core issues in West Indian children's experience in school. Both contribute more to attitudes and adjustment, the expectations surrounding the children, and their achievements (or lack of them) than any other factors, and yet there has been very little attention to them.

Assessment

The same sort of process operates in the testing of children's abilities. Ferron[22] in his analysis of the intelligence test performance of 'coloured' children from many different parts of the world, concluded that:

> ... As far as one can make out, poor test performance of coloured children is fundamentally the outcome of emotional and motivational problems involved in the assimilation of Western culture ... Where circumstances are such as to ensure that white and coloured groups share a common way of life and have equal educational opportunities differences are small or non-existent.

However, in this country, white and black groups do not have a common way of life, and while equality of opportunity exists in principle, the kinds of processes described earlier prevent its realization in practice. Not surprisingly, 'under-achievement' in school is a serious problem for immigrant children, West Indians in particular. Here, unspoken assumptions about the intellectual correlates of low caste disguise the role of cultural factors in performance, like the culture-bias of the tests, for example. Thus failure on tests which may be solely due to caste or cultural factors may be interpreted *in a caste climate* as evidence of intellectual inferiority. Culture-bias in tests operates in a variety of ways which are not at all obvious. Apart from the issues of bias in verbal tests because of language difficulty and in non-verbal tests through lack of familiarity with spatial relations, bias extends even to the concrete materials of the test – it has been pointed out that many children are simply unaccustomed to the use of pencils and paper as these seldom appear in their homes. Similar consideration apply to the ordinary week-by-week assessment of schoolwork. Where the society propagates a notion of a group's inferiority it is unreasonable to expect the teacher to be totally immune from it. Unwittingly, judgements are coloured and prophecies fulfilled. And even the social scientists' 'kinder' term, cultural 'deprivation', only adds to connotation of inferiority.

Certainly factors like culture-bias and caste-tinted assessment contribute to the disproportionate representation of West Indian children in schools for the educationally subnormal. For even apparently 'culture-free' tests can discriminate against the minority child to some extent, but the resulting poor performance is unremarkable if that is what is expected of a child from an 'inferior' group. Unless it is held that a group is genetically inferior it is reasonable to say that poor performance of whole groups and disproportionate ESN classification are simply measures of inappropriate teaching and assessment.

Fortunately ESN classification only affects a minority of children. Less dramatic labelling occurs through 'streaming', affecting the majority. Goldman and Taylor, in their survey of immigrant educational problems[23], point out that 'although immigrant children are not being segregated, they are generally in the 'C' streams or remedial classes because of their *linguistic disabilities*' (my italics); they add: ' ... this may not be due to low ability since few authorities have evaluated their ability levels. Once in these streams, though, it may be difficult to avoid conforming to the achievement level of that stream. Jackson[24] studied 660 schools in Britain and found that changes of stream were very rare. Moreover, Douglas[25] found that over a three-year period the relative attainments of the children in the upper streams improved, while those of the children in the lower stream deteriorated. So what may start off as a mis-assessment of ability may become a self-fulfilling prophecy. This chain of events is even more disturbing in the light of Goldman and Taylor's hypothesis that immigrant children may have *above average* potential in view of their parents' initiative and resourcefulness in making the emigration.

So caste status creates a climate of inferiority around the child which tends to assimilate other evidence to support it. This picture structures the interpretation of quite unrelated aspects of the child's behaviour to 'fit' with the overall evaluation. It goes without saying that these are largely unconscious processes; sometimes, however, they are given very explicit support. The Jensen–Eysenck hypothesis of racial differences in intelligence is a case in point. This gives quasi-scientific support to the notion that certain disadvantaged racial minorites are innately intellectually inferior to whites. Of course, this is a theory that the prejudiced layman has held for years. And so it is naïve in the extreme to maintain, as the authors have done, that this hypothesis is proposed as pure social science with no political intention. This does not absolve them from some responsibility for the inevitable politicals *effects*, whatever their innocent motivations. A science of race relations does not exist in a social vacuum, and views such as these proposed by respected scientists are seized upon by the mass media and given wide exposure. Obviously they reinforce the idea of 'inferiority' associated with the minorities by giving it a scientific legitimacy; and all the processes we have described – teachers' low expectations, the misinterpretation of cultural differences, and, most of all, the belief in the significance of caste status – are intensified as a result. In this light the propagation of disputed hypotheses as scientific fact becomes far more reprehensible.

British policies

There is no uniform policy for the education of immigrant children in this country, a great deal being left to the discretion of the individual Local Education Authorities. Realization of the need to make special provision for immigrant children has lagged well behind the need itself. The range of LEA provisions, surveyed by Townsend[20] include the following:[26]

1 Reception centres which provide orientation and cultural adjustment

together with basic training. The shock of migration on the child cannot be overestimated; in the space of two or three days many Asian children pass from peasant villages to the crowded classrooms of one of our nineteenth-century inner city schools, receiving any number of cultural and emotional jolts *en route*. It is no exaggeration to say that they move from one reality to an entirely different one. In this context the need for a cushioning phase before total immersion in the new situation seems absolutely essential, yet only two LEAS in England automatically pass all immigrant children through a reception centre.

2 Full- or part-time language centres, and full- or part-time language classes within normal schools. Because language difficulties have been identified as the immigrants' most pressing educational problem, more resources have been devoted to this aspect than to anything else. There is tremendous variation in the type of instruction given under each type of provision, some concentrating narrowly on linguistic competence, others giving extra tuition in other subjects in which the children are less advanced than native children. One of the main problems seems to be that, even when the focus of the effort is restricted to language teaching, it is difficult to adequately prepare the child for the language demands made on him, particularly at the secondary-school level. Although the child may be able to converse reasonably well, the more specialized subject vocabularies he will require to progress further in school demand the reaching of 'second stage English' as it has been called. It seems that very few authorities have tackled this. Further, the statistics confirm that the overwhelming majority of pupils in the language centres and classes are Asians, for the reasons we have discussed. The West Indians' language needs are not being adequately catered for, so that once again the LEA language provision seem to neglect an important part of their constituency.

3 A third policy is included under the official rubric of 'language provision', although it is arguable whether it should properly be so. This is the policy of *dispersal* of immigrant children from their own neighbourhoods into surrounding areas in order to reduce the proportion of immigrants in 'ghetto' schools. In the original Department of Education and Science circular describing the policy (DES Circular 7/65) it was depicted as partly a response to immigrant language difficulties, and the need to spread the load of extra teacher-attention needed to meet them. However, many people felt that the policy was more a capitulation to the fears and prejudices of white people who were concerned about supposed deterioration of educational standards or who simply opposed the idea of majority-black schools. Such anxieties were fanned during this period by those politicians lobbying for further immigration control. There were some indications in the circular itself that the policy was directed to this group:

> It will be helpful if the parents of non-immigrant children can see that practical measures have been taken to deal with the problem in the schools, and that the progress of their own children is not being restricted by the undue preoccupation of the teaching staff with the linguistic and other difficulties of the immigrant children ... it is to everyone's disadvantage if the problems within the school are allowed to become so great that they cause a decline in the general standard of education provided.

This explains why 'immigrant' children were dispersed, irrespective of whether they were immigrant or not, irrespective of whether they had language difficulties or not, including among them some West Indian children, who, in contrast to what we now know, were then thought *not* to have language difficulties of the same order as the Asians. In other words, the children were dispersed solely on the basis of colour, and despite some educational and social motives (like 'integration') the main purpose of the policy was to assuage white anxieties.

Much of the earlier discussion of de-segregation and 'bussing' in America applies here with equal force. The benefits of inter-racial schooling are mixed benefits, and we need not re-iterate the reasons for this. Even in areas which bus immigrant children this is acknowledged:[27]

> When children are taken from their local environment by coach the integration which takes place at school can never be complete. Friendships formed at school cannot be followed up in the children's leisure hours. Children who come by coach are inclined to form groups within a school. If they also have a different language, culture or colour this danger is greatly increased. The immigrant children who are dispersed may experience a deeper sense of isolation from the native community than they would if they had remained in their neighbourhood school – even though that school might be almost all-immigrant.

'Bussing' also militates against the involvement of children in their own community, and formation of neighbourhood friendships, and against involvement of parents in the school. Some research on rural English children[28] showed that children who travel long distances to school seem more prone to maladjustment; how much greater the damage in the case of black children when they are made to travel great distances which necessarily involve a degree of alienation from the home and the community.

Policies like dispersal institutionalize the recognition of the disparity between the races. They allow that white people's wish to remove immigrants from their neighbourhood schools is a permissible sentiment;

by actually implementing this desire they confirm the immigrants' second-class status and officially endorse the prejudice.

Of course, multi-racial education is the ideal. But, as we have argued, this can only be successful on the basis of equality between the races, which, here as in America, does not exist. Without it all the pressures of caste and colour, working through prejudice, rejection, and lowered expectations in the minds of teachers and pupils, combine to damage the black child's performance, adjustment and fulfilment. Education authorities, schools and teachers are only slowly realizing that these pressures operate in this country also. Not surprisingly, then, there has been little official acknowledgement of the effects of prejudice on the child's performance and adjustment, and even less action.

Notes

1 US Commission on Civil Rights (1967) *Racial Isolation in the Public Schools* Washington: US Govt. Printing Office

2 O'Reilly, R.P. (1970) *Racial and Social Class Isolation in the Schools* New York: Praeger

3 Coleman, J.S. (1966) *Equality of Educational Opportunity* Office of Education, US Department of Health, Education and Welfare, US Govt. Printing Office

4 Passow, A.H. (ed) *Reaching the Disadvantaged Learner* New York: Teachers College Press, Columbia University

5 Wilkinson, D.A. (1970) 'Compensatory Education Programmes across the Nation', A.H. Passow (ed) *Reaching the Disadvantaged Learner*, op.cit.pp 1–17

6 Weinberg, M. (1968) *Desegregation Research: An Appraisal* Bloomington: Phi Delta Kappa

7 Silberman, C.E. (1970) *Crisis in the Classroom* New York: Random House

8 Katz, I. (1968) 'Factors Influencing Negro Performance in the Desegregated School' in Deutsch, Katz and Jensen, *op.cit*

9 St John, N. (1970) 'Desegregation and Minority-Group Performance' *Review of Educ. Res.* 40 (i) pp.111–33

10 Gordon, E.W. (1968) 'Programs of Compensatory Education', in Deutsch, Katz and Jensen, op.cit

11 Adam, R. (1969) 'Project Headstart LBJ's One Success' *New Society* 14 no. 370 pp. 681–3

12 WESTINGHOUSE LEARNING CORPORATION AND OHIO UNIVERSITY (1969) *The Impact of Head Start* Bladensburg, Maryland

13 STALLING, F.H. (1959) 'A Study of the Immediate Effects of Integration on Scholastic Achievement in the Louisville Public Schools', *J. Negro Educ.*, 28, pp. 439–44

14 BARATZ, S.S., and BARATZ, J.C. (1970) 'Early Childhood Intervention: The Social Science Base of Institutional Racism', *Harvard Ed. Rev.*, 40, pp. 29–50

15 FORBES, J.D. (1971) The Mandate for an Innovative Educational Response to Cultural Diversity in J.C. STONE and D.P. DeNevi (eds) Teaching Multi-Cultural Populations Van Nostrand

16 GINSBURG, H. (1972) *The Myth of the Deprived Child* Prentice Hall

17 VALENTINE, C.A. (1968) *Culture and Poverty*, Chicago: Univ. of Chicago Press

18 FRAZIER, E.F. (1966): *The Negro Family in the US*, Chicago; Univ. of Chicago Press

19 MOYNIHAN, D.P. (1967) 'The Politics of Stability', speech to National Board, Americans for Democratic Action, 23 September 1967

20 TOWNSEND, H.E.R. (1971) *Immigrant Pupils in England*, Slough, National Foundation for Educational Research

21 BHATNAGAR, J. (1970) *Immigrants at School,* London, Cornmarket

22 FERRON, O. (1965) 'The Test Performance of "Coloured" Children', *Educ. Res.*, 8, (i), pp. 42–57

23 GOLDMAN, R.J., and TAYLOR, F.M. (1966) 'Coloured Immigrant Children: A Survey of Research Studies and Literature on Their Educational Problems and Potential', *Educ. Res.*, 8, (iii), pp. 163–83

24 JACKSON, B. (1964): *Streaming: An Educational System in Miniature*, London: Routledge & Kegan Paul

25 DOUGLAS, J.W.B. (1964) *The Home and School*, London, MacGibbon & Kee

26 Note: British 'compensatory education' programmes will not be considered here, for they have not yet been adopted on a wide scale as LEA policy, many still being at the 'research and development' stage. Chazan (1973)[29] has recently reviewed their progress so far

27 EDUCATION COMMITTEE, EALING INTERNATIONAL FRIENDSHIP COUNCIL (1968): *The Education of the Immigrant Child in the London Borough of Ealing*

28 LEE, T. (1957) 'On the Relation between the School Journey and Social and Emotional Adjustment in Rural Infant Children', *Brit. J. Ed. Psych.*, 27, (ii), pp. 107–14

3.2 Racist textbooks

Chris Proctor

Part I

How do we decide what is racist and pernicious in a text-book? The most basic fact that emerges from the modern school experience is that, in the school, the biggest influence on the child's attitude to race, as with all other social standards, is, and will continue to be, the teacher. Thus, it is of the greatest importance that the teacher is aware of racist or possibly racist content in what he is teaching. If he can identify it he has three courses open to him; to point out the inadequacies, to use the passage for discussion, or simply to refuse to use the particular book. The problem arises with books when the situation is either accepted or not recognised, and racist sections are merely passed over or ignored.

It is often difficult to say if a passage or expression is racist and the teacher has a duty to be permanently on watch for this. Often it is just the language that is used, often it is racist by omission (especially when only white people are seen doing the 'nice', bourgeois jobs), or because the individual portrayed is a stereotype: it is a real problem to decide how to come to a conclusion about what is racist and what is not. We now offer various methods suggested by people who have written on this subject.

Rae Alexander, in an article in *Interracial Books for Children* (Autumn 1970), suggests that her criteria for calling a book racist were:

1 if it was likely to communicate to either a black or a white child a racist concept or cliche
2 if it failed to give some strong characters to serve as role models with which black youth can identify and find fulfilment
3 if it could give pain to even one black child
4 if it could not be equally well used in an all-black classroom, an all-white classroom, or an integrated classroom

The Schools Council/NFER Project 'Education for a Multiracial Society' offers the following draft criteria for discussion:

Source: NUS Publications (1974), pp. 9–25.

Working draft

Criteria for the selection of learning experience

Teachers need time to consider criteria for the selection of learning experience for children growing up in multiracial Britain.

The criteria that follow are offered for discussion.

1 People from British minority groups and from other cultures overseas should be presented as individuals with every variety of human quality and attribute. Stereotypes of minority groups in Britain and of cultures overseas, whether expressed in terms of human characteristics, life-styles, social roles or occupational status, are unacceptable and likely to be damaging.
2 Other cultures and nations have their own validity and should be described in their own terms. Wherever possible they should be allowed to speak for themselves and not be judged against British or European norms.
3 Contemporary British society contains a variety of social and ethnic groups, this variety should be made evident in the visuals, stories and information offered to children.
4 Children under thirteen should have access to accurate information about racial and cultural differences and similarities.
5 Because people and cultures of African descent have been undervalued by Western writers and historians, it is reasonable to correct that imbalance by showing black characters in positive roles and by selecting for study a variety of African societies.
6 Because antagonism and tensions do exist among children from different ethnic and racial groups, it seems unwise to make available books or materials which reinforce the influences of the mass media by giving currency to expressions of prejudice.

These two sets of suggested criteria together form a very useful base. The first is a rough guide as to the rejection of a book, the second is a draft of proposals as to the type of book one would consider appropriate to use in the development of a multiracial society. Rae Alexander's suggestions are, I feel, an excellent potted summary to bear in mind. Of course, the NFER proposals will continue to be contentious, especially perhaps point 5 about the necessity to redress the balance with reference to African people and culture. I would agree with the proposals and consider that the mass of literature which has been produced that is detrimental to Africa must be balanced, and that this can only be done by positive effort. How many of us discovered in school that Africans had any sort of culture at all? We were all shown pictures of Africans performing strange dances, but surely never equated this with 'culture'? 'Culture' was something vague and holy, and involved dressing-up, art-galleries and Beethoven and was certainly not something to be participated in. Neither did we ever hear of the frequent communal way of life of many African people, or if we did, it was something alien, unrealistic and retrogressive, far removed from anything which related at an equal level in any way to ourselves. To study the way of life of African societies would not only correct an imbalance but would also be a fruitful exercise for all pupils. The present failure to do this, except on a superficial basis, is a positive injustice to immigrants of African or Asian descent in this country. It is also necessary that white children should not be segregated for this exercise, as they should know as much of African culture as African children, or British children of African descent, need to know of British culture. At the present time, serious problems are caused for immigrants who see their own culture rejected, and perhaps then reject their own identity and culture, consciously or unconsciously. As the NFER introductory pamphlet has it, 'it is a psychological truism that a positive self-image is a prerequisite for academic success, mental health and fulfilment in adulthood.'

Point 6 of these draft suggestions is also a matter for some debate, concerning the desirability of restriction of expressions of prejudice. Those who argue against this proposal say that children are likely to hear expressions of prejudice on television, in the street, in the home, everywhere they are likely to go, so that it is better to air them at school as well, so that they can be discussed and explained. I would think that this is nonsense, and would only add validity to these expressions. It does not matter what motive lies behind the production of television programmes such as the Alf Garnett series, it still serves to spread the language and attitudes of bigotry and prejudice. There are books written for use in schools which are written with the best of intentions using the Garnett-type stock-phrases and usually ending with the black persons being accepted by the white neighbours but I feel that these are counter-productive. One should be prepared to, and must be prepared to, discuss the ethnics of racialism with one's pupils, but this cannot be conducted in the Garnett-type phraseology. As soon as a teacher lowers himself to discussing 'Coons' or 'sambos', these words become valid in the eyes of the pupils. This reinforces and perpetuates the prejudice and must not be allowed. It is the language of prejudice, not of reason, and it is basically impossible to conduct a reasoned discussion with prejudiced language.

The largest single problem in text books is the stereotype. Entire races are assumed to have exactly the same appearance (crinkly hair, shiny teeth, thick lips) characteristics (lazy, warlike, uncivilized) and potential (non-whites are inevitably seen doing manual jobs). Thus, in *Teaching Prejudice – a View from Canada* (Education and Community Relations, May 1972) a survey was conducted to find the adjective usually applied to certain minority groups. The top one in each group was as follows: Christians (devoted); Jews (great); immigrants (hard working); Moslems (infidels); Negroes (primitive); and American Indians (savages). Again, a survey of pictures in text-books was carried out with similarly interesting results. For example the following percentages were found for various groups who were pictured naked or half-naked: Canadians (0); Asians (11); American Indians (42); Africans (39). The following were the results of pictures showing skilled or professional work; Canadians (22); Asians (7); American Indians (0); Africans (1). This shows a very clear trend towards stereotyping. Nothing needs to be actually stated, but, nevertheless, an impression is conveyed of a person's status and position in that society. Look at Longman's *Mining in South Africa* (1962) and the implications of 'European labour is necessary for the more skilled jobs. Thousands of African labourers do the heavy unskilled work'. The very existence of such stereotyping should be a warning to the teacher.

The other main fault all too easily found in text books is information which is either misleading or utterly false. The whole myth of white superiority is rebuilt in schools as the whole history of Europeans encroaching on the rights, aspirations and land of any inhabitants is once again painted as the great imperial crusade against ignorance. History seems to begin only when a white man arrives and then he is painted as the great philanthropist. It is never mentioned that for every arrival concerned with philanthropy there were thousands interested only in material exploitation. There is also seldom, if ever, any examination of the culture before the arrival of whites. The white culture is assumed as the norm. For example, the case of Manhattan Island being bought from the American Indians for a few dollars and a calculation of what it is worth today is often used to scoff at the stupidity of the Indian. The other side of the coin, however, is far more revealing. To the Indian the notion of a person *owning* the land was ridiculous. The land cannot belong to one person, and why should one want to own it? Use it by all means, but the sale of Manhattan Island was a joke in Indian eyes. Somebody gave them four dollars to buy what cannot be possessed. It was like buying the sun to a European and seems, to me at least, to say a great deal more for Indian culture than for European. Yet this aspect is not discussed, and usually the intolerant laughter at the episode is suffered, if not encouraged. Enter the 'thick Indian' myth. The question of who owns the land is taken a step further by works such as *Britain in the Modern World – The Twentieth Century* by E. N. Nash and A. M. Newth (Penguin Education, 1970). It is explained that 'at the end of the nineteenth century the European countries became interested in building empires for themselves in Asia and tropical Africa and agreed to share out the continent'. Because there is no questioning of the right to do this, the young reader can easily just accept this right, with all the implied superior/inferior relationships. Certainly it must become obvious that in selecting criteria by which to evaluate school books all such unquestioned moral assumptions must be condemned, and all books using them must be classifed as dangerous. I feel that the importance of this and stereotyping amply justified the length of the treatment they have been allocated.

Perhaps one other broad item worth considering is the way that colonializm and Western expansion is protrayed. There is usually a portrayal of war and conflict which is assumed as soon as black meets white. This can suggest to the child that there is something unnatural about peaceful co-existence between races, and the reasons for the constant battles are not explained. There is frequently some element of necessity implied in the constant warfare. Instead of showing colonialism as the process of removing natives' rights and land and economically exploiting them, the natives (of no matter what part of the globe) are seen as mindless, heathen aggressors, attacking the white man who has come to help them. Status values are implicit here; the white man sets off with 'good' motives, he is civilized; he is always the victor (or when he does lose he and his men are 'slaughtered' or 'butchered'). There is so much bias by implication in so many books, especially history books, that it is a serious problem. The difficulties of saying 'this book is racist' or 'this one is not' are now becoming more apparent. Often the offensive passage can be a very small section of an otherwise useful book, and often, taken out of context, can seem quite trivial. However, when all these impressions from books on all subjects are accumulated, the problem becomes real. One very useful series of questions to ask in looking at children's books was produced by the National Union of Students. It reads as follows:

> The most important thing to remember in examing children's books is to note the date of first publication and the dates of reprinting. It is particularly obvious in history books and certain social history or 'topic' books that a failure to update factual information is the cause of gross distortion in the picture presentation of other countries. Only the oldest books really contain glaring misrepresentation, but these are still in regular use in primary and junior schools; an attempt to simplify often distorts. For reference we have drawn up a list of primary questions. They are not meant to be comprehensive, but a starting point; pure vocabulary and language use is left out.

1 **Reference books and Encyclopaedia for children's use** (for prime examples see 'Junior World Encyclopaedia' Sampson and Low), under 'race':

(a) how is race defined?
(b) how are different races illustrated?
(c) is there an implied social milieu for each race?
under 'Asia', 'Africa', etc:
(d) what kind of description is given of their history? e.g. is the emphasis on white 'exploration' or 'discovery' or black independence and present development?
(e) who are the 'personalities' mentioned in these references?

2 Subject text books – Geography, History, 'topic' books
ask again questions d and e, from number 1.
(f) Have facts about independence of former colonies been updated with reprinting
(g) Is the writer's attitude objective? (This is really a question of language and asides).
(h) How is S. Africa portrayed? as a white state? a black/white state? is any judgement of apartheid made? What social relationships implied?
(i) Are the continents of Africa and Asia implied to be single states or is there proper examination of individual countries?
(j) Is any country wrongly identified with only one racial/ethnic group?
(k) Does the description of each social/ethnic group imply one social milieu or more than one?
(l) In descriptions of people living in Africa and Asia is the emphasis on urban and rural development, on tribalism, on traditional 'custom'?
(m) Are 'typical' personality traits attributed to any group.

3 Subject text books – Religious instruction
(n) Look at the hymns and prayer books used at assembly. Look for nineteenth century compositions about missionary work to the primitive people abroad.
(o) In RE text books, are non-christian religions mentioned? Discussed? If so, what attitude towards them is encouraged?
(p) Are the words 'heathen', 'pagan' used? If so, in what sense?
(q) In any comparison of religions, what concepts are used as the basis of any 'moral' distinctions made?

There are plenty of story books available about children in other countries, and plenty of collections of foreign folk tales etc. There are fewer books set in Britain containing both black and white characters, these are correspondingly more difficult to deal with, in that the distortions arise through omissions.

I feel that this set of questions can provide a very fair overall survey, but that it is impossible to attempt to draw up a definitive list, mainly because of the last point raised by NUS, that of omission. Also, these points cover all the major kinds of ways that racial bias is conveyed. One hopeful note could be included here in relation to religious instruction which is often one of the most progressive subjects taught. Certainly these points are a very useful guide-line to a teacher, or preferably a group of teachers, who were prepared to conduct a survey of the books in their own school or college.

Thus we finally arrive back at our point of departure, which was our assumption that it is the teacher who will play the largest role in any attempt at the implementation of education for a multiracial society. He has particularly great reponsibilities with regard to which books he will use, and how he will use them. I feel that using Rae Alexander's point of 'Could this give pain to even one black child?' as a general rule, and then expanding on this, makes an individual start possible.

On a collective basis, the NUS is building up a list of books which act counter to the aim of creating a true multiracial and multiethnic society. We urge your participation in order to make this as full and comprehensive as possible.

Part II

In this section we will merely list some easily found examples of racially dangerous statements, with as little comment from ourselves as possible. We often find some of these examples amusing on a first superficial reading, as no doubt you will also. However, to the child who is slowly becoming aware of the world about him, they are very dangerous indeed. Often they give the child an impression of himself as an Anglo-Saxon English (superior) person completely apart from and better than all other forms of humanity. People from other countries seem so widely different from him that they are impossible to relate to, having such strange habits and ways of life. Certainly, they cannot be considered as equals, possibly not as human beings, having such 'uncivilized' traits. This can leave a permanent scar on the child's formation and development, and one which even adult rational argument cannot later remove because of awakened prejudice at this early stage.

We will begin with non-African references, and deal with the African ones later as they abound even more in quantity as well as intensity. Let us look at Marguerite Turnbull's *Other People's Homes* (Hulton Education Publications Ltd., reprinted 1968.) This whole book is the ultimate in the uniformed stereotype. For instance: 'If you were Japanese, you would not think it at all strange to live in a house made mostly of paper'. I imagine the inhabitants of Tokyo would be not only surprised but fairly concerned! In this book, too, we have Spaniards living in boats 'on a creek of the great Yangtse river' (no doubt the reason that Chairman Mao is always swimming to the shore!).

The only Scotsman portrayed in the book is a 'crofter'. They 'keep sheep and a cow or two and grow oats and potatoes. Many of the men and boys also go fishing'. Fortunately, they are kept 'warm and cosy all through the year' by 'a peat fire'. Wonderful stuff! In three sentences she manages to write off Glasgow, Edinburgh and the Scottish NUM! The Swiss, of course, live in chalets, the ground floor being for the inhabitants 'cattle, sheep and goats' and with a special room for 'making butter and cheese'. Whatever happened to Zurich? In Canada there are inevitably Eskimos building igloos, page after page. Are these examples really racist? I do not think they are so intentionally, by any means. But to the young child they are confusing enough to sow the seeds of prejudice and racialism. How can one identify with these unusual phenomena? How can one consider oneself on the same level as a Spaniard, who lives in a cave? Marguerite Turnbull does not mention that most of these people live in houses exactly like those in Britian (for better of for worse), and does not concede that her information refers only to a minority. In fact, it is out of date, irrelevant and misleading. This kind of 'information' alienates and separates.

In the chapter 'Albert the Aborigine' from *This is your Neighbour* (Johnston and Bacon, 1967) by A. Elliott-Cannon and Derek Stewart, 'He is a little afraid of the giant plane that comes to collect the meat the white Boss has stored in the great refrigerators'. Happily it goes on 'there are still thousands of "abos" left'. Then is the really condescending 'many aborigines are in fact clever people ... ' and goes on to commend those clever abos who 'have accepted the white man's way of life'.

There is an interesting piece on Clive of India in Rowland W. Purton's *Days of Adventure* (Collins, reprinted 1967). In all his stories, and in most books about explorers, the white man is seen as some kind of international philanthropist, going out of his way to help these strange people. Clive of India 'is one of the greatest men in the history of India'. He 'stopped trouble' and 'defeated Indian princes'. The rather important fact that had it not been for Clive and other English imperialists there would have been no trouble to stop is omitted. It leads to a biased half-truth being expounded which is both derogatory and dangerous.

Let's Visit Rhodesia (Burke 1970) by Guy Winchester-Gould could easily have been written by the Rhodesia propaganda machine. 'Among the countries of the African continent it (Rhodesia is second only to South

Africa in economic progress and advancement. This is a remarkable achievement considering that only eighty years ago the land was inhabited by savage people who were always at war with one another. Wild animals roamed the open plains and forests. There were no roads or towns, only widely scattered tribal villages'. Rhodesia, we are assured 'is a multiracial country'. What does this involve? 'This means that different races work and live there together.' There is no mention of the inhuman system of apartheid that exists there at all.

The history of this land begins in 1853 'the year that Cecil John Rhodes was born'. (Exactly what was there before is vague; perhaps Rhodes created the land out of nothing?) The land was 'occupied by wild animals and savage African tribes which belonged to the Bantu family'. (Note the juxta-position of animals and man, and the use of the word 'savage'). However, good old Cecil did his bit; after his defeat of the Mashona 'there was no further trouble from the native inhabitants. From then on development in Rhodesia was rapid'. What kind of development is this? Development is synonomous with Europeanization, as can be seen as Winchester-Gould scoffs at the Batonka tribe. Until a few years ago they had never seen a white man or a motor car! – which makes them 'the most primitive tribe in Rhodesia'.

The use of 'primitive' and 'savage' are very evocative, especially to the young reader, but the Europeanization is even more explicitly stated later when it is reported as an example of social progress in Rhodesia that 'every school child, no matter of what race or belief, is given instruction in the Christian religion'. The final sentence of the book summarizes the whole: 'From a wilderness to a republic – in only 80 years – that is the story of Rhodesia.'

There is no mention of colonialization, of apartheid of the inhumanity of white to black, merely the overall assumption that what the white man does in Africa is for the Africans' good, and that before the white man was savagery, butchery and degradation. It assumes the inherent superiority of white over black, the kind of attitude that leads A. Elliott Cannon and D. Stewart to write in *This is Your Neighbour* (*op. cit*) the following about Toma the Bushman: 'Here is a story about a man with no neighbours. He lives deep in the Kalahari Desert, in Africa. But we ought to take a neighbourly interest in him. If we do not, his race may die out before long'. What did Africans ever do before the arrival of the white man? He did very well to exist for so long.

What is South Africa like? J. C. Gagg tells us in the Young Learner Book *People of the World* (Chatto and Windus, 1970) that it is 'interesting', 'it has many white people, but they speak two languages, English and Afrikaans, and they do not always agree about things. Then there are the black-skinned people, who lived there in the first place.' Note the relegation of the indiginous people by the juxtapositioning, and also the statement about 'many white people'. Many in relation to what? Certainly not in relation to the natives of South Africa. Also, there is one picture of the 'black-skinned people'. Pickin' oranges, naturally. At least it's a change from cotton.

F. G. Moss gets stuck in right away on his section on Africa in *People and Homes in Many Lands*. This is published by Harrap, who first produced it in 1930 and went about 'revising, enlarging and resetting' it in 1966. It rambles on for two pages about wild animals, and then enlightens us with: 'Besides being the home of many wild animals, the African grasslands are the home of many different tribes of Negroes'. This juxtapositioning is inexcusable as is the parallelism of the different kinds of animals and tribes of Negroes. Equality between the two is clearly suggested. intentionally or not. This pernicious book continues with two examples of scandalous paternalism:

'The Zulu homes and villages, which have been described are in parts of South Africa called "reservations" where the people are allowed to live just as their ancestors did without interference.' And again: 'The government, which in this part of Africa is run by people of European ancestry, has helped the Zulu to improve their farms and cattle, and sees that they have medical care.'

There is no mention that the government also sees that they have no freedom in their own country, nor of how the Europeans came to run a government in a country not their own in the first place or of why people should have to be 'allowed' to live as they want in their own land. It gives the young pupil an impression, hard to destroy later, that when a white man rules a coloured man, this is an ordained, natural and correct situation, a desirable situation. It is a logical step to take this further to personal relationships, where the situation would seem to be that a white person is the natural leader and the coloured person is the servant.

Yet a further example of this suggested relationship occurs in the afore mentioned *Days of Adventure* (Collins, reprinted 1967) by Rowland W. Purton. In his section on Livingstone he says 'always his faithful negro friends stood by him for they loved this great white traveller'. It suggests the relationship between man and dog. The slogan for this section is 'Helped People to Know More about Africa'. Which people? Europeans, of course, the only ones who seem to matter to Mr Purton.

His slogans for Mary Slessor are equally bland and paternalistic. They are: 'In Africa for 36 years' which is fair enough, then 'changed Some Bad Customs'; 'Helped the Africans' and 'Stopped Some Fighting'. Completely without any back-up information he says 'Many times she was able to get evil ways (?) changed' and 'once, she was able to stop a war between two tribes of Africans by showing the chiefs how silly it was to fight.' A few million people might not have been blown to bits if this good lady had been around London in 1914 and 1939. Or possibly we Europeans would have been too civilized to heed her advice.

The same misconceptions, value judgments and misleading information occur time and time again. L. F. Hobley writes about *Tropical Forests of One Earth* in the *Introducing Earth* series (Macmillan 1970). He says of the pygmies of the Congo forest: 'Some of these primitive people have come into contact with other tribes in recent years, and they have learned from them. They often wear more clothes, and use cloth instead of bark. They exchange meat for iron tipped arrows, and for matches or flint and steel'. Again, 'very few white people lived for long in these colonies, for the climate is exceedingly unhealthy and uncomfortable'. Everything is judged by the European norm.

He has some interesting information to proffer about pygmies. 'African pygmies are very fond of bananas, and they sometimes go to the banana plantations of the negroes on the edge of the forest, take some bananas and leave some meat in exchange'. This is technically known, we are assured, as 'silent trade'. Another dreadful stereotype like the stiff upper-lip Englishman with his brolly and brief case. Enter the banana stuffing pygmy!

Even when countries become independent, the paternalism does not stop: the white man is still needed. Speaking of the West African coast, Hobley says: 'The countries in this area are now independent, and white men are no longer the rulers and "Bosses", but the white man's inventions, such as refrigerators and air conditioned houses make life much pleasanter and healthier for those Europeans who help the Africans to modernize their countries'.

Colonialism gradually becomes an exercise in benevolent good-will towards our coloured brothers. For example, we have the following reference to Ghana, 'Before the country became a British colony, most of the people grew crops mainly for their own use, and there was not much trade. Gradually this changed under British influence and encouragement and many people began to grow crops for export to the rest of the world.' Again: 'Tin has been mined in northern Nigeria for centuries and this was developed by the British. It is still an important export.' All this leads to a complacency in European superiority, a feeling of pride that we helped these unprotected Africans on the road to some form of civilization. The omissions are obvious.

Ladybird books as a whole tend to have a political line slightly to the right of Ghengis Khan. This example from the *Book of Travel*

Adventures, Flight Five: Africa, helps to build up all the old myths about the lazy slothful black man. Again it cannot be sufficiently stressed that this is exactly the time when children's ideas start to be formulated.

The following is a portrayal of a Zulu family. 'Mr Van Meetznan told them that the Zulus are the descendants of a proud warrior race. Now they live peaceably farming their land. The women work in the fields and look after the homes, the boys herd the cattle, and spend most of their time playing in the sunshine, while the men take it all easily.' This hardly comprises an in-depth overall survey of Africa.

In *Africa and Southern Asia* by Martin Simons (Hulton 1964) we see more of the myth that nothing existed in Africa before the arrival of 'great white travellers': 'only people who lived in East Africa before the white man explored it were dark-skinned African tribes like the Masai and the Kibuyn.' This really derogatory statement strongly implies dismissal of the 'dark-skinned Africans' and applauds the arrival of the whites. On page 23 of our edition Simons continues: 'So many different races living close together have created serious problems'. This suggests implicitly that different races cannot live close together, and sows the germ of an idea which can easily grow in a young reader's mind. Also, once having approached this theme, he abandons it completely. There is no development or elaboration, no mention of land – ownership, apartheid or of the many different tribes in Africa who have always lived side by side. A prime example of biased and selective reporting, wholly out of context.

Arnold Curtis' contribution on Africa in Vol. IX of *The Oxford Reference Library for Children* (Oxford University Press, 1969) does attempt to be informative and to refer to Africa's rich cultural past, but paternalism still creeps through the text, and European norms are assumed throughout. 'Africa is full of vigorous determined people who mean to reach the heights, even if they make many mistakes in doing so.' Other extracts are even sillier: 'Though they were pagans, the kings ruled their country well....' This must come as a surprise to those of us who believed that all good men are Church of England. Also 'Bushmen belong to the past and have very little to do with the modern world; for example – wait for it – they hardly wear any clothes, as almost all Africans do nowadays.' Presumably, using the same logic, as soon as one divests oneself for a bath, one has little to do with the modern world. A sobering thought to all progressives! But behind it is a serious and incorrect assumption, that if you do not adopt European culture, then you are not 'modern', you belong to the past. Thus, you are inferior and wrong. It is an unfortunate deviation in what might have otherwise been a relatively useful article.

One final remark on this section is the prejudice often caused by sheer chauvinism. In a Ladybird Key Word Easy Reader by W. Murray entitled

Some Great Men and Women (all caucasian, of course, and including such noteable progressives as Nelson and Churchill) is a section on Sir Francis Drake: 'one of Sir Francis Drake's *small* ships attacks a *large galleon* of the Spanish Armada' – showing that we British can do it even with inadequate weapons. However, it is in the text that the misconceptions appear. 'Francis Drake was a great man' it is asserted. Why? 'Ships went from Spain to the New World to take gold back to Spain. Francis Drake sailed with ships from England to take this gold from them.' This is all the explanation required. It is an assertion of the assumption that it is the right of the British to rob and plunder any other country unfortunate enough not to be British and/or without British strength of arms. It is also an assumption of national superiority, which easily translates to racial superiority.

The examples referred to in this chapter are not the worst examples to be found in text books in our schools, but they point out the kind of problem that we are facing in the fight against racism. We hope that a realization by our readers of the effects on young children of reading such books will encourage those readers to look more carefully at what they give to children to read, and encourage teachers to expose this kind of literature publicly.

3.3 What the British school system does to the black child

Bernard Coard

Some time ago a white boy of thirteen in the school for Educationally Subnormal children where I teach, asked my permission to draw a picture of me. I had been his class teacher for one year. I had a very good relationship with him, and he was very fond of me. He enjoyed drawing. The picture he did of me was quite good. He had included my spectacles, which he always teased me about, and he also drew my moustache and beard while he made great jokes about them. When he was finished, he passed me the paper with the portrait of myself, looking very pleased with himself at having drawn what he considered a near-likeness. I said to him: 'Haven't you forgotten to do something?'

'What?' he said, looking curious and suspicious.

'You forgot to colour my face. My face and cheeks, etc. – they are not white, are they?'

'No, no! I can't do that!' he said, looking worried.

'Well, you said you were painting a picture of me. Presumably you wanted it to look like me. You painted my hair, moustache and beard, and you painted them black – which they are. So you have to paint my face dark brown if it is to look like me at all.'

'No! I can't. I can't do that. No. No,' he said, looking highly embarrassed and disturbed. He then got up and walked away, finding himself a hammer to do woodwork with in the corner of the room far away from me.

This same boy, along with one of his white school friends, had waited outside the school gate for me one afternoon the previous week. When I approached, one of them said: 'People are saying that you are coloured, but you aren't, sir, are you?' This was a rhetorical question on their part. They both looked very worried that 'some people' should be calling me

Source: *How the West Indian Child is made Educationally Sub-Normal in the British School System* (1971), pp. 26–31.

'coloured', and wanted my reassurance that I was not. They both liked and admired me, and hated thinking that I might be coloured! I explained to them then, as I *had* done many times before in class, that I *was* black, that I was from the West Indies, and that my forefathers came from Africa. They obviously had mental blocks against accepting me as being black.

This white boy, who did not even know who 'coloured people' were, obviously had the most fearful image of what black people were supposed to be like, even though his favourite teacher was black, and one of his closest friends in class was a black child. I happened to know that his house-mother at the children's home where he lives has never discussed race with him, and does not display any open prejudice to black people. In fact she has, over the years, been an excellent foster-mother to two West Indian boys. Yet he picked up from somewhere a sufficiently adverse image of black people, that he couldn't bear to have his favourite teacher be 'coloured', and could not bring himself to draw me as I was – a black man. He had to have my face white!

This experience of mine gave me an idea; if this is how two white boys in the class felt about me, then perhaps they felt the same way about their close friend, Desmond, a black boy of eleven from Jamaica. So I gathered together all the drawings and paintings which the children had done of each other, and sure enough, Desmond got painted white by all the white children! What's worse, Desmond and the other four black children had painted each other white also!

A week later, Desmond, the West Indian boy, asked me to draw a picture of him. I drew the outline, as he watched, making critical comments from time to time. Having completed the outline, I began shading his face black. He immediately said: 'What – what are you doing? You are *spoiling* me!'

I said: 'No, of course not. I am painting you as you are – black; just like *I* am. Black *is* beautiful, you know. You aren't ashamed of that, are you?'

At that he calmed down, and I completed shading his face black. Then I did his hair. His hair was black, short, and very African in texture. I drew it exactly as his hair really was. When he saw it, he jumped out of his chair and shouted: 'You painted me to look like a golliwog! You make me look just like a golliwog!' and he was half about to cry, half about to pounce on me for having done so terrible a thing as to have drawn his hair like it was, instead of making it long, straight and brown, as he had drawn himself in the past!

After I had calmed him down, again by pointing out that my hair was exactly the same as his, and that *I* liked mine, he decided to retaliate by drawing one of me. He drew my hair black and African-like, he drew my moustache and beard, but he, like the white boy before, refused to shade my face dark brown or black even though I had done his that way. When I asked him to draw my face the colour it really was, rather than leaving it white, he said very emotionally: 'You do it yourself', and walked out of the room.

Obviously in an English classroom it is terrible to be black. The white child is concerned lest his best friend be considered black, and the black child is more than concerned that he should be considered black!

And this is what this society, with the aid of the school system, is doing to our black children!

The examples I have given above are not isolated ones. There is the Indian girl in my class who wears Indian clothes to school and whose mother wears her caste-marks and sari when going anywhere, and yet this girl once denied she was Indian when speaking to her English friends in the class. Or there is the case of the Jamaican girl in my class who pretended not to know where Jamaica was, and stated indignantly that she was not from 'there' when speaking to some of the other children one day. Both conversations I overheard by accident. I could give case after case, for they are endless. In fact, none of the West Indian children whom I taught and ran clubs for over a period of three years, have failed to reveal their feelings of ambiguity, ambivalence, and at times despair, at being black. Many have been made neurotic by their school experience.

How the system works

The black child's true identity is denied daily in the classroom. In so far as he is given an identity, it is a false one. He is made to feel inferior in every way. In addition to being told he is dirty and ugly and 'sexually unreliable', he is told by a variety of means that he is intellectually inferior. When he prepares to leave school, and even before, he is made to realize that he and 'his kind' are only fit for manual, menial jobs.

The West Indian child is told on first entering the school that his language is second rate, to say the least. Namely, the only way he knows how to speak, the way he has always communicated with his parents and family and friends; the language in which he has expressed all his emotions, from joy to sorrow; the language of his innermost thoughts and ideas, is 'the wrong way to speak'.

A man's language is part of him. It is his only vehicle for expressing his thoughts and feelings. To say that his language and that of his entire family and culture is second rate, is to accuse him of *being* second rate. But this is what the West Indian child is told in one manner another on his first day in an English school.

As the weeks and months progress, the black child discovers that all the great men of history were white – at least, those are the only ones he has been told about. His reading-books show him white children and white adults exclusively. He discovers that white horses, white rocks and white unicorns are beautiful and good; but the word 'black' is reserved for describing the pirates, the thieves, the ugly, the witches, etc. This is the *conditioning effect* of what psychologists call *word association* on people's minds. If every reference on TV, radio, newspapers, reading-books and story-books in school shows 'black' as being horrible and ugly, and everything 'white' as being pure, clean and beautiful, then people begin to think this way on racial matters.

Several months ago in my class I was reading one of S. K. McCullagh's story-books for children, *The Country of the Red Birds*. This author is world famous, and she has written numerous story-books and reading series for children, used in schools in many parts of the world. She is actually a lecturer in psychology. In this story, these two white children went out to the 'island of Golden Sands'. They got to the 'white rock', where the very helpful 'white unicorn' lives. When they met the unicorn, 'the first thing that they saw was a black ship, with black sails, sailing towards the white rock'.

'The black pirates! The black pirates!' cried the little unicorn. 'They'll kill us! Oh, what shall we do?'

Finally they escaped from the white rock, which the 'black pirates' had taken over, and went to the island of the 'red birds'. There, 'a black pirate stood on the sand, with a red bird in his hand', about to kill it. The white boys and the white unicorn, along with the other red birds, managed to beat off the black pirate, and the red birds in gratitude to the white boys and white unicorn state: 'We will do anything for you, for you have saved a red bird from the black pirates.'

For those who may be sceptical about the influence of word association on people's minds, it is interesting to note that when I said 'black pirates' in the story, several of the white children in the class turned their heads and looked at the black children, who in turn looked acutely embarrassed.

When the pictures, illustrations, music, heroes, great historical and contemporary figures in the classroom are all white, it is difficult for a child to identify with anyone who is not white. When in addition the pictures of blacks are golliwog stereotypes, about whom filthy jokes are made; when most plays show black men doing servant jobs; when the word 'black' in every story-book is synonymous with evil, then it becomes impossible for the child to want to be black. Put another way, it would be unnatural of him not to want to be white. Does this not explain why Desmond and the other black children draw themselves as white? Can you blame them?

But this is not the end of the picture, unfortunately, for the black children know they are black. Whenever they might begin in their fantasy to believe otherwise, they are soon reassured on this score by being told they are 'black bastards' whenever there is a row in the playground – and even when there isn't.

The children are therefore made neurotic about their race and culture. Some become behaviour problems as a result. They become resentful and bitter at being told their language is second-rate, and their history and culture is non-existent; that they hardly exist at all, except by grace of the whites – and then only as platform sweepers on the Underground, manual workers, and domestic help.

The black child under these influences develops a deep inferiority complex. He soon loses motivation to succeed academically, since, at best, the learning experience in the classroom is an elaborate irrelevance to his personal life situation, and at worst it is a racially humiliating experience. He discovers in an amazingly short space of time the true role of the black man in a white-controlled society, and he abandons all intellectual and career goals. Remember the four-year-old black girl in America, mentioned earlier, who said to Mary Goodman: 'The people that are white, they can go up. The people that are brown, they have to go down.' When two other psychologists in America (Radke and Trager) investigated 'Children's perception of the social roles of Negroes and Whites',[1] the 'poor house' was assigned to Negroes and the 'good house' to whites by the great majority of white and Negro children aged five to eight years.

Note

1 *Journal of Psychology*, 29: 1950.

3.4 Performance of children from ethnic minority backgrounds in primary schools

Alan Little

The issues

Over the past twenty years the characteristics of the school population in certain local education authorities have changed with the arrival of immigrants to the United Kingdom from the New Commonwealth.[1] Their children (both those who arrived with their parents, came later, and more recently growing numbers born in this country) have needs in common with other pupils, and they also have special needs stemming partly from the fact of their or their parents' recent arrival, partly from cultural differences, as well as specific language needs; on top of this there is the majority population's reactions to them and in particular their colour.[2] The key issue facing educationalists is the extent to which the conventional educational system and its practices require modification to ensure equality of opportunity and performance for these pupils and ways in which necessary modifications can be best achieved.[3]

At the outset two major points must be emphasized:

1 Although pupils with 'New Commonwealth' backgrounds constitute a small proportion of the total school population in the country as a whole, their concentration is such that in certain areas – especially urban areas – they account for a large proportion of the relevant population. Townsend[4] has shown, for example, that these pupils constituted 3.3% of the total school population in the country on the basis of the Department of Education and Science definition; and he calculated that on a wider definition the figure is about 4.5%. This small proportion, however, conceals the uneven distribution. The London area accounts for slightly more than half followed by South Lancashire and the West Midlands. In fact two local authority areas have more than 25% of their pupil roll

Source: *Oxford Review of Education* (1975), vol. 1. No. 2. pp. 117–35.

defined as immigrant, five between 20–25% and a further six 15–20%. Furthermore the number of individual schools with heavy concentrations is growing. Nearly 1,000 schools out of 33,000 now have over one quarter immigrant pupils, and some authorities with few children of minority groups overall have one or two schools with very large percentages.[5] This uneven distribution means that some areas and schools are faced with a greater need to cope with the educational issues which pupils from minority backgrounds present than others and in these areas a twofold response is called for. The first requirement is a commitment to positive policies, an admission that the education of minority group children is an important issue, a move away from the 'we-have-no-problem-here' approach found in some areas. Secondly the need is for more resources to be made available to such areas, both from the local education authorities and as a result of positive action by central Government.

2 A second consideration which is relevant concerns the extent to which the educational needs of these pupils and those of under-privileged sections of the indigenous community are similar.[6] Similarities exist because many with New Commonwealth backgrounds live in depressed areas with whites; further some of them share the characteristics of the socially and economically disadvantaged groups in society. Yet these similarities do not override important differences. For one thing, not all recent settlers come from economically disadvantaged homes nor do they all reside in depressed areas. Beyond this, two important factors must be recognized. Firstly the different ethnic background of these settlers and the fact that they do not share the common English language heritage sets them apart from the indigenous community. Their values, attitudes and behaviour differ in important respects from those of the indigenous population and it should be possible to preserve these differences. Secondly, because of their colour they are a visible minority and are often subject to the hostility of the host community as well as frequent discrimination in such areas as housing and employment.[7] Furthermore, the low economic and social status which New Commonwealth immigrants are frequently accorded in our society must affect the 'identity' these groups have of themselves and the self concept they can pass on to their children. These factors determine the character of the educational issues which emerge in the schools and must, in turn, influence the responses which the schools and local authorities adopt, and it is in view of these factors that such educational issues require serious consideration in their own right.[8]

One point should not be lost sight of as far as the school population is concerned. In the late 50s and early 60s virtually all Asian and West

Indian pupils were born and frequently started their education outside the United Kingdom. During the second half of the 60s the number of minority group pupils born in this country increased. By the end of the 70s virtually all black pupils in primary schools and an increasing proportion in secondary schools will have been born here. This means that the nature of the educational issues will change, one aspect of this is the type of cultural conflict and clash that is created for a black person, simultaneously living in the majority world of school and the minority world of home. In principle the problem is common to all minority groups, in practice its nature and intensity will differ between groups.

Opportunity

For some people the arrival of large numbers of black settlers was seen exclusively as a problem or series of problems. Schools and their staffs were sometimes guilty of the same stereotyped 'problem' view. There is little doubt that new issues were raised and old problems intensified by the presence of black pupils in schools and in the community but equally important (and often neglected) are the opportunities proffered by their presence. The presence of one and a half million black people in Britain does not make it a multi-racial society either in the numerical sense (it is actually 3% of the total population) nor in the strictly scientific sense (it would be inappropriate to see the various minority groups in this country as racial or race groups) but what is beyond doubt is that areas and schools with ethnic minorities have the opportunity of creating the conditions within which equal relationships can exist between groups and equal opportunities proffered to minority groups. To achieve this would be no mean achievement and would require a widening perspective and educational experiences of pupils from majority backgrounds. The United Kingdom has become more differentiated by the presence of a black community(ies). In consequence the educational experience offered to the majority population should be modified and in certain respects radically changed to enable them to cope adequately with the facts of cultural, national and racial diversity. Clearly this implies changes in the curricula and teaching methods, not least important eliminating the xenophobia and cultural blinkers that permeate much history, geography and literature teaching.

Sources of school performance

It must be emphasized that the findings reported in this paper do not indicate the potentiality of children from minority groups, they are based upon conventional tests of performance within the existing primary schools and therefore they are culturally limited in two senses:

1 They are related to the traditional primary school curriculum and are largely concerned with basic skill acquisition, reading, English and mathematics.
2 The tests themselves, and especially the reading and verbal tests, require various cultural experiences (in and out of school) in order for the pupil to perform adequately upon them. Such experiences may have been denied to many minority group pupils.

What the test results do indicate is the performance of pupils from minority backgrounds within the existing school system[9] and results from three separate sources are reported:

1 an analysis of the distribution of performance of 4,269 'immigrants' and 22,023 non-immigrants entering secondary schools in the autumn of 1968. At that time all pupils in the ILEA due to transfer to secondary schools were placed in one of seven 'profile' groups for English, mathematics, and verbal reasoning (a separate group for each subject) by the primary school. For English and mathematics the primary school ranked its own pupils in order of merit and provisionally assigned each to a group. Each child was then tested in the two subjects anonymously in the school. The tests were marked in the school and the results collated centrally. Schools were then informed of the number of pupils, who, compared with all pupils in the Authority, would be expected to fall into each of the seven groups. In the light of this information the Head then made his final decision on the groups to be assigned to each pupil. The procedure for verbal reasoning was different. Pupils took probably two standardized tests in the autumn term and in January all pupils took the same test which was marked by the school. A conversion table was provided for converting numerical marks into the seven groups. The Head then decided the group for each pupil using the test results and his own assessment of the pupil's ability. Theoretically 10% of the pupils should be in Group 1, 15% in Group 2, 15% in Group 3, 20% in Group 4, 15 % in Group 5, 15% in Group 6 and 10% in Group 7. For the purposes of this report, this survey will be called survey or project A.[10]

2 an analysis of the reading standards of 32,000 pupils in the first term of their second year junior schooling in October 1968 in the ILEA. The test used was a sentence completion test (involving silent reading and comprehension) devised by the NFER for their streaming project. Several points must be made about the test: it was a group test and not an individual one and inevitably a relatively blunt measure of reading attainment. Further, it measured reading comprehension and not other

aspects of literacy (reading fluency, oracy, etc.). Other basic primary skills (writing and numeracy) have been ignored, as have other aspects of the curriculum (social adjustment and personal relationships). More varied and comprehensive testing might have produced different results. For the purpose of this paper it is necessary either to assume a high correlation between the reading skill measured by the test used and other cognitive skills and/or that the reading skill is of such intrinsic importance that the results are of intrinsic interest. This survey will be called survey or project B.[11]

3 one of the areas used as part of the national Educational Priority Area/ Project was in central London and amongst the information collected about pupils were the following measures of performance:

(a) a test of reading standards (SRA)
(b) a test of passive vocabulary (English Picture Vocabulary Test)
(c) a test of psycholinguistic functioning (Illinois Test of Psycholinguistic Abilities)
(d) a test of basic skill performance in primary schools (Bristol Achievement Tests).

In all 3,000 pupils attended the schools in the area and the schools were recognized by both the DES and the ILEA as an EPA school (e.g. teachers in seven of the twelve schools received the £75 allowance for teachers in EPA schools, and all were included in the ILEA's own schemes to aid EPA schools). As one pupil in six was defined as an immigrant, the results provided a unique opportunity to compare performance of under-privileged and immigrant pupils. This study will be referred to as survey or project C.[12]

Note The definition of immigrant is the DES one, i.e. an immigrant pupil is a child either (a) born outside the United Kingdom, but now living with parents, relatives, or guardians in the country or (b) born inside the United Kingdom to parents whose country of origin was abroad and who have been in the United Kingdom for less than about 10 years. (The definition excludes those from Northern Ireland and Eire.)

Results

IMMIGRANT PERFORMANCE AND LENGTH OF EDUCATION
(Source: survey A)

Table I shows how far the performance distributions of all immigrants were markedly different from both the theoretical and actual ILEA distributions. For example, fewer immigrants than expected were placed in the top two groups (e.g. 8% on the English) and more in the bottom two groups (53%), compared with an expected 25%. The performance distributions of the non-immigrants, on the other hand, were either the same as or better than expected (more in Groups 1 and 2, less in 6 and 7). For example, again on the English, 25% of non-immigrants were in Groups 1 and 2, 23% in Groups 6 and 7. These examples are typical of results on all three tests, the non-immigrants had better distributions than the immigrants.

Table 1 Performance of pupils at transfer to secondary school

	English		Mathematics		Verbal reasoning	
Distribution	% 1+2	% 6+7	% 1+2	% 6+7	% 1+2	% 6+7
Theoretical	25	25	25	25	25	25
Non-Immigrants	25.0	23.2	22.9	25.6	19.8	28.9
Immigrants	8.1	53.0	8.0	53.5	6.7	58.9
West Indian	5.0	57.9	3.8	61.6	3.6	66.6
Indians/Pakistani	14.1	44.9	16.2	42.2	13.4	48.4
Greek Cypriot	8.1	50.3	10.1	46.1	5.9	55.6
Turkish Cypriot	2.2	65.2	4.7	64.8	3.5	70.0
Other Immigrant	15.3	41.6	15.2	37.5	12.9	41.6
Long-stay	12.4	37.9	11.7	41.5	10.0	46.1
Short-stay	5.5	61.8	6.0	60.6	4.7	66.8

None of the nationality groups studied had distributions similar to the theoretical or actual ILEA or non-immigrant distributions. Each of the given nationality groups (West Indian, Indian and Pakistani, Greek Cypriot and 'Others') had smaller percentages in Groups 1 and 2, higher percentages in Groups 6 and 7, than the comparative distributions. For example, on the English test these ranged from 2.2% (Turkish Cypriots) to 15.3% ('Others') in Groups 1 and 2, compared with 25% of the ideal and 23.7% of the actual ILEA. The distribution of the 'Others' and Indians/Pakistanis came 'closest' to all the nationality groups, to the theoretical and actual ILEA distributions (i.e. relatively the highest percentages in Groups 1 and 2 and the lowest in Groups 6 and 7). The opposite was true of the West Indians and the Turkish Cypriots. Greek Cypriots were in the mid-position. On the English test, for example, more than 30 times as many Turkish Cypriots were in Groups 6 and 7 as in Groups 1 and 2; the West Indians had more than 11 times as many in Groups 6 and 7 as in Groups 1 and 2, the Greek Cypriots more than 6 times as many, the Indians/Pakistanis more than 3 times as many, and the 'Others' more than twice as many. For non-immigrant pupils the ratio is roughly 1:1. For all but the West Indians, the distributions on the mathematics were closest to the non-immigrant distribution. It seems then that for pupils from non-English speaking countries performance was, not surprisingly, best on the least verbal of the tests. Differences between the immigrant groups and the actual ILEA distributions were generally most marked on the verbal reasoning test.

Immigrants who had a full education in the United Kingdom did better than the newly arrived immigrants. On the English, for example, 5.5% of the more recent arrivals were in Groups 1 and 2, compared with 12.4% of these who had a full United Kingdom education. Comparative percentages for the bottom two groups were 62% and 38%. It is important to note that distributions of the immigrants with full United Kingdom education were by no means the same as the distributions of the non-immigrants (for example 25% of the non-immigrants were in the top two groups for English compared with 12% for long stay). Given the importance attached to the actual process of immigration it was expected that the long-stay immigrants born here would do better than the long-stay immigrants arriving during infancy. This, however, was not the case; in fact the distribution of those born here and those arriving before the beginning of infant schools (1956–1959, or 1960–1961) were very similar. Performance on the English may again be taken as an example, as the pattern is the same in mathematics and verbal reasoning. On the English, perçentages in Groups 1 and 2 varied from 11.8% (1956–1959 arrivals) to 12.6% (born here), while percentages in Groups 6 and 7 varied from 36.9% (1960–1961 arrivals) to 38.4% (born here); in neither case is the difference educationally significant. The critical factor, then, seemed to be the amount of the pupil's education in the United Kingdom. A full education in the United Kingdom seemed most important in determining performance, but even with a full education, performance of the immigrant was not the same as that of the non-immigrant. The relationship between performance and amount of United Kingdom education seemed to be almost linear where the more recent arrivals were concerned; as the amount of the education decreased from 'some infants and full junior school' experience to 'less than one year junior school', percentages placed in Groups 1 and 2 decreased, while those in 6 and 7 increased. For example, on the verbal reasoning percentages placed in Groups 1 and 2 ranged from 7% (1962–1964 arrivals) to 3.6% (1965–1967 arrivals) to 2.4% (1968 arrivals).

Table 2 Percentage of pupils fully educated placed in upper quartile on transfer to secondary school

	English	Mathematics	Verbal reasoning
West Indian origin	9.2	7.4	7.2
Asian origin	19.3	20.2	21.1
Indigenous	25	22.9	19.8

Table 3 Mean reading score of UK children in schools with varying proportions of immigrants

Immigrants (%)	UK
0	99.0 (1,104)
1–10	97.7 (10,578)
10.1–20	95.3 (5,267)
20.1–30	95.6 (2,348)
30.1–40	94.4 (1,440)
40.1–50	96.5 (397)
50.1–60	93.7 (429)
60.1–70	88.9 (73)

A further point is worth making about pupils with full education in the United Kingdom: although the distributions of West Indians with a full education in the United Kingdom were better than the distributions of new arrivals, they were still far from the indigenous. Table 2 shows that 9% in English and over 7% in mathematics and Verbal Reasoning were placed in the upper quarter. By contrast the distributions of Indians/Pakistanis with full United Kingdom education were only slightly different from the actual ILEA distributions, around 20% on all three tests placed in the upper quarter.

From this analysis three points should be emphasized:

1 The 'immigrant' population is a heterogeneous one, both in national origin and performance in primary schools. On the whole pupils from

India and Pakistan do better than other immigrants, and West Indian and Turkish Cypriot children appear to do rather worse.

2 Length of education in the United Kingdom appears to be a more important determinant of performance than length of residence. This finding underlines the existing efforts of school staffs and perhaps suggests the need for pre-school; facilities for under-privileged pupils generally and minority pupils in particular.

3 There is a high inter-correlation in performance on all three measures of the primary curriculum.

SOCIAL AND ETHNIC MIX OF SCHOOL AND ATTAINMENT

(Source: survey B)

In this section the effect on reading attainment of children of different social/ethnic backgrounds in schools of varying social and immigrant composition is examined. The attainment data used in this paper is derived from a survey of eight-year-olds and the measure of attainment used is the mean reading quotient (RQ) for groups and sub-groups. The test was standardized on a national sample with a mean of 100, standard deviation of 15 and range of 70 to 140. The mean RQ for the London survey was 94.4. Mean scores can be very roughly converted into reading ages. A mean score of 90, for example, is equivalent to a reading age roughly one year below chronological age. Overall, London children had a reading age roughly six months behind their chronological age, and immigrants about one year below. When considering the effect on children's attainment of immigrant concentration it is important to examine the effect on the performance of both immigrants and non-immigrants. In order to simplify presentation non-immigrants and immigrants have been dealt with separately. Furthermore for the non-immigrants I have excluded the Irish and concentrated on children born in the United Kingdom.

Table 3 indicates that there is a fairly marked relationship between attainment and immigrant concentration in the school. The total range in attainment between low and high concentration is 10 points, which is approximately one year's reading age. There is a fall in attainment of children in schools with more than 60% immigrants; excluding this last group the range is six points, which is equivalent to six months' reading age. But there is not a smooth progression. There is very little difference, for example, in the mean scores of children in schools of between 10% and 50% immigrant concentration and, in fact, the mean of the 40–50 group is marginally higher than those of the three previous groups, suggesting that it is the extremes of immigrant concentration (i.e. less than

10% and more than 50%) that is related to the performance of the indigenous population.

This analysis can be taken a step further by examining the effect on different ethnic groups' mean performance of varying per cent from different socio-economic and other backgrounds. Three important points emerge from this analysis (see Table 4). First, for nearly all occupation groups there seems to be a trend of lower performance with higher immigrant concentration. For most occupational groups a marked fall in performance seems to occur when the immigrant concentration is greater than 10% and in schools which have 50% or more immigrants (although this latter is not true of the professional or the semi-skilled group). Secondly, it should be noted that *within* each occupational group the differences in mean score are not so great as the range shown in Table 3 (even allowing for the merging of the 60–70% immigrant groups). For most groups the range is in the order of four and a half points (except among the semi-skilled where the range is of one and a half points only). Thirdly, it is worth noting that parental occupation appears to be more important than the immigrant concentration of the school. Further support for this proposition can be obtained from the fact that in most cases a child whose parent is in a high status occupation but is himself in a school of high immigrant concentration attains at a higher level than the child whose parent has a lower (occupational) status but is in a school with few immigrants. One example of this is that the mean score of children of professional parents in schools with more than 50% immigrants is 104.9 while there is a mean score of 102.0 for the children of other non-manual parents who are in schools with under 10% immigrants. It is interesting to note that the effect of immigrant concentration on performance is virtually identical with the effect of lower working class concentration on the performance of children from different social backgrounds.

The discussion of the impact of social characteristics on performance can be extended by including an examination of the general social and community characteristics of the school neighbourhood (i.e. an index of social deprivation). This was developed by the ILEA (and it included measures of economic and housing stress, teacher and pupil turnover as well as measures of immigrant concentration and social composition which are important here).[13] Table 5 presents the variation in performance when schools are grouped by scores on an EPA index, but due to the small numbers in some sub-groups the analysis is presented for non-manual and manual groups and not for each occupation group separately. Amongst children from non-manual backgrounds, none of the differences shown is statistically significant, and, more important, there is no clear trend such as has emerged in previous tables, except possibly in the lowest priority group (4).

Table 4 Mean reading score of UK children classified by guardian's occupation and school's immigrant concentration

Immigrants (%)	Professional	Other non-manual	Skilled	Semi-skilled	Unskilled
<10	109.0 (1,159)	102.0 (1,973)	98.1 (3,800)	94.5 (2,335)	91.9 (2,109)
10.1–30	106.6 (617)	100.1 (1,054)	96.1 (2,579)	92.9 (1,745)	89.8 (1,348)
30.1–50	105.5 (124)	99.4 (228)	95.6 (660)	92.8 (383)	89.6 (308)
>50	104.9 (22)	97.3 (81)	93.7 (159)	93.1 (112)	87.6 (98)

However, it should be noted that in the third priority group (3) there is a trend but it is in the *opposite direction*, i.e., performance appears to improve with increasing immigrant concentration. For the high priority groups there is no clear pattern. Further, it can be seen from Table 4 that the general indicator of social and educational problems is a more important factor than simply that of immigrant concentration. This can be deduced from the fact that in nearly all sub-groups the mean scores of children in a low priority group are higher than those of children in a

Table 5 Mean reading score of non-immigrant children in schools of varying education priority rank and immigrant concentration

Immigrants (%)	Education priority rank 1	2	3	4
		Non-manual		
<10	97.5 (67)	96.1 (174)	100.2 (613)	106.2 (2,429)
10.1–30	96.6 (77)	99.4 (317)	101.7 (679)	104.8 (737)
30.1–50	94.2 (36)	101.3 (138)	101.2 (224)	103.9 (58)
>50	96.1 (35)	99.1 (47)	104.1 (17)	–
		Manual		
<10	89.3 (371)	90.2 (712)	93.8 (2,821)	97.0 (4,881)
10.1–30	88.3 (730)	91.2 (1,732)	94.2 (2,615)	96.0 (1,248)
30.1–50	92.6 (128)	91.8 (698)	94.1 (617)	94.5 (83)
>50	89.5 (203)	91.8 (178)	98.5 (26)	–

higher priority group whatever the immigrant concentration. For example, the mean score of children in priority group (2) in predominantly immigrant schools is 99.1 as compared with mean of 97.5 of those in schools of less than 10% immigrants but in priority group (1). Among the manual children such trends as there are would seem to point towards high performance being related to high immigrant concentration. In summary it would seem from this analysis that when account is taken of other factors, in particular, parental occupation and the school's educational priority rank, the factor of immigrant concentration is of negligible importance in determining non-immigrants' performance.

Fewer West Indians (who account for half of the immigrants in the survey (B)) are in schools of low immigrant concentration and more in schools of high concentration than 'other' immigrants. This is important since West Indians perform on average much less well than the 'other' immigrants. For this reason it was necessary to carry out the analysis for each nationality group separately. However, the resulting numbers in some sub-groups were so small that many of the tables presented only the West Indians and 'other' immigrants have been included. Among West Indians, Greek Cypriots and Indians attainment is very similar regardless of immigrant concentration, with the exception that there is a lower attainment in schools with over 60% immigrants. Among the Pakistanis and Turkish Cypriots there is no clear pattern but the differences between sub-groups are much larger. However, the numbers of children involved are small and there is no clear trend discernible. Among the 'other' immigrants there appears to be a trend similar to that shown for the non-immigrants, i.e. declining attainment with increasing immigrant concentration. However, this trend appears to be reversed in the group of 50–60% immigrants (see Table 6).

Again the effect of general social characteristics of the school and the area need examining and Tables 7 and 8 show their impact on West Indian and other immigrant pupils. The most significant point in Table 7 are the small differences in mean score between the sub-groups; it does not matter whether one reads across or down the table (varying priority rank or immigrant concentration), differences are small. The largest difference is of only six points. Furthermore, it is not possible to discern any clear trend; in schools of the highest and lowest priority there is no trend and in schools of the two middle priority groups there is a *slight* trend of increased attainment with increased concentration, and if anything the pattern appears to be less clear among the 'other' immigrants. The differences shown in Table 8 are, in fact, greater than those among West Indians, being in some cases as much as 10 points. However, the only difference which is statistically significant is that in the highest priority

Table 6 Mean reading score of immigrant children classified by nationality in schools of varying immigrant concentration

Immigrants (%)	West Indian	Indian	Pakistani
>10	88.1 (228)	90.5 (48)	90.7 (26)
10.1–20	89.1 (401)	90.2 (70)	92.1 (43)
20.1–30	87.3 (364)	89.8 (48)	94.3 (33)
30.1–40	87.4 (343)	89.6 (33)	87.3 (15)
40.1–50	88.0 (203)	89.9 (15)	83.1 (7)
50.1–60	87.6 (330)	87.9 (14)	88.3 (9)
60.1–70	84.7 (57)	75.4 (8)	78.7 (6)

Immigrants (%)	Greek Cypriot	Turkish Cypriot	Other
>10			
10.1–20	86.8 (63)	87.1 (32)	96.0 (230)
20.1–30	86.4 (81)	85.5 (48)	93.1 (256)
30.1–40	88.7 (100)	82.2 (39)	94.1 (173)
40.1–50	85.6 (51)	84.3 (73)	91.3 (120)
50.1–60	86.1 (22)	79.2 (25)	86.5 (43)
60.1–70	85.6 (50)	81.5 (30)	93.3 (54)
	88.5 (14)	81.3 (17)	85.1 (14)

group between children in schools of 10–30% immigrants and those in schools of 30–50% immigrants; 92.1 as compared with 82.6. Furthermore, in no priority group is there a clear trend discernible. Finally, for the 'other' immigrants (unlike the West Indians) education priority rank would seem to be an important factor. The differences between some sub-groups are large, for example, there is a range of 22 points between children in schools of 30–50% immigrant concentration as between the lowest and highest priority schools.

Table 7 Mean reading score of West Indian children in schools of varying immigrant concentration and educational priority

	Educational priority rank			
Immigrants (%)	1	2	3	4
<10	85.1 (19)	85.6 (52)	87.5 (81)	89.9 (107)
10.1–30	86.5 (110)	86.1 (279)	87.7 (370)	90.7 (172)
30.1–50	84.5 (72)	86.2 (271)	88.2 (273)	88.7 (27)
>50	84.3 (197)	87.8 (214)	90.9 (34)	

In conclusion it would seem that with the exception of very high and very low concentration there is no evidence to support the hypothesis that non-immigrant (or immigrant) children are adversely affected in their reading attainment by being taught in a school of varying immigrant concentration, nor conversely is immigrant children's attainment higher if they are taught in a school of low immigrant concentration. Compared with parental occupation and the index of multiple deprivation (education priority rank) the factor of immigrant concentration would appear to be of small and inconsistent importance. Children in high concentration immigrant schools are likely, however, to attain at a lower level than their peers because they are more likely also to come from a less advantaged home background and – regardless of immigrant concentration – the school is more likely to be a disadvantaged school. More specifically the following points emerge from survey B:

1 ILEA junior schools present considerable variety in the degree of both social and ethnic mix. Something like 40% of ILEA pupils are in schools

Table 8 Mean reading score of 'other' immigrants in schools of varying immigrant concentration and education priority ranking

	Education priority rank			
Immigrants (%)	1	2	3	4
<10		89.8 (19)	90.8 (53)	97.6 (174)
10.1–30	92.1 (34)	90.7 (93)	92.9 (182)	95.2 (162)
30.1–50	82.6 (30)	88.2 (53)	89.4 (75)	104.6 (19)
>50	88.3 (27)	92.0 (38)	94.0 (7)	

with a social or immigrant concentration comparable (within 10% limits) to the Authority as a whole. About one quarter of middle-class children are in predominantly middle-class schools (i.e. 50% or more middle-class), nearly a half of all lower working-class children are in schools which are predominantly lower working-class (50% +), while one sixth of the immigrant children are in predominantly immigrant schools (50% +).

2 The effect of immigrant concentration on educational performance is less important than the degree to which schools are experiencing multiple deprivation. As far as immigrant children are concerned their performance is only marginally affected by the immigrant concentration in the school. Non-immigrant children appear to be affected at the extremes of concentration: children in schools with less than 10% immigrants have a reading age approximately one year in advance of those children in schools with over 60% immigrants. However, the variation between these

extremes is slight: children in schools of between 10 and 50% immigrants attain at very much the same level. Furthermore, the relationship between immigrant concentration and performance is complicated by the fact that children in schools of low immigrant concentration come from predominantly higher status occupational backgrounds and the schools are furthermore low on the index of multiple deprivation, whereas children in high concentration schools are predominantly working-class and the schools are high on the index of multiple deprivation.

3 When social and ethnic mix appear to be closely related to performance it is at a level which an explicit policy directed towards encouraging and supporting such social and ethnic mix could not achieve in an area with a large number of recent settlers. For example, immigrant proportions of less than 10% cannot be achieved in an Authority in which the overall percentage of immigrants is twice that.

4 We are confronted, then, by a situation in which no matter how desirable for other social and educational reasons social and ethnic mix may be, it cannot be justified in terms of the performance measures used in this paper. Either the gains are too small to warrant the policy effort or the objectives are unrealistic in terms of the characteristics of the population. Improved educational performance of under-privileged children might be achieved if appropriate action was taken based on an examination of the social and psychological dynamics which underpin the index of multiple deprivation referred to in this paper and the mobilization of suitable resources to alleviate the situation. This conclusion should not be allowed to deflect attention from the minority of children in highly a-typical school situations, especially when such extreme concentrations are deviant not simply from the Authority of borough population but from smaller, more local areas. Nor to the possibility of encouraging dispersal out of areas of heavy concentration (for example two out of three West Indians are in the Greater London area) into other parts of the country. Again whether larger gains could be achieved by a policy directed towards greater social and ethnic mix, or by national, regional and local policies of positive discrimination in educational resources towards the disadvantaged schools, is at least debatable. The pay-off in terms of educational attainment of greater mix is perhaps indicated in this paper and may be small. How far dramatic redistribution and proper utilization of scarce educational resources would have a more significant impact is not known but such a policy is consistent with the strong influence shown in this paper of 'multiple deprivation' on attainment.

These conclusions are so important that it is worth looking at survey (A) in a similar way to see whether it is consistent with these results. When the percentage of immigrants in schools was related to performance (see Table 9) the distribution of immigrants' performance was closest to non-immigrants in schools with less than 10% immigrants, though even these distributions had a negative bias when compared with actual ILEA distributions. The distributions of those in schools with 10–19% immigrants were slightly more negatively biased than those of the 0–10% immigrant roll schools, but the first marginal drop in performance came for those in schools with 20–29% and 30–39% immigrant concentration. Performance improved to about the level of those in 10–19% roll schools for those in schools with 40–49% immigrants, but dropped sharply for those in schools with 50–59% immigrants, to 'level off' for schools with

Table 9 Performance of immigrant and non-immigrant pupils by class and ethnic concentration of the school

		English		Mathematics		Verbal reasoning	
Immigrants		1 + 2(%)	6 + 7(%)	1 + 2(%)	6 + 7(%)	1 + 2(%)	6 + 7(%)
1 Immigrants in	<10	9.5	47.4	9.9	44.6	8.0	52.6
school(%)	10–49	8.4	54.5	8.4	54.7	7.2	59.8
	>50	6.0	50.4	5.3	54.6	3.6	59.6
Non-immigrants							
1 Immigrants in	<10	27.9	20.4	25.9	22.6	22.9	25.8
school(%)	10–49	23.9	24.4	21.1	26.4	18.6	30.0
	50	18.0	30.7	14.3	33.9	12.7	37.3
Immigrants							
2 Semi-unskilled in	0–49	11.5	47.2	11.4	47.0	9.3	52.4
neighbourhood	50–59	5.3	56.4	4.9	58.8	4.3	63.5
(%)	>60	5.9	57.3	6.2	57.5	5.3	63.3
Non-immigrants							
2 Semi-unskilled in	0–49	29.1	19.9	27.2	21.6	23.7	24.7
neighbourhood	50–59	20.7	24.0	17.1	27.8	15.1	30.1
(%)	60	21.7	27.8	20.0	29.7	16.9	33.7

60% + immigrants. These differences in performance based on immigrant concentration remained when different patterns of length of stay or nationality of pupils in schools were controlled. It is important to remember that the differences discussed here are in English, mathematics and verbal reasoning. There was greater variance in performance based on immigrant concentration for the non-immigrants than for the immigrants. When non-immigrants in schools with no immigrants are included for comparison, the pattern which emerged was one of very high performance amongst non-immigrants in schools with no immigrants and slightly less good performance in schools with 0–10% immigrants; an identifiable drop in performance for those in schools with 10–19% immigrants (but no differences between these groups and schools with 20–29, 30–39, 40–49 percentages) – though performance was still better than the actual ILEA. This is followed by two large drops in performance for those in schools with 50–59% and 60%+ immigrants. The largest differences in performance were in the 'extreme' schools (there were either no immigrants at all or those with over 50% immigrant rolls): non-immigrant pupils in the former having distribution superior to the rest of the Authority, non-immigrants in the latter having distributions inferior to the remainder of the Authority. When immigrants and non-immigrants in the same schools (controlling both the immigrant and class composition of the school) were compared, in no instance did the immigrants do as well as the non-immigrants. However, the performance of certain groups (long-stay, Asian immigrants) is at least equal to the indigenous population.

Concerning the relative importance of per cent immigration roll and concentration of working-class in determining performance:

1 For both immigrants and non-immigrants, the 'social' composition of the neighbourhood seemed to account for more of the differences in performance than did immigrant composition of the schools.

2 Immigrant composition seems to be an important influence of the immigrant and non-immigrant performance when the percentage of immigrants reaches 50%, and although such situations are not frequent they are the ones in which a formal or informal dispersal policy might have effect.

3 Having no immigrants or very few (less than 10%), seems to be related to relatively high levels of performance for both immigrants and non-immigrants but as the per cent increases from 10–19, 20–29, 30–39, 40–49 only slight and sometimes inconsistent changes occur. There is some evidence that the increases affect non-immigrant more than immigrant performance. But low immigrant proportion was closely related to low working-class concentration of the neighbourhood, and it is therefore related to the inter-action of social and ethnic mix.

A COMPARISON OF IMMIGRANT SCHOOL PERFORMANCE WITH UNDER-PRIVILEGED INDIGENOUS CHILDREN

(*Source: survey C*)

The comparison of immigrant and non-immigrant performance within the same category of school is worth examining with reference to the reading ages found in project (B). Table 10 gives the mean reading scores for non-immigrants from semi- and unskilled working-class backgrounds and for West Indians. All the comparisons suggest that West Indians in similar school categories are performing at a lower level than the under-privileged white pupils and this finding is confirmed by the EPA study (project C). The mean reading standards of all pupils on the SRA test was nine points (nearly one year in reading age) below the national mean: the mean score of non-immigrants was 93.4 and of West Indians 89.4 points and the other immigrants 90 points. Within the area defined as 'under-priviliged' the indigenous pupils' mean reading achievement was four points above that of the West Indian settler pupil population.

Table 10. Mean reading score of lower working class and West Indian pupils by immigrant concentration

Immigrants in school (%)	Semi-skilled	Unskilled	West Indian
−10	94.5	91.9	88.1
−30	92.9	89.8	88.0
−50	92.8	89.7	87.6
50+	93.1	87.6	87.2

Confirmation of the same points can be obtained from the analysis of the English Picture Vocabulary Test (see Table 9). This test has two levels, one for infant school pupils (level 1) and the other for pupils in the junior range (level 2). Several interesting points emerge from this analysis: pupils in schools defined as EPA score over five points below the national norm on level 1 and nine points below on level 2. West Indians in infant schools (and therefore pupils who are likely to have a full United Kingdom education in the future) score 13 points below their national age peers and 11 points below their indigenous classmates. In junior schools the gap between them and their national age peers is nearly 15 points and with class peers over seven points. What stands out is that even at a very young age (i.e. infant schools) the indigenous white pupil in an EPA school is performing at a significantly higher level than his black classmate but at a significantly lower level than his national age peer. It is worth noting that this finding is confirmed by a study completed in another EPA area using the pre-school version of the English Picture Vocabulary Test: 63 non-immigrants in the area (mean age of four years five months) had a standardized score of 95.2, 23 immigrants (mean age four years seven months) a standardized score of 84.1. This indicates that the gap in passive vocabulary pre-dates school entry.

Table 11. Score of pupils on the EPVT in EPA schools

	Level 1			Level 2		
	N	Mean	SD	N.	Mean	SD
All pupils	1341	94.5	14.8	1551	90.9	13.8
Non-immigrant	957	97.9	13.8	1162	92.9	13.0
West Indian	298	86.9	12.8	250	85.5	13.1

The English Picture Vocabulary Test is a test of passive vocabulary. As a broader measure of language skills the study used the Illinois Test of Psycholinguistic Abilities. The test was administered individually to a sample of classes with second year junior pupils in some of the EPA schools. The test was used as part of a language programme evaluation to draw a psycholinguistic profile of the language skills of EPA children. Unfortunately it had no English norms. Detailed results are given in Table 12 but three main general findings are significant. When considering these results the small numbers of pupils involved in this aspect of the project must be remembered (i.e. 101 non-immigrants, 27 West Indians and six other immigrants).

Table 12. Mean scores on individual items on the ITPA

	Non-immigrant	West Indian	Other immigrant
1.* Auditory reception	30.7	23.9	26.8
2. Visual reception	21.0	20.6	23.3
3.* Auditory association	26.9	24.5	23.7
4. Visual association	23.6	21.3	22.2
5.* Verbal expression	31.0	27.4	27.3
6. Manual expression	28.5	27.1	24.3
7.* Grammatical closure	28.0	18.4	19.0
8. Visual closure	25.0	22.3	22.0
9.* Auditory memory	30.9	32.4	27.5
10. Visual memory	20.1	18.5	18.5
N	101	27	6

Table 13. Mean standard score of EPA pupils on Bristol achievement tests

	Non immigrants	West Indians	Other Immigrants
	N	N	N
	202	54	21
English	91.5	87.6	86.8
Study skills	93.2	86.5	85.2
Mathematics	96.9	91.0	88.1

1 The overall 'psychological profile' of the group of children tested was below and different from American norms. On the information available it is impossible to attribute this to differences between groups of English and American children or between normal English and English EPA groups of children.

2 Relative to the other areas of their psycholinguistic functioning, EPA children appear to have perception difficulties (i.e. they have difficulty deriving meaning from stimuli presented to them either visually or orally); on the other hand they seem to have little difficulty in expressing themselves either verbally or manually.

3 The West Indian sub-group of children have a 'psycholinguistic profile' which is different from that of non-immigrant EPA children when the auditory vocal channel of communication is being used. Half of the 10 IPTA sub-tests concentrate on skills involving this communication channel (those marked with an asterisk in Table 12); on four of them West Indian children had significantly different and lower scores than their other non-immigrant EPA classmates. On sub-tests involving the other communication channel tested on the IPTA – the visual-motor channel – there was no significant difference between the non-immigrant and West Indian groups. One of the sub-tests involving the auditory-vocal channel (the Grammatic Closure Test) West Indian children had particularly different scores from the non-immigrant children.

These findings confirm many teacher statements about West Indian children; namely that they are deficient in areas where language must be used as a directive tool but when visual-motor skills are necessary their performance is not different from their non-immigrant peers and combined with the EPVT finding (the passive vocabulary of the immigrant groups was significantly smaller than that of non-immigrant groups) provides a starting point for developing teaching programmes designed to meet the special needs of West Indian pupils.

A final series of data is available from project (C): one of the main curriculum schemes was an environmental studies exercise for fourth year junior pupils in the EPA schools. As part of this evaluation the Bristol Achievements Tests were used (which gave pupil performance in English, mathematical and study skills). Table 13 summarizes the scores of pupils at the beginning of the project: on English the indigenous pupils scored over eight points below the standardized scores and West Indian pupils over 12 points below. On mathematics the difference was three points and nine points; on study skills nearly seven points for the indigenous and over 13 points for West Indians. Children of new settlers in this country are performing at a level (on English, mathematics and study skills) not only below their age peers in the rest of the country but below the indigenous under-privileged children in EPA schools. Four main results stand out:

Main results of these comparisons and implications for education

1 The immigrant population is differentiated in terms of its adjustment to and performance in the English education system. Of the two main groups of New Commonwealth settlers (Asians and West Indians) the Asians appear to be performing at a higher level than the West Indians.

2 Length of education in the United Kingdom appears to be a more important factor in determining primary school performance than length of residence or being born in the country. But even with full education the performance of pupils from certain backgrounds is below the indigenous population.

3 With the exception of extremes social and ethnic mix of the school appears to have little influence on the performance of either the indigenous or the settler population. Where it does have an effect (where there are very few or very many settlers) it appears to influence the privileged pupils more than the under-privileged (middle-class rather than working-class, white rather than black). Further, positive gains in performance take place at a level of minority and class composition outside the possibility of policy changes in areas of heavy settlement.

4 The relatively poor performance of minority pupils is across the curriculum (passive and active vocabulary, verbal reasoning, reading, English, mathematics, and study skills) although some differences can be found in certain parts of the curriculum. Finally under-privileged white children perform at a higher level than West Indian settlers and this appears to be true of pupils before and in the early years of their primary education.

It is important to clarify what these broad generalizations mean: they refer to the relative performance of various sections of the population. Of course many children from minority backgrounds are performing at a level above many children of the indigenous population and differences within groups are far greater than that between groups. Just as the educational system has in a sense failed to meet the needs of the child from a working-class background, so now, to an even greater extent, it is failing to meet the needs of the child from a different cultural background and this is demonstrated by differences in mean levels of attainment. Various reasons can be advanced for these differences. The comparative newness to the United Kingdom educational system of certain groups is one, the educational consequences of social deprivation and the effects of cultural differences between minority and majority populations are others. However, it is the inability (or unwillingness) of the existing system to modify its practice to meet the needs of new types of pupils that should be stressed. There are two reasons for emphasizing the importance of modifying the existing school system; first what goes on in school is a factor determining differences in performance and second (and perhaps more important) is the fact that educational policy and practice is under the control of educational policy makers whereas the other factors are not. Therefore, it is suggested that what is required is a careful and critical examination of current educational practice and its modification as a means of improving the levels of achievement reached.

In particular these five implications for action need emphasizing:

1 It is the child from the West Indian background whose needs in terms of basic skill performance should be given highest priority. Further indications of some of the differences can be detected at or before school entrance.

2 Without positive action these needs are unlikely to be seriously reduced in short run: neither being born here nor having a full education bring performance levels up to the indigenous population. As a higher proportion of pupils from minority home backgrounds are born in the United Kingdom, so the mean levels of performance will improve, but certain sub-groups will continue in the immediate future to be below the indigenous population and even socially disadvantaged white groups.

3 That changing the social and ethnic mix of schools (i.e. bussing or dispersal) in areas of minority settlement is unlikely to change the performance of minority pupils with the possible exception of basic training in English for non-English speaking pupils.

4 The need for early intervention into development (certainly at the beginning of infant schools and more desirably earlier) of minority pupils.

5 The need to develop programmes especially designed to meet the disadvantages (and particularly the language needs) of children from the West Indian backgrounds, and expand language programmes for pupils from non-English speaking backgrounds.

Notes

1 Statistics of Education, Vol. 1, published annually.
2 Community Relations Commission (1974) *Educational Needs of Children from Minority Groups.*
3 See, for example, Community Relations Commission (1974) *Teacher Education for a Multi-Cultural Society.*
4 TOWNSEND, H.E.R. & BRITTAN, E. (1972) *Organization in Multi-Racial Schools* NFER.
5 Statistics of Education, *op. cit.*
6 HALSEY, A.H. (ed) (1972) Educational Priority, Vol. 1, *EPA Problems and Policies:* Vol. 2, *EPA Survey and Statistics* London HMSO
7 See, for example, Political and Economic Planning, Vol. XL, Broadsheet No. 547, *The Extent of Racial Discrimination.*
8 These points have been described in an article by Alan Little, in Richard Rose (ed) (1973) *Lessons from America: an Explanation*, London, Heinemann.
9 HAYNES, J. *Educational Assessment of Immigrant Pupils*, NFER.
10 Unpublished research at ILEA.
11 These results were reported in an article by A. N. Little & C. Mabey, in D. Donnison & D. Eversely (eds) (1973) *The Inner City*, London, Heinemann.
12 These results were reported by BARNES, J. (1975) *Educational Priority*, Vol. 3. London, HMSO.
13 This index is described by A. N. Little & C. Mabey, in A. Shoufield & S. Shaw (eds) (1972) *Social Indicators and Social Policy*, London, Heinemann.

I wish to thank Jack Barnes, Marjorie Clegg, Christine Mabey, who were colleagues of mine at the Inner London Education Authority, and Vivien Stern at the Community Relations Commission, for help with this paper.

4 Children and teachers

Introduction

In this final section we have gathered together four papers under the heading of Children and Teachers. The article by Kellmer-Pringle (4.3) describes the children she sees as being 'at risk'. Drawing on a wide-range of research she identifies an array of children (many of whom are likely to be found in urban areas) as being most vulnerable – the children from low-income families; those with only one parent, from broken homes etc., and she assesses the cumulative and long-term consequences of such disadvantage. Cicerelli (4.2) examines the various models for the disadvantaged that have been offered, reviewing the approaches and the assumptions on which these educational strategies were based, especially during the 1960s. He points a way forward to, what he believes are the possibilities open in the 1970s to close the achievement gap between the urban poor and the middle-class child. Eisenberg (4.1) draws out the *difference* and *defect* argument of educational disadvantage pointing out that we need to recognize the assets as well as the liabilities of the so-called disadvantaged group of children by creating a system in which the differences can be used to advantage.

The final paper (4.4) is taken from Gerald Grace's book *Teachers, Ideology and Control* (Routledge and Kegan Paul, 1977) one of the few works which has dealt systematically with the role of teachers in the development of schooling in urban areas. We have chosen here an extract which deals with the radical tradition among urban school teachers. The conservative and liberal critiques of urban schools are dealt with elsewhere in the course (see Unit 16 of the Education and the Urban Environment course in which other parts of Grace's work are discussed). We therefore end the section with questions about the role of the teacher and about changes in teacher consciousness in urban schools.

4.1 Strengths of the inner city child

Leon Eisenberg

The view that poverty is the result of stupidity or indolence is like saying that large shoes cause big feet. The key issue in looking at the strengths of the inner city child is the importance of not confusing difference with defect. Any teacher who has taught a grade in the middle-class section and a grade in the lower-class section of the city can certainly testify to the difference. Inner city children's clothes, their accents, their activity level, their classroom behaviour, their type of verbalization, their health standards, all do differ. Depending upon the type of test you use, they do test defective – notice that I said 'depending on the type of test.'

If we look at what we are and what they are as an anthropologist might, and total up the assets and the liabilities in the patterns of each group, then we find that all of the virtues are not on our middle-class side.

Some inner city children show positive attributes that we don't succeed in conveying to ours. Let me make it clear: I don't mean to suggest that the inner city child is a paragon of all virtue.

I'm calling attention to the positives because they're so often overlooked, but I don't suggest these children are without their difficulties. For, surely, they enter our schools poor in vocabulary, limited in ability to abstract, hampered even in capacity to sit still. They are children who are angry – angry perhaps for a good reason, but with an anger that takes it out on them and on us as well.

The behaviours the inner city child displays, however, are not entirely inside him. They emerge in response to the setting and values we supply and there is a way to alter what comes out. There is the possibility of change in the presence of what one might call an educational or a therapeutic environment.

For instance, the Harlem Project in the New York City Schools put extra services in a high school for a three-year period. As a result, it was

---

Source: *Baltimore Bulletin of Education* (1963–4), 41 (2), 10–16. A transcript of a taperecording of Dr Eisenberg's talk to the elementary staff of the Baltimore City Public Schools.

possible to lift the group IQ ten points, to triple the number of graduates, and to double the number who went on to take some further type of education. If this can be done in high school where the children are certainly in worse shape, think of what could be accomplished at an elementary school level. The success of the programme stemmed from a saturation of educational services; just a little bit here and there will not get the job done.

Cooperativeness – mutual aid

If we are to succeed in changing these children, we have to build on what their strengths are. And what are some of them?

To begin with, the family of the inner city child is marked by a degree of cooperativeness and mutual aid between family members that extends beyond the nuclear family typical of the middle class. It embraces uncles, aunts, grandparents, cousins, and so on. The child has a sense of being part of a large and extended family which becomes as large as the community in which he grows up, and these are people available to him as a resource in times of crisis.

In our work in the Children's Psychiatric Service, it is not uncommon to have a child brought to the clinic by someone who is not a blood relative of the child but has taken him in. This goes back to customs in the rural South, customs which still characterize some of this area, whereas in the neighbourhood in which I live, it's almost unknown to take in children who aren't within the immediate family.

In consequence of the cooperativeness and mutual aid in the lower-class family, these children display a feeling for people which may be more extensive and widespread than is found in the group we're used to. Inner city children frequently enjoy each other's company more freely and fully than do children who are more individualistic and self-oriented. As a rule, they show less sibling rivalry than do middle-class children. There isn't the struggle for mother's or father's love – the family situation is more diffuse.

Family and group values

Psychologically, these youngsters are less marked by an individualistic competitive orientation, a characteristic which may be either a deficit or an asset. It does mean that you have to find other ways of challenging them in the classroom, ways that differ from the ones suitable with the middle-class child who's out to start his bank account of grades and money as soon as possible. You need a different approach with the inner city child who doesn't think of himself as setting aside wheat in his granary so that he can eat while others have to struggle.

Inner city children tend to have collective, that is family and group values, rather than individualistic ones. Again, this is a clue to what the teacher has to strive to work for with them. These children come from families where the parents feel that if there's to be any advance, it has to come out of social group forces, not individual activity. They're not oriented toward individual success because, in general, there is a feeling that you can't succeed anyway; the odds are stacked against you. There is a feeling that if we are going to get anywhere, all of us have to do it at one time. We've got to act as a group. A kind of fellow-feeling comes out of that which you don't get from people who feel 'I'm going to make it on my own'.

I might point out that collective or group values can have an extremely potent motivating force if you can tackle them and put them together. There is good evidence that one nationalistic group has succeeded in rehabilitating a number of people who had criminal records, were drunks, or addicts, thus indicating the potency of belonging to something which is meaningful.

Also, evidence is pretty impressive that during the bus strike in Montgomery, Alabama (the first shot in the current Negro resistance campaign), the rate of crimes committed by Negroes dropped sharplv. Once people had a collective, socially positive way of expressing their antagonism, it was channeled to this constructive goal; people didn't commit the individual acts of violence which represented their antagonism, anger, futility, and defeat. Here is a tremendously potent educational force, if we can find a way to catch the child up into it so that his aggressive energy is channeled into positive classroom work, not into throwing stones at the school after classes are out.

Equalitarian values

Inner city children and their families are less readily taken in than are we by status and prestige. They have more genuinely equalitarian values.

This is part of your problem, too. My child, having been raised to believe that teachers are good and should be respected, is likely to listen and to believe the teacher, to assume that what the teacher did was for the right kind of motive. On the other hand, the inner city child feels that people are what they are on the basis of what they show and not on the basis of their titles. This child, when the teacher walks into the classroom, is likely to think, 'Who is this woman? Is she like all the other adults I have known? The ones who slapped me, punched me, didn't give me candy, failed to provide dinner, threw me out of the candy store, etc., etc.?' What I'm saying is the inner city child isn't so readily taken in by a person who has all the right credentials but isn't a genuinely deserving person. You've got to prove yourself.

Responsibility for family chores

Typically, inner city families are somewhat disorganized. The parents have so much to do, they can't watch over their children the way we watch over ours. Consequently, inner city children are free from parental overprotection. They are more ready to accept responsibility and many begin babysitting at the age of five, six, and seven, and keep the baby out of trouble. They'll make mistakes because no seven-year-old ought to have to take care of the baby. But they often show more responsibility for family chores than I see in my child – it's my fault not his.

In effect, these children learn to negotiate the jungle of the slums. If we put 100 children from the inner city and 100 children from the suburbs into the slums of another city, our children wouldn't make it because they haven't learned something that inner city children have. Some of the things inner city children have learned are terrible – how to steal candy from the store and so forth. But on the other hand, there is a certain kind of know-how for survival, and this is an intellectual art, not just an exercise in an Oliver Twist environment.

Some years ago, a prominent psychologist went to Africa to study the chimpanzee. He took along some geometric form tests which are standard for cross-cultural studies. During the rainy season, he tested his native guides on the form tests. He found, as had been demonstrated by others before him, that primitive peoples do poorly on the form boards. If you were to use American standards, they would be mentally defective. When the rains stopped, he went out with his guides to look for the chimpanzees. Day after day, the native guides deduced where the chimps would be found that day and led him to the right spot. They did this by observing details of the environment that the psychologist could not learn to see in all the time he was there.

Obviously these people were not mentally defective as you might have concluded from the test score. They hadn't learned the geometry of Euclid that is in our environment from the beginning – houses with square corners, streets built in straight lines – they hadn't seen triangles and diamonds. What they'd learned is a kind of non-Euclidean geometry with relation to Nature about them.

Concreteness without flexibility

Likewise, a Guatemalan eleven-year-old girl, who can't put circles and triangles in place on a form board, can weave geometric designs on a rug – she's learned to do it one way but not the other.

This is another characteristic of the inner city child to which you have to pay attention – the concreteness of his learning and the lack of flexibility in mental sets. Having learned to do something according to way 'A', he can't do it according to way 'B', at least not until he's been given extensive experience. This is something to which the teacher has to be alert.

Let's not jump to the conclusion that the inner city child is inadequate because, having lacked the early experiences our children have had, he cannot do the things that our children do. The inner city child is responsive, he has learned, but the trouble is that we haven't yet got a curriculum that pegs the things that he has learned so as to start from where he is.

Another point about these youngsters is that they're angry. It's anger expressed directly and not in devious ways. If one can get anger expressed verbally rather than physically, it can be channeled and redirected. These children are less verbal and this is one of our serious problems. But it's also true that they're less word-bound, they don't sit around just talking and not doing.

Physical skills

Finally, these children show superior physical coordination and skills. They have had to learn to survive by doing rather than talking; they possess a kind of body language and grace, a style that is physical rather than verbal. This was demonstrated as long ago as the 1920s at Teachers College, Columbia, when groups comparable to inner city children, although they fell way down on verbal items, had higher test results on performance items than did middle-class children.

Other traits could be listed. Perhaps such a list misses the point. The issue isn't who is better, but what are the differences. Teacher understanding of the differences provides the basis for more effective teaching.

What we need, and some day we'll get, is teacher training that prepares teachers to use Methods A, B, and C for Children of Category 1; Methods D, E, and F for Children of Category 2; and so on, instead of feeling that it's got to be one way. No system works for all children. You have to know a variety of methods so that you can reach the child with his particular needs.

Physically and visually oriented

As I've indicated, the inner city style of orientation to the environment is physical and visual rather than auditory. You can sit here and listen to me talk. I've caused sound waves and they are more or less effective. For other groups of people, this would be a total waste of time.

The style of inner city children is physical and visual. To engage these children in watching a movie where they see it, or a class play where they act it out, or a role-playing exercise where they pretend to be the storekeeper and customers if you want to teach them behaviour in a store – these techniques have been demonstrated to be effective. There is much greater likelihood of getting the children to be able to give you verbal descriptions of what happened than if you simply challenged the children with a verbal stimulus.

If you say, 'Johnny, what do you think about George Washington?', you'll get an 'OK' if you're lucky, or nothing. If you get Johnny to play George Washington in a little drama in the classroom or watch somebody else play it, he may not give you a very accurate picture of George Washington, but you'll get him involved, it'll matter to him, he'll care. George Washington will have seemed to have been a real person. Johnny will begin to talk and talk around something constructive, and then you have your avenue.

Experiences concrete

Just reading stories is not enough. If you read stories, you have to have pictures, the children have to have something to do. What they can see is better than what they can hear, at least as a beginning to build on. People have examined this by asking children to tell stories under different circumstances and counting the number of words. The response to 'tell me a story' is absolutely minimal in these youngsters, whereas with a middle-class child you can get a fair amount.

The more clues you give them, the more you show them, the more you make it a personal kind of experience, the better the inner city child's response. Some of the apparent verbal poverty disappears when the conditions are changed. Then the teacher can work with the child's inner world, which he could not have done while the child was sitting there mute, sullen, and unresponsive. But the primers and the readers will have to deal with the issues of slum life and not a lily-white fairybook family the like of which he's never seen.

Externally oriented

These children are externally oriented rather than introspective. Questions about how people feel and think are less meaningful to them than questions about what people do. The lower-class society, in general, is a doing society. These children have had relatively little training toward thinking about the self, meditating about one's feelings. These children are all on the outside; they're doing. If they feel angry, they run; they don't talk about why they're angry. This is unfortunate because talking to some extent would help them.

This action rather than word and feeling orientation suggests that play and games with children like this are a more effective spur to thinking and finally to talking than are verbal exercises. It's a challenge to design games that really do lead the child in a kind of direction.

The thinking of inner city children tends to be concrete rather than abstract. The logic they display is inductive rather than deductive. These youngsters have to be taught something very specifically, then after a number of specific teachings led on toward the generalization.

Thinking concrete not abstract

In a study being carried out at New York Medical College, a simple test is applied to lower-class and middle-class children. The child is given picture cards which have a number of objects on them. Commonplace objects are chosen so that both the lower-class and the middle-class children can describe them with about equal adequacy. The first card in the series has a doll, a ball, a toy gun, a drum, and so on. Then you say, 'Tell me what's on the picture.' Then you take away the card and you give it to the child again. This time you say, 'Give me a *title* for the picture.' The word 'title' means 'what class' the objects in this picture belong to, only that would be too complicated an idea for the first-grader, so you say 'give me a title.'

The middle-class child will call it 'toy,' 'things I like, ' 'things for children,' or something like that showing the subsumption of objects under a generic term as a generalization. The lower-class child will say 'drums,' because there was a drum on the picture, or 'balls,' because there was a ball on the picture. Usually, he cannot see that all of these objects have in common some abstract characteristic. This inability to abstract from the particular the characteristics of the general class constitutes a major barrier to learning in school. And we have to give the inner city child this ability which the older children come into the classroom with. Of course, it would be great if we did it at three and four, but until we get that, we've got to do it in kindergarten and first grade.

Slow not facile cognitive style

The cognitive style of inner city children tends to be slow, careful, and patient as opposed to clever and facile. A conclusion that the child is stupid is easily drawn by an examiner who will not wait to let the child arrive at the goal toward which he may be slowly progressing. What's your rush? You know he's got sixty-five years ahead. It's true you've got a certain amount of work to get done in the classroom. But when you cut him off from a path at which he would have arrived, you tell him he can't get this and he becomes convinced of what you were convinced of in the first place, that he's stupid. Then he acts stupid, and you're on your way to defeat, and he will be, too.

So these children need time. Holding up a flash card to see who's the first one to shout out the right answer isn't an appropriate exercise for them. They do poorly, particularly if there are some facile and clever children in the classroom. They have to be protected from the kind of competitiveness where speed is the major requirement. Certainly, we all agree we'd prefer to have the child arrive at the right answer even if it takes him longer than give the wrong answer quickly.

These and other characteristics that could be listed suggest a need for modification of the classical educational methods which have been developed on the pattern of the middle-class child.

These are children with insufficient verbal and experiential stimulation who have not yet formed the learning sets necessary before formal learning in school can begin.

The principle of learning sets is illustrated in the work of Harry Harlow at the University of Wisconsin.

Lack of learning sets

Harlow presented to a hungry monkey in a cage a little tray on which there were three geometric objects, two triangles and a circle. If the monkey lifted off the circle, the one that was different, there was food underneath the circle. Harlow brought in a tray with two squares and a triangle. Again, the food was under the one that was different, the triangle.

Isn't this what you do with the first-grader in reading readiness? Which is the one that's different?

Since you can't ask the monkey and the monkey can't tell you, you put food under the one that's different and he has to learn how to pick out the one that's different. He will learn although it takes an inordinate amount of time. It's really easier working with people than with monkeys when you're trying to teach them something. But psychologists are very patient people and finally the monkey learns the problem.

If you then give him another problem of the same general class but with different constituents, it will take him a long time, but not as long a time. By the time you get to the two hundredth problem with the monkey, he will be able in one or two trials to solve that problem where it might have taken him 500 trials to solve the first problem. He has acquired, in Harlow's terms, a 'learning set' – he has learned how to learn.

That is what inner city children don't know how to do, because of lacks in their experiences. They learn other things outside the classroom, some things we wished they didn't learn. But in a classroom setting they have to learn how to concentrate, how to look, how to narrow attention, how to abstract from the situation its general properties, and so on. Each thing you try to teach isn't as important in itself as it is as preparation for learning more.

The teacher of the inner city child needs more than techniques, though I've talked at some length about techniques. Above all else, the teacher needs a respect for and serious interest in the child and his family, demonstrated not by word but by dedication to service of the child and patient interest in his family. If the principal or the teacher says, 'Oh, how nice to have you here, Mrs Jones,' but really hoped Mrs Jones never showed up because her dress isn't the finest and her language isn't the best, Mrs Jones will get the unspoken message and she will disappear. They're better judges of motives than we are. I don't mean to put all the responsibility on the teacher, but I do mean to suggest that the teacher's attitude is a very important variable in this.

Impact of teachers

A significant change was reported to me in the case of some children who are bussed into one of the schools in the northwest section of the city. Several weeks ago, the children were behaving well but were silent, there were not many smiles, and not much output. A group of PTA parents organized a carpool to bring in the mothers of these children because they didn't have cars. And so some thirty or forty mothers whose children were bussed in came to the gathering. The next day the change in the atmosphere of the school was remarkable in terms of the behaviour of the children who finally felt that someone cared about them. This story illustrates a point that has been demonstrated elsewhere.

You will have respect for inner city children if you understand the relationship of their behaviour to their environment. Teaching these children is the most effective form of psychiatric therapy that I can imagine in terms of making constructive people out of them. The rates of mental illness and antisocial problems are very high among this population, but they don't need a psychiatrist, they need good education. Of course, you'll need not only yourself but the help of more teachers, and more specialists, than the school system at the moment is providing. It is only this, a knowledge of competence, that can restore the child's self-respect and give him a sense of potency. The most dreadful thing about these youngsters and young adults is the feeling, 'There's just no use in this world, no matter what I do it's not going to make any difference. If I have the chance to make a quick buck, I might as well take it. Why be a fool?'

The only way to change that is to create the reality that will give the child the feeling that he can do something. Obviously, part of this task is beyond the public schools. If you have good vocational education and he learns to do a job but when he comes out he can't get in a labour union or he can't be hired in a factory, then it's going to feed back negatively. But we have a job, too. It requires that we involve the child in direct activities that make sense to him as producing benefits to his family, to his neighbourhood, and hence to himself.

The effective teacher is one whose concern for these children extends beyond classroom activities to citizen participation in efforts to upgrade the neighbourhood, to abolish discriminatory practices, to provide more recreational facilities, to support social action for human betterment. Such a teacher will have an impact on her pupils and engage them to the end that they realize the talents they have in the same measure as children elsewhere, but that they cannot develop without her help.

It is no trick to teach the middle-class child – the odds are all with the teacher; and I suspect that even if we took the teachers out, the middle-class children would learn, but a little more slowly and a little more clumsily. The real challenge is to lead forth the disadvantaged child to a place in the sun, because he isn't learning by himself and he isn't learning in the way we have been teaching him. Here is the challenge. If you accept it, if you use your ingenuity, if you have faith in the child's capacity for growth, you will succeed. And society will owe you a debt that money and prestige can never repay.

4.2 Educational models for the disadvantaged

Victor G. Cicirelli

For many years in the United States, most children of the urban poor have been inferior in academic achievement to middle-class children and have suffered the consequences of being rejected by teachers, becoming school dropouts without jobs, and contributing excessively to welfare rolls and incidence of crime, drug addiction, and mental illness. The cost for the individual and society has been staggering.

What was new in the sixties was the greater awareness of and concern for the urban poor – especially the education of their children. Out of the many approaches to the problem have emerged three broad viewpoints about the cause of the achievement gap and the means to eliminate it; for convenience, these may be labeled deficit models, school-disparity models, and de-actualization models. The deficit models assert that something is wrong with the children of the poor; they are intellectually retarded or limited in some way and hence cannot attain middle-class levels of achievement without appropriate remedial or preventive intervention programmes. The school-disparity models assert that something is wrong with the schools; the children of the poor are different from middle-class children but not inferior, and the schools must change their present ineffective approaches in order to use these children's talents for achievement while simultaneously maintaining their subcultural indentities. The de-actualization models assert that something is wrong with society; society has a false conception of human nature, and the so-called achievement gap between middle-class and poor children is really a pseudo-problem. Each child is a unique individual whose goals for achievement should be determined by his own needs and interests rather than by the imposition of external goals and standards; the disadvantaged child is restricted in the self-actualization of his potential and needs

Source: Walberg H. J. and Kopan A. T. (eds) *Rethinking Urban Education* (1972), pp. 31–48.

developmental programmes allowing him the freedom to release his potential and develop to the fullest.

This paper will consider each of these models in greater detail as a basis for making recommendations for the seventies.

Deficit models

Common to all deficit models is the notion that the child is lacking in something essential to his achievement in the mainstream middle-class society; that something must be corrected, improved, or prevented from occurring if the child is to achieve in school and later in life. Hence, diagnosis and prescription become important for remedial intervention programmes, and a theory of mental development becomes important to guide selection of appropriate experiences for preventive intervention programmes.

Three deficit models can be distinguished: the environmental-deficit model, the nutritional-deficit model, and the genetic-deficit model.

Environmental-deficit model

Of all the theoretical models, the environmental-deficit model is undoubtedly the most pervasive; it underlies the bulk of compensatory intervention programmes in existence today. In essence, this model asserts that the achievement gap between poor and middle-class children is caused by intellectual (and accompanying emotional-social) retardation in the children of the poor – retardation resulting from lack of appropriate stimulation in the developing child's environment. This position rests on the idea that intelligence is not fixed but 'plastic' and that environmental stimulation plays a major role in intellectual development (Hunt, 1961, 1964).

Also, some hold that critical (Hunt, 1964) or optimal (Bloom, 1964; Deutsch, 1964) periods exist early in life; if the stimulation needed to develop certain intellectual functions is not present at these periods, remediation of the resulting deficits is impossible or quite difficult. Others hold that mental growth is cumulative in nature, building on what has gone before; later development, therefore, will be difficult if earlier development is deficient (Elkind, 1970). Inappropriate early experiences may inhibit new learning through the mechanism of negative transfer (Jensen, 1966) or 'harden' the individual in certain intellectual channels, so that new learning is difficult (Ausubel, 1965). Because of the great difficulty involved in obtaining adequate measures of supposed impoverished environments, evidence in support of this model is largely correlational; causal relationships have not been established to the extent needed to confirm the environmental-deficit model.

Those who espouse the environmental-deficit model assume that the deficits can be remediated or even prevented if intervention begins early enough. With the broad objective of remediating the disadvantaged child's cognitive deficits, a dazzling variety of intervention programmes have been mounted, ranging from small experimental efforts to the nationally implemented Head Start programme. Such programmes or 'treatments' have largely been based on common sense, trial and error, traditional nursery school approaches, Piaget, O. K. Moore, Montessori, S-R approaches, and a smattering of theories of learning, motivation, and individual differences. Many of the programmes are quite eclectic in approach.

While the majority of the programmes begin intervention in early childhood, the less than satisfactory outcomes of the early-childhood programmes have led to extensions of the compensatory-education approach both upward into the elementary school (Follow-Through, Title I programmes) and downward into infancy (Gordon, 1969; Lambie and Weikart, 1970), where mothers are trained to teach the infants at home or the infants are taught directly.

Most of the intervention programmes formulate specific or multiple cognitive objectives, attempt to identify deficits, and devise strategies to overcome these deficits. Just how well the various programmes have succeeded is another matter. Many programmes have reported improvements in cognitive areas as measured by tests of intelligence, school readiness, and achievement. For example, most of the Head Start centres reported small to moderate pre-test to post-test gains, and such experimental programmes as Klaus and Gray (1968), Karnes (1969), and Bereiter and Engelmann (Engelmann, 1970) reported IQ gains of up to twenty-five points. These apparent successes have been dimmed by findings of a fadeout effect in the elementary grades, where these children either regress or stay at a plateau while control groups of children who have not had the intervention treatment make a spurt and catch up (Gray and Klaus, 1970; Westinghouse, 1969). Some argue that one cannot expect long-term effects from intervention programmes without continuing special environmental stimulation, but such a view implies that more needs to be done than merely remediating certain deficits. In any event, even if long-range effects can be demonstrated, educators must still judge whether the results are worth the costs.

Comparative experimental studies (Karnes, 1969; Spicker, 1971; Weikart, 1969) have provided some valuable information about the merits of the various treatment approaches of compensatory-education programmes. Approaches stressing cognitive or academic-skill development produced the largest IQ increases; other programmes produced IQ gains when they were highly structured and incorporated language development as an important objective.

Beyond this, we still know little about what constitutes the 'appropriate' environmental treatment, the sequencing of curriculum materials within the treatment, the timing of such treatment, or the kinds of treatments needed for individuals with particular kinds of cognitive deficits. Infant, nursery, pre-school, and parent-education programmes continue to proliferate at a rapid rate, in spite of our present ignorance about proper treatment and doubts about the outcome. Whether such approaches can ever enable the urban poor to 'catch up' to more affluent segments of society remains to be demonstrated.

Genetic-deficit model

Another variant of the 'something is wrong with the child' hypothesis is the genetic-deficit model, most recently propounded by Jensen (1969) and Shockley (1971). The main (and greatly oversimplified) argument is that existing data (largely from twin studies) show individual differences in IQ to be largely hereditary and that, as a result, differences in IQ between socio-economic-status groups or between racial groups are also largely hereditary, since the environmental contribution to the variance in IQ is insufficient to explain such group differences. According to Jensen, one can expect little gain in IQ from environmental manipulations such as the many types of compensatory-education programmes now in existence. Shockley's main concern is that disproportionate reproduction in lower socio-economic Negro subgroups is dysgenic for the entire population, and Herrnstein (1971) argues that we are moving not toward a classless society but one of increasing social stratification based on inherited IQ differences.

While a summary of the arguments advanced in opposition to the genetic model is beyond the scope of this paper, these range from arguments that the question is not a proper or valid one for study ('Is Intelligence Racial?' 1971), to Bereiter's (1970) contention that even within the strictures of Jensen's model substantial differences in IQ can be accounted for by environmental variables. According to Bereiter, a fourteen-point increase in mean IQ (without necessarily changing the population variance) can result from environmental changes; such an outcome would place the attainment of basic academic skills needed for gainful occupation within the capabilities of the great majority of those presently disadvantaged.

While Jensen feels that compensatory-education programmes are of little use to disadvantaged pupils, he does not feel that educational efforts should be abandoned. Instead, the educator should consider a broader spectrum of abilities and design curricula suited to these children's stronger abilities. As an example, he cites his own two-level model of abilities; according to this model, low socio-economic children achieve as well as high socio-economic children at the first (associative) level of abilities but not at the second (conceptual) level. Low socio-economic children, then, should be taught in a way that makes use of their associative abilities.

Nutritional-deficit model

The nutritional-deficit model asserts that inadequate protein intake or synthesis during brain development could result in some loss or change of function. Inasmuch as 60 per cent of brain growth is complete by the end of the first year, and 90 per cent by age five, early nutritional adequacy is important. Inadequate nutrition during pregnancy is also implicated in higher incidence of prematurity and complication of pregnancy in low socio-economic populations (Pasamanick and Knoblock, 1966; Pasamanick, 1969). Just how extensive or severe malnutrition might be among America's urban poor today is not known, but 'there exist subclinical states of poor nutrition throughout the world that go unrecognized and may be perpetuating silent destruction upon the learning skills of the world's population' (Kappelman, 1971, p. 160).

Harrell, Woodyard, and Gates (1955), in a classic study, provided nutritional supplements to experimental groups of pregnant women and gave placebos to control groups; later they gave intelligence tests to the offspring. Significantly higher IQ's of experimental-group children resulted in two of the three areas where the studies were carried out; in New York City, this amounted to an IQ difference of eight points at four years of age. Cravioto (1966, 1968) found IQ gains of up to eighteen points in studies of severely malnourished Latin American populations – provided nutrition therapy was instituted by two years of age; he found no change in response to nutrition therapy after four years of age.

If previous research is correct, the time for prevention or remediation comes well before the schools are concerned with the child. School nutrition programmes for the children of poverty, while laudable for humanitarian reasons, may thus not be expected to remediate early damage. Effects of improved health and vigour on motivation and school achievement (and long-range effects on the next generation) are of course another matter.

In addition to nutritional problems, children of the poor suffer from a host of health problems, which prevent the children from effective school performance. According to A. F. North, Senior Pediatrician with Project Head Start: 'Children living in poverty have more frequent and more severe illnesses and are less likely to receive adequate health care than are more advantaged children, so health assumes an even more important role in the development of socially disadvantaged children' (1968, p. 195). (Children of the poor, particularly in aging sections of large cities, have higher incidence of lead and other heavy-metal poisoning, with its attendant CNS damage.) However, the difficulty of obtaining good data relating to health problems of young children precludes exact documentation of this claim. In a study of 1,467 Head Start enrollees given medical and dental screening in Boston in the summer of 1965 (Mico, 1968), 77 per cent were referred for further diagnosis or treatment for one or more reasons; however, in spite of these difficulties, 80 per cent of the enrollees were given general-health ratings of from good to excellent. Certainly evidence is needed as to whether these health problems can be effectively treated and whether the treatment results in improved intellectual functioning.

School-disparity models

These models all have in common two basic ideas. First, the urban poor child is not inferior to the middle-class child, although he may be different in various ways. Second, the schools are responsible for the achievement gap between the poor and the middle-class child, since they fail to reach the different child. The school-disparity models vary in their conceptions of just how the urban child differs from the middle-class child and also in how the school is at fault.

Cultural-difference model

The cultural-difference model, as presented by Baratz and Baratz (1970) and Stewart (1968), refers to language differences between American Negro cultural groups and the middle-class culture, although the model can be extended to other ethnic groups and cognitive functions. Proponents of this model argue that the schools – instead of attempting massive intervention procedures with culturally different children – must eliminate their archaic and inappropriate procedures for dealing with cultural differences. Intervention programmes have failed, according to this view, because they are based on nonexistent deficits, black dialect is not a defective linguistic and conceptual system, as charged by many interventionists, but a structurally coherent although different system. In other words, it has all the components of an adequate grammar. Education for these children should not attempt to destroy the experience and cultural forms with which the child is familiar, but use culturally relevant methods and procedures to teach new materials. Thus, in the Baratz programme, instruction is begun in the child's dialect and extended to standard English and mainstream culture.

Culture-of-poverty model
The culture-of-poverty model (Banfield, 1971; Gladwin, 1961; Lewis, 1966) refers to a way of life or style of living that is handed down across generations of the poor and transcends social, racial, regional, and national boundaries; thus, urban poor the world over have much the same system of values and style of living.

Presumably, ghetto children have acquired the basic values and attitudes of their subculture early in life, which accounts for their differences in behaviour and achievement compared to the middle-class child. These values and attitudes include strong feelings of fatalism and belief in chance, strong present-time orientation and short time perspective, impulsiveness or inability to delay gratification or plan for the future, concrete rather than abstract thinking processes and concrete verbal behaviour, feelings of inferiority, acceptance of aggression and illegitimacy, and authoritarianism. Such people have little interest or motivation for schooling and achievement, and are supposedly resistant to change no matter how it is advanced.

Riessman (1962) suggests that a recognition of this different culture can aid the teacher to structure his social-emotional relationships with the child in such a way as to make use of the child's in-group loyalties, informality, humour, and so on, and to structure his teaching so as to take advantage of the child's particular abilities and style of learning.

The idea of a culture of poverty has been sharply criticized (Allen, 1970), in that this position implies a consensus and homogeneity of values and styles of living within the poor that is not borne out by empirical studies. Studies supporting the culture-of-poverty idea have been observational and anecdotal in nature and involved extremely small samples of people; further, values derived from observations of behaviour are used circularly to explain that same behaviour. Finally, the definition of the poor is not clear-cut; the model may apply only to a small number of extreme poor and not to the majority of ghetto residents.

Bicultural model
The bicultural model, as expounded by Valentine (1971), refers to the ghetto Negro, although it could apply to other ethnic groups as well. According to this view, blacks are simultaneously committed to both black culture and mainstream culture (the two are not mutally exclusive, as often assumed); ethnic socialization comes from the family and other primary groups, and mainstream enculturation comes from such sources as television, mass marketing, and public institutions and amusements. A good deal of the mainstream cultural content remains latent and potential,

since there is little opportunity to practice mainstream behaviour patterns in everyday life. (For instance, the black may comprehend standard English, even though he uses dialect.) There may nevertheless be psychological allegiance to mainstream cultural values, aspirations, and role models.

If educators, instead of assuming that the black child lacks mainstream culture, would realize that he has acquired a good bit of mainstream culture but may be too inhibited to demonstrate it, they could provide real aid to the biculturation process through attitudes of acceptance and awareness. Those blacks who have genuine difficulties in adjusting to mainstream cultural institutions need special guidance and help in removal of obstacles to biculturation.

Institutional-prejudice model

Proponents of this model (Clark, 1965; Rosenthal and Jacobsen, 1964; Stein, 1971) regard the achievement gap as the consequence of an institutional prejudice against the children of the poor, and not due to any inherent deficiencies on their part. Teachers and administrators prejudge these children as incompetent and difficult to handle; and their low expectancies of poor children's success may act as self-fulfilling prophecies. To discourage the achievement of ghetto children administrators may formulate devious policies, such as tracking, watered-down curricula, non-academic goals, assignment of ill-qualified teachers to ghetto schools, encouragement of dropping out, excessive suspensions and expulsions, and a policy of accountability to no one for lack of success in teaching. Such an atmosphere discourages both the children and the few teachers who are sincerely trying to teach. Stein terms all of the above 'strategies for failure', which may be accompanied by the setting up of many ineffective compensatory programmes in the schools. A way out of the situation is seen in the rise of parent groups who seek to control the education of their children.

De-actualization models

De-actualization models all have a humanistic underpinning: The individual is unique, and his subjective experiences and self-concept are basic determiners of his behaviour and development. Human nature is basically good; the individual has the capacity for insight and for sustained motivation to actualize his potentials. The individual is constantly growing and 'becoming,' and his primary motivation is to actualize his potential and develop into the best version of a person he could become relative to his own values and goals.

The traditional nursery school embodies many of these ideas (Elkind,

1970), such as individualized instruction, discovery learning, and use of intrinsic motivation. This extension of the traditional nursery school overlaps in its viewpoint with progressive education, Piagetian theory, British Infant School approaches, today's youth movement, certain neo-Freudians, and the humanist-existentialist viewpoint toward human nature and development.

The children of the poor differ in achievement from middle-class children because they have not been motivated to actualize their potentials; instead, they have been frustrated and alienated so that they do not have the basic trust and autonomy necessary to take risks, reach out, grow, and attempt to learn in a meaningful way. A diagnosis-prescription approach is not what is needed to help these children, but rather a self-prescription. What they need is a warm, accepting environment, a prepared environment of many alternatives and opportunities, and freedom to choose accordingly (to play, ask questions, explore, manipulate, and experiment to see what happens). Teachers are to supply the warm interpersonal relations and the environment, and then consult, tutor, advise as the occasion demands. When the children of the poor gain emotional security, they will become free to choose and to release their learning powers and actualize their potential. (At times they may need help, such as specific instruction or drill, but always within the context of ongoing meaningful learning for them.)

Since each child is basically unique, it makes no sense to compare his achievement as he actualizes his potential to that of other children through standardized tests or other normative criteria. Thus, comparison of urban poor children with middle-class children in terms of achievement is really a pseudo-problem.

Lack of evaluation and systematic research into educational practices is one of the major criticisms of this approach. There seems to be an overemphasis on arts and crafts, with an isolation from real problems of the outside world. In general, educational goals are vague and ambiguous. Proponents of this approach assume that free selection implies interest and sustained motivation and that teacher selection implies lack of interest and motivation. As yet there is no evidence for this, nor for the goodness of human nature and self-insight. Such programmes leave much to chance, for the individual may never get beyond superficial interests or random activities.

New directions

The problem facing educators in the seventies remains much the same as it was in the sixties: to account for the achievement gap between the urban poor and middle-class children and to find ways to close it. What is new is a growing disillusionment with many approaches tried in the sixties, and with the capabilities of urban school systems to deal with the problem at all. What, then, is the future course of the various approaches discussed here?

Environmental approaches

These models have led to the development of conpensatory-education programmes whose objectives are to diagnose deficiencies and to remediate or prevent them, if the programmes are started early enough. In the early seventies, although Head Start has retrenched somewhat, other programmes are proliferating at a rapid rate, with government-sponsored day care soon to become a reality. At this point, we do not know whether these programmes will be any more successful than they were in the sixties, although their very proliferation assures their continued existence.

In the sixties these programmes were not successful in producing long-range effects or in producing effects at acceptable levels of efficiency (size of effects relative to time and cost). In addition, a successful 'delivery system' was lacking, one that could transmit promising experimental programmes for wider or mass applications.

Since we still do not know what makes for a successful programme, it is imperative that intervention programmes be kept experimental, with well-designed evaluation procedures. Many questions can and should be researched in order to determine the limits of modifiability of the human organism and to formulate a prototype programme (Sigel, 1971). The most effective time for intervention, the duration of the intervention, and the type of programme that is most effective with children of different racial/ethnic backgrounds or with different cognitive deficits are all of great importance. Also, the possible inhibitory or facilitating effects of the same training stimulation at different points in the curriculum sequence or at different ages must be determined (Sigel, 1971; White and Held, 1967). This kind of research will be time-consuming, but there is no alternative unless we are to be satisfied with compensatory programmes at their present levels of development.

Various programmes are now operating at different age levels; but there is no genuine continuity, since such programmes are not articulated with each other. (The abrupt discontinuity of the transition from compensatory preschools into traditional elementary programmes – with their different values, expectations, and regimentation – is frequently blamed for fade-out effects.) As everyone knows, intelligence continues to develop at least through the teens without any abrupt shift at puberty. If follows that we need, at least experimentally, articulated programmes of sustained duration from infancy through high school graduation. Such planned continuity can best be carried out within the structure of the established urban school system, which could be extended downward to include infant and nursery programmes. Such an administrative unit would make it more feasible to carry out longitudinal studies with proper controls and evaluation.

Urban systems must take seriously the employment of an evaluation expert for each school, one who is well versed in research design, measurement, and statistics, and who can involve the faculty in continuing and constructive evaluation of the success of their work.

Nutritional approaches

Although we have been made aware of the importance of adequate nutrition for prenatal and early development, and of the high incidence of nutritional and health problems among the urban poor, it seems unlikely that any great gains will be made without an extensive government commitment to public health and a programme that will attract ghetto mothers and children. Educators can help by giving their junior and senior high school students information on the importance of prenatal care and nutrition. Also, well-articulated programmes from infancy to high school graduation can provide a vehicle for associated health and nutritional care.

Genetic approach

This model has stimulated no programmes in the sixties, but it has stimulated thought to the point where we must take the question of the hereditary background of the learner more seriously. Do different social and ethnic groups have inherently different patterns of abilities and hence require different educational programmes? Intergroup profile differences (Jensen, 1970; Lesser, Fifer, and Clark, 1965; Westinghouse, 1969) – although they cannot be attributed solely to differences in heredity – at least suggest that some attention must be focused on these questions.

According to Herrnstein (1971), if compensatory programmes succeed in creating equivalent environments for all children throughout their development, then heredity will account for all differences between individuals and we will develop an aristocracy far more permanent than anything in the past. We may then need to take more seriously the notion of genetic engineering (or some sort of sophisticated eugenics programme) to attain an egalitarian society.

If, on the other hand, as Bereiter (1970) suggests, we can – through compensatory education alone – succeed in lifting the IQs of the genetically most poorly endowed to a level that would permit them to undertake a gainful occupation and enjoy a reasonable standard of living, we will have eliminated a major social problem.

School-disparity approaches

Advocates of these models have made us aware that schools in the sixties have not met the challenge of recognizing the cultural differences of the children of the poor and teaching them accordingly; indeed, school practices may actively interfere with and inhibit the children's ability to learn.

If it is correct that something is wrong with the schools and not with the children, then certain recommendations for the seventies emerge. First, a major research effort (given government support of a magnitude at least equal to that given the deprivation hypothesis) should be made to discover the specific subcultural differences of importance to education and the ways of gearing teaching methods and curriculum to these differences to produce relevant educational outcomes. Since most of our major cities contain a number of minority subcultures, this may well imply a much more individualized approach to education than heretofore employed.

Second, if one accepts the school-disparity models, it must be noted that early intervention is not implied. (If there are differences, not deficits, early education has no priority.) Instead, the massive funds now devoted to early intervention programmes could be channeled into improvements and research at the primary and secondary levels.

Third, the charge that school administrators and teachers treat ghetto children so prejudicially as to doom them to failure must be investigated and met, where needed, with major reforms. Administrative policies can be changed through administrative reorganizations, with ghetto parents and teachers participating in the decision making. Most would agree that we must improve, rather than eliminate, our public schools.

Actualization approaches

Programmes that strive to promote self-actualization are less explicitly advanced and identified than are the various compensatory programmes. The very fact that such programmes seem to be in tune with both the youth movement and the traditional nursery approach makes it likely that we will see more of them in the future. However, unless we are to accept on faith that such programmes will have more desirable outcomes than alternative educational measures, we must have careful evaluations of their worth. Such evaluation, combined with research aimed at discovering the most worthwhile learning options to offer the child at a particular stage of development, is strongly needed in the seventies.

Common trends and recommendations

All of the models – whether they are trying to correct or prevent deficits, to teach to the cultural differences of students, or to release self-actualizing tendencies – seem to be converging on the idea of individualized instruction. If we are indeed moving in the direction of individualized instruction, then it seems important to integrate all three positions as effectively as possible. Thus, students should be given as much freedom as they can handle from infancy through high school; but teachers, armed with knowledge of the students' deficits and differences (where these exist), can use this information to advise, consult, and intervene at the right moment to aid.

Since early-education programmes evidently are going to be with us for some time, every effort must be made to develop an articulated total education programme, with particular emphasis on improvement in the elementary and secondary programmes. Again, all models imply such a need.

Educators must seriously consider the relationship of school achievement to later success on the job and in life. Evidence from a variety of sources indicates that IQ and school achievement are poorly correlated with job success (Jensen, 1970; Kohlberg and the Mayer, 1971), although the correlation is greater between these factors and occupational status. It is likely that opportunities for employment and advancement in later life are now too strongly tied to educational qualifications. What is needed is to identify just what is really important and relevant for success in life, and to make sure that proper priorities are established in the schools.

In conclusion, the seventies must be a decade of improvement in the education of the urban poor. The schools themselves can do the job, and they should attempt it. Even if schools have been doing a questionable job in the past, they should not be eliminated in favour of other institutions or reduced in significance, as some would have us believe (Holt, 1965; Illich, 1971). On the contrary, with some measure of relief from the enrollment pressures and scarcity of qualified teachers which characterized the sixties, this is the ideal time to concentrate on quality education for all.

References

ALLEN, V. L. 'Theoretical Issues in Poverty Research.' *Journal of Social Issues*, 1970, *26*, pp. 149–167

AUSUBEL, D. P. 'The Effects of Cultural Deprivation on Learning Patterns.' *Audiovisual Instruction*, 1965, *10*, pp. 10–12

BANFIELD, E. C. (1971) *The Unheavenly City*. New York: Harper & Row

BARATZ, S. D., AND BARATZ, J. C. 'Early Childhood Intervention: The Social Science Base of Institutional Racism,' *Harvard Educational Review*, 1970, *40*, pp. 29–50

BEREITER, C. 'Genetics and Educability: Educational Implications of the Jensen Debate.' In J. Hellmuth (ed.), *Disadvantaged Child*. Vol. 3. New York: Brunner/Mazel, 1970 pp. 279–299

BLOOM, B. (1964) *Stability and Change in Human Characteristics*. New York: Wiley

CLARK, K. B. (1965) *Dark Ghetto*. New York: Harper & Row

CRAVIOTO, J. 'Nutrition, Growth, and Neurointegrative Development: An Experimental and Ecologic Study.' *Supplement to Pediatrics*, 1968, *38*

CRAVIOTO, J. 'Nutritional Deficiencies and Mental Performances in Childhood.' In D. Glass (ed.), (1968) *Environmental Influences*. New York: Rockefeller University Press, pp. 3–51

CROW, J. 'Genetic Theories and Influences: Comments on the Value of Diversity.' *Harvard Educational Review*, 1969, *39*, pp. 301–309

DEUTSCH, C. P. 'Auditory Discrimination and Learning: Social Factors.' *Merrill-Palmer Quarterly*, 1964, *10*, pp. 277–296

ELKIND, D. 'The Case for the Academic Preschool: Fact or Fiction?' *Young Children*, 1970, *25*, pp. 132–140

ENGELMANN, S. 'The Effectiveness of Direct Instruction on IQ Performance and Achievement in Reading and Arithmetic.' In J. Hellmuth (ed.) (1970) *Disadvantaged Child*. Vol. 3. New York: Brunner/Mazel, pp. 339–361

GLADWIN, T. 'The Anthropologist's View of Poverty.' In *The Social Work Forum*, (1961) New York: Columbia University Press

GORDON, I. 'Early Child Stimulation through Parent Education: A Final Report to the Children's Bureau.' Gainesville: University of Florida Press, 1969

GRAY, S. W., AND KLAUS, R. A. 'The Early Training Project: A Seventh-Year Report.' *Child Development*, 1970, *41*, pp. 909–924

HARRELL, R. F., WOODYARD, E., and GATES, A. I. *The Effects of Mothers' Diets on the Intelligence of Offspring*. Bureau of Publications, Teachers College, New York, 1955

HERRNSTEIN, R. 'IQ.' *Atlantic Monthly*, September 1971, pp. 43–64

HOLT, J. 'How to Help Babies Learn – Without Teaching Them.' *Redbook*, 1965, *126*, pp. 54–55

HUNT, J. MC V. (1961) *Intelligence and Experience*. New York: Ronald Press

HUNT, J. MC V. 'The Psychological Basis for Using Preschool Environment as an Antidote for Cultural Deprivation.' *Merrill-Palmer Quarterly*, 1964, *10*, pp. 209–248

ILLICH, I. (1971) *Deschool Society*. New York: Harper & Row

'Is Intelligence Racial?' *Newsweek*, May 10, 1971, pp. 69–70

JENSEN, A. R. 'Cumulative Deficit in Compensatory Education.' *Journal of School Psychology*, 1966, *4*, pp. 37–47

JENSEN, A. R. 'How Much Can We Boost IQ and Scholastic Achievement?' *Harvard Educational Review*, 1969, *39*, pp. 1–123

JENSEN, A. R. 'Another Look at Culture – Fair Testing.' In J. Hellmuth (ed.), *Disadvantaged Child*. Vol. 3. New York: Brunner/Mazel, 1970. pp. 53–101

KAPPLEMAN, M. H. 'Prenatal and Perinatal Factors Which Influence Learning.' In J. Hellmuth (ed), *Exceptional Infant*. Vol. 2. New York: Brunner/Mazel, 1971, pp. 155–171

KARNES, M. B. 'Research and Development Programme on Preschool Disadvantaged Children.' Final Report, Vol. 1, University of Illinois, Contract No. OE–6–10–235, US Office of Education, 1969

KLAUS, R. A., AND GRAY, S. W. 'The Early Training Project for Disadvantaged Children: A Report after Five Years.' *Monographs of the Society of Research in Child Development*, 1968, *33* (4)

KOHLBERG, L., AND MAYER, R. S. 'Report to the Office of Economic Opportunity.' Cited in *Report on Preschool Education*, July 14, 1971, p. 6

LAMBIE, D. Z., AND WEIKART, D. P. 'Ypsilanti Carnegie Infant Project.' In J. Hellmuth (ed.), *Disadvantaged Child*. Vol. 3. New York: Brunner/Mazel, 1970. pp. 362–395

LESSER, G. S., FIFER, G., AND CLARK, D. H. 'Mental Abilities of Children from Different Social-Class and Cultural Groups.' *Monographs of the Society for Research in Child Development*, 1965, *30* (4)

LEWIS, O. 'The Culture of Poverty.' *Scientific American*, 1966, *215*, pp. 19–25

MICO, P. R. 'Head Start Health: The Boston Experience of 1965.' In J. Hellmuth (ed.), *Disadvantaged Child*. Vol. 2. New York: Brunner/Mazel, 1968. pp. 187–215

NORTH, A. F. 'Pediatric Care in Project Head Start.' In J. Hellmuth (ed.), *Disadvantaged Child*. Vol. 2. New York: Brunner-Mazel, 1968. pp. 95–124

PASAMANICK, B. 'A Tract for the Time: Some Sociobiologic Aspects of Science, Race, and Racism.' *American Journal of Orthopsychiatry*, 1969, *39*, pp. 7–15

PASAMANICK, B., AND KNOBLOCK, H. 'The Contribution of Some Organic Factors to School Retardation in Negro Children.' In S. W. Webster (ed). *The Disadvantaged Learner: Knowing, Understanding,*

Educationing. San Francisco: Chandler Publishing Co., 1966. pp. 286–292

RIESSMAN, F. (1962) *Culturally Deprived Child*. New York: Harper & Row

ROSENTHAL, R., AND JACOBSON, L. F. 'Teacher Expectations for the Disadvantaged.' *Scientific American*, 1964, *218*, pp. 19–23

SIGEL, I. 'Developmental Theory: Its Place and Relevance in Early Intervention Programmes.' Paper presented at biennial meeting of the Society for Research in Child Development, Minneapolis, April 1971

SPICKER, H. H. 'Intellectual Development through Early Childhood Education.' *Exceptional Children*, 1971, *37*, pp. 629–664

STEIN, A. 'Strategies of Failure.' *Harvard Educational Review*, 1971, *41*, pp. 158–204

STEWART, W. 'Continuity and Change in American Negro Dialects.' *The Florida FL Reporter*, 1968, p. 6

VALENTINE, C. A. 'Deficit, Difference, and Bicultural Models of Afro-American Behaviour.' *Harvard Educational Review*, 1971, *41*, 137–157

WEBER, E. (1970) *Early Childhood Education*. Worthington, Ohio: C. A. Jones Publishing Co

WEIKART, D. P. 'Comparative Study of Three Preschool Curricula.' Paper presented at biennial meeting of the Society for Research in Child Development, Santa Monica, California, March 1969

WESTINGHOUSE LEARNING CORPORATION/OHIO UNIVERSITY. *The Impact of Head Start: An Evaluation of the Effects of Head Start on Children's Cognitive and Affective Development*. Vols. I and II, Springfield, Virginia: Clearinghouse for Federal Scientific and Technical Information, Sales Department, US Department of Commerce, 1969

WHITE, B. L., AND HELD, R. 'Plasticity of Sensorimotor Development in the Human Infant.' In J. Hellmuth (ed.), *Exceptional Infant*. Vol. 1. New York: Brunner/Mazel, 1967. pp. 291–313

4·3 Children who are 'vulnerable' or 'at risk'

Mia Kellmer Pringle

The myth of childhood being a carefree, happy time persists despite scant evidence to substantiate it. On the contrary, there is much that frustrates, frightens and baffles the growing child just because of his inevitable lack of experience and power. The younger he is, the more he lives solely in the present and his time perspective is limited so that he does not even have the consolation that anxieties and unhappiness will pass. Nor does he know that his frequent feelings of uncertainty, his lack of confidence and his failure to understand adults' reactions, are shared by many, if not most, of his contemporaries. This awareness comes largely with maturity except for the fortunate minority whose parents and teachers have the gift of remembering these feelings and, by using their memories, enable the young to cope with them more easily.

In one sense, then, all children are vulnerable and likely to experience unhappiness and stress. In addition, certain groups are made doubly vulnerable because of the presence of specific, potentially detrimental personal, family or social circumstances. It is such children who should be regarded as being 'at risk'. The idea that certain individuals or groups may be at high risk of future misfortune or malfunctioning has for long been accepted and acted upon in the world of life or accident insurance. The concept of being 'at risk' psychologically, educationally or socially is beginning to gain currency, following its successful application in the medical field.

The Perinatal Survey (Butler and Bonham, 1963; Butler and Alberman, 1969), emphasised the danger signs which place a baby at high risk of dying. These were shown to be not only abnormalities of pregnancy and complications of labour, but also biological factors, such as extremes of maternal age, and social circumstances, such as low socio-economic

Source: *The Needs of Children* (1974), pp. 107–17.

K

status. Moreover, adverse social and biological characteristics tended to reinforce one another. There is evidence too that an unfavourable socio-economic environment continues to exert and adverse effect on the growing child. That this is so, at least until the age of eleven years, has been shown by the *National Child Development Study*.

To ensure the earliest diagnosis of defects, local health authorities were encouraged to keep 'at risk' registers of those babies thought to be vulnerable because of adverse circumstances before, during or after birth. Though some doubt has recently been cast on their effectiveness, there is evidence that they can be of considerable value (Davie, Butler and Goldstein, 1972); this is particularly so if it leads to the differential allocation of resources between 'high' and 'low' risk children – in other words, positive discrimination in favour of the most vulnerable.

Whether it is either desirable or practicable (or both) to keep a register of children who are psychologically, educationally or socially at risk is a controversial question. Undoubtedly, such a suggestion is fraught with difficulties, not least because of its political implications. Also knowledge regarding likely physical consequences is much better established than the understanding of psychological concomitants.

In essence, the issue is this: if later malfunctioning or handicap can be predicted early with a satisfactory degree of probability, then three consequences could follow as a matter of practical politics: first, to assess, and where necessary to refine, methods for identifying 'vulnerable' or 'at risk' groups at the earliest possible time; secondly, to devise procedures to prevent the harmful effects altogether if possible, or else to mitigate their severity; and thirdly, to evaluate the short- and long-term effectiveness of any interventionist procedures.

There are five groups of children who are particularly 'vulnerable' or 'at risk' of becoming stunted or damaged in their psychological development because of personal, family or social circumstances. They are: children in large families with low incomes; children with physical or mental handicaps; those in one-parent families; children who have to live apart from their parents for longer or shorter periods; and those belonging to some minority groups. There are, of course, other stressful circumstances such as living in a home where there is a chronically sick or disabled parent or a step-parent; or where the father is unemployed or follows a criminal career, spending long periods in prison; or where the child has been in a natural disaster. However, these five groups have been chosen because they include the great majority of children 'at risk'.

The various kinds of potentially harmful circumstances are not, of course, mutually exclusive. The exact proportion of children affected by one or more of them is not known. It could well be as high as 15 or 20 per cent but the proportion depends to some extent on the definitions and borderlines which are chosen.

It must also be stressed that none of these circumstances inevitably leads to psychological damage. To some extent, the concept of vulnerability is a statistical one, being rather like an actuarial prediction: it is concerned with likelihood, not certainty, in respect of any individual child. Indeed, there are many who triumph, apparently unscathed, over severe and prolonged environmental handicaps.

Large families with low incomes

In Great Britain at least three million children – or nearly a quarter of the child population under the age of fifteen years – are growing up in families of four or more children. As a group, they tend to be on average, relatively under-privileged whatever the socio-economic level of their parents, but here we are concerned with families of limited means.

Some of the measurable effects

The most recent evidence from the *National Child Development Study* demonstrates that the handicapping effects begin before birth and affect subsequent physical, psychological and educational development. This was so both at the age of seven and eleven years (Davie, 1972; National Children's Bureau, 1972; Prosser, 1972; Wedge and Prosser, 1973).

Family size was found to have an adverse effect on both height and educational attainment. For example, the difference between a child who has no older siblings and one who has three or more was 2.8 cm height and fifteen months of reading attainment at the age of seven years. By the age of eleven years the difference had increased to 4.0 cm for height and twenty-nine months for reading. These findings applied irrespective of the father's occupation, the mother's height or the number of younger children in the family. It used to be thought that children's social adjustment in school was better when they came from large than from small families; more recent evidence, including the above study, has shown the opposite to be the case.

Children from large families with low incomes may also be at greater risk right from conception onwards because of their mother's smoking habits. It is now widely accepted that maternal smoking during pregnancy is associated with both a reduction in birthweight and an increase in perinatal mortality. In the *National Child Development Study* a higher proportion of mothers from working-class homes were smoking during pregnancy and, irrespective of social class, more mothers with large families (three or more children) were doing so while pregnant. After allowing for these factors, this had a measurable effect both on height and on educational attainment. Its size was the same at the age of seven and eleven years, namely 1.0 cm and four months in reading (Butler and Goldstein, 1973).

There are likely to be additional disadvantages since large families tend to occur more often in the lowest socio-economic groups. For example, in the *National Child Development Study* $5^1/_2$ per cent of children in Social Class I and 32 per cent in Social Class V came from families with five or more children. Irrespective of family size, the income of semi- and unskilled workers is substanially lower than that of the other socio-economic groups (Central Statistical Office, 1972). Hence financial hardship is virtually inevitable despite various allowances and benefits where there is a large family. According to official figures (DHSS, 1971), there were 135,000 families with four or more dependent children, where the wage earner was in full-time employment, whose income was less than five pounds above the Supplementary Benefit level, allowing for housing costs.

The disadvantages of belonging to a large, low income family are further magnified by the consequences of suffering from other associated shortcomings. The parents' own education, parental interest shown in the child's scholastic progress, housing, play space, household amenities such as indoor sanitation or running hot water – all these and many other circumstances are more frequently unfavourable in such homes. Furthermore, a whole range of adverse factors is often found together so that the resulting consequences on the child's development are in most cases both multiple and interrelated.

Some results from the Bureau's longitudinal study will illustrate this interlinked pattern of continuing and cumulative disadvantage. When both the father and mother stayed on at school beyond the minimum school-leaving age, they were likely to have a smaller family; also they were more likely to show a greater interest in their children's education (at the age of eleven years). In turn, both parental education and parental interest were, separately and measurably, associated with the children's actual level of scholastic attainment – the effect of each being the equivalent of, for instance, almost a year's reading age and a combined effect of nineteen months at the age of seven years.

At this early age, the overall effect of social disadvantage, and hence readiness to respond to educational expectations, is already clearly evident. After two years of schooling, the chance of a seven-year-old's being unable to read was fifteen times greater for a child from an unskilled working-class home (Social Class V) than from a professional (Social Class I); and the proportion of children from the former who would – in the opinion of their teachers – benefit from attending a special school was forty-five times larger than for those from a professional home.

Another example relates to housing. To begin with, there is a relationship between family size and over-crowding: the larger the former, the worse the incidence of the latter is likely to be. Thus whereas 57 per cent of children from families with five or more children were over-crowded, the incidence fell to only 4 per cent where there were not more than four children. Over-crowding remained a problem, so that by the age of eleven (i.e., in 1969), as many as one in eight of this nationally representative group lived in such conditions. Next, there was a very marked social class difference: children from unskilled working-class homes were ten times more likely to live in an over-crowded home than those from professional-class parents. Thirdly, the larger the number of children the less likely the family was to enjoy the sole use of such amenities as a bathroom, indoor lavatory and hot water supply.

Clearly stress and hardship are further magnified the larger the number of children. Cramped conditions which deny privacy, space for play and quiet for homework readily lead to irritability, restlessness and bad temper all round. Inevitably the brunt of the burdens are carried by the mother who is rearing a family without the basic amenities which are taken for granted by the more fortunate majority.

These problems are further aggravated because outdoor play space is at a premium in practically all urban areas. The poverty of recreational provision is indicated by the fact that nearly three times as many mothers expressed dissatisfaction with available amenities as were dissatisfied with housing conditions (33 per cent compared with 12 per cent); a recent government study corroborated our findings (Department of the Environment, 1973). This situation is likely to be worse for children living in deprived city areas where houses and flats are commonly without a private garden or yard.

Again, over-crowding and a lack of amenities had considerable and measurable effects on educational attainment, social adjustment and health. For example, at the age of eleven years, over-crowding was associated with a retardation of about seventeen months in reading age and of twelve months where amenities were lacking – a combined effect of almost two and a half years. This is more marked than the effects had been at the age of seven years (nine months' retardation in relation to over-crowding and nine months also in relation to amenities).

Taken together these findings point to three conclusions. First, many children growing up in large families whose income is low, are beset by multiple, interrelated and interacting disadvantages which have a detrimental effect on the level of their educational attainment, social adjustment in school and probably also on their physical development, in

K 2

particular height. Secondly, these effects usually work in combination and are cumulative. Thirdly, their adverse influence seems to increase over time so that the gap between the most advantaged and the most disadvantaged grows wider as the child grows older.

At least, this is the case in the Bureau's longitudinal study; for example, the combined effect of social disadvantage on reading attainment showed itself in a four-year gap at the age of seven (a good reader having attained the level of an average nine-year-old while five years is usually taken as the level of a non-reader). By the time the children were eleven years old, it had risen to a difference of eight years between the most advantaged and disadvantaged respectively (Davie, 1973; National Children's Bureau, 1972).

This finding of a widening gap in reading attainment during the junior school years confirms the results of an earlier study (Douglas, 1964). It also reinforces the view that equality of opportunity will not come about through changes in secondary or higher education. Rather it is during the pre-school and early school years that ways must be sought to overcome or compensate for the effects of environmental disadvantages on children's development. Limiting the initial gap is likely to be the most effective way of reducing the gap at later stages.

Effects on family relationships and on personal development

There is a tendency to paint a rather rosy picture of lower working-class life, according to which mutual self-help and support in child rearing, as well as in general family and financial matters, play a major part. It is doubtful whether this is in fact the dominant pattern in areas of high social need. In reality, more often than not, all members of the extended family in deprived urban neighbourhoods suffer from multiple disadvantages which stem from low income, poor housing and a limited ability to cope. Poor health and irregular employment not infrequently add to the difficulties.

For those at the lowest rung of the social and economic ladder, even collective resources have little to offer. Shared misery may temporarily lighten the weight of the burden but it is unlikely either to reduce its effect materially or to alleviate its causes. Grandparents may add another dimension to children's lives by providing a three-generation perspective; yet they also make heavy inroads on very limited family budgets. Other relations may contribute some cast-off clothes or a little cash in times of financial crisis, but usually they can do little to improve grossly inadequate housing or income (Leissner, 1972).

Another study concluded that:

> there was no doubt that individual and social handicaps marched together remarkably closely ... It does not follow, of course, that because they are found together that personal maladjustment is caused by poverty; on the contrary, it could be argued that, under present day conditions, to be conspicuously poorer than one's neighbour is a consequence of personal inadequacy (West, 1969).

While favourable socio-economic conditions do not necessarily ensure that children's psychological needs are met, it is much more difficult to do so in circumstances of severe socio-economic strain. Moreover, to be able to give and receive love it needs to have been experienced and many parents have themselves been unloved if not rejected in childhood.

The need for security may also remain unsatisfied because parental behaviour is unpredictable and contradictory. On the one hand, discipline tends to be autocratic; also physical punishment may at times be more of an outlet for parental anger and frustration, generated by the pressures of the daily struggle rather than a means of ensuring the child's conformity to desired standards of behaviour. Chastisement of this kind only succeeds in teaching its recipient to respect and to use force himself; even a verbal berating, coupled with threats of being 'put away', is more likely to make a child feel rejected than to enable him to understand what is expected of him and why.

On the other hand, living in a state of perpetual crisis and chronic frustration, the parents' capacity to deal with their own anxieties is often so limited that they feel helpless and overwhelmed by the problems of sheer existence. Hence they are unable to provide the necessary emotional support to their children at times of anxiety and conflict. Yet the children are in great need of such support just because family stability is inevitably so precarious.

The pressures of life in the most disadvantaged homes also prevent the parents from being adequate models for their children. The unskilled labourer, whose earnings are low and irregular and who leaves all family responsibilities to his wife; the mother who scorns or fears him, and who is herself weighed down by the burden of home-making and child-rearing – neither is able to present a picture of adult life and behaviour which is likely to evoke their children's respect or a desire to become like them. Worse still, as the children grow into adolescence they will become increasingly aware of how limited their chances are of escaping from the constricting net of their multiple disadvantages.

Thus many youngsters from severely disadvantaged families, being thrown back upon their own resources, come to look to their siblings and to their peers in the street for emotional support and for model figures. Is it justified to argue that turning to contemporaries and to gang life because parental support is so limited, shows early independence and self-sufficiency? At the same time, when faced with outside criticism, such youngsters show highly ambivalent attitudes, expressing strong feelings of family loyalty and affection. Probably this is because they have never known security or acceptance elsewhere. It is similar to the loyalty shown by children who have been neglected or even abused by their parents. 'The attachment of children to parents who by all ordinary standards are very bad is a never-ceasing source of wonder to those who seek to help them' (Bowlby, 1951).

Having had to adapt to precarious relationships as well as inconsistent or otherwise unsatisfactory parental models, and having lacked a predictable framework of discipline, the child will expect other authority figures, such as teachers, to behave in a similar fashion.

Because his needs for new experience, and for praise and recognition will probably have been inadequately met too, he comes to school ill-prepared to respond to what will be demanded of him. Even if aware of the value of play and of fostering language development, his parents will rarely have had the emotional or physical resources to provide either to a satisfactory degree. A limited range of experiences and limited language skills will make him an unrewarding, because unresponsive, pupil. From the outset, he confronts his teachers with both behavioural and educational difficulties so that they may soon come to expect low standards from him while he will be aware of their disappointment in him. And so all too often their mutual expectations will eventually become self-fulfilling prophecies.

He in turn will be bewildered by the, to him, alien achievement-orientated climate of the class-room; by the conflicting standards of behaviour expected at home and at school; by the displeasure and disappointment shown by his teacher towards his ineffective efforts; and by her disapproval and punishment of his lack of progress. Her assessment of him as 'hopeless' will make him feel 'hopeless' too. And so he may well come to view school life with the same attitude of resigned or resentful helplessness with which his parents view their own fate. Thus his educational experience only confirms the attitudes formed earlier by parental handling:

> unable to identify with or to beat the system, he will expect nothing nor will he be equipped to do anything about it. Thus the child born into the lowest social bracket has everything stacked against him, including his parents' principles of child upbringing (Newson, 1972).

The fourth need, for responsibility, is often forced upon the child prematurely. He may have to fend for himself, both before going to school and when returning to an empty house afterwards. If there is a large family, he may have to assume pseudo-parental roles by taking care of younger siblings, to the detriment of his own development. When he fails to control them or when accidents occur he is likely to incur punishment. Yet he is given little chance to exercise responsibility appropriate to his age and ability level and with appropriate adult guidance.

Thus, on the one hand, being given responsibility is likely to be a source of anxiety and a burden, instead of an enjoyable opportunity which becomes increasingly challenging with age. On the other hand, in terms of his own personal life, his freedom of choice will be severely circumscribed by his lack of educational skills and social know-how. At best, a boring, poorly paid job with few prospects and fewer opportunities for exercising responsibilities lies ahead. At worst, there will be unemployment with its destructive effect on self-respect and self-confidence.

Social handicap and delinquency

Though the total and abject poverty of fifty years ago is now rare, today's greater general affluence may make a barren life and relative deprivation more difficult to bear: when the ownership of material possessions is widely advertised and equated with the good life; when having fun at parties, on yachts and at exotic beaches abroad, is featured prominently as the desirable way to spend one's leisure; then is it not likely that the dull, dead streets of inner cities and of redevelopment areas, as well as the windy deserts below high-rise tower blocks, feel even duller, deader and more frustrating by comparison? When everyone is poor or in danger, a shared fate makes for fellow feeling and solidarity. The more glaring the inequalities, the greater divisiveness, resentment and hostility.

Yet, contrary to public fears, the majority of youngsters from severely disadvantaged homes are not angry and militant but apathetic and unassertive.

> Far from challenging the world around them, they seem personally and socially incarcerated; their talents are consistently under-rated, their vision constricted, their most personal modes of expression stifled. Each self-image they have created for themselves has been repeatedly deflated, all futures prematurely and permanently foreclosed (Davies, 1969).

On the other hand:

> For statistical purposes, basic social factors will undoubtedly prove the most effective predictors of delinquency, but cause and effect is

another matter. This Study has also shown the remarkable concentration of parental pathology, in the shape of unsuitable discipline, unfortunate attitudes to children, personality deviations, etc., among the socially handicapped group. Personal inadequacies and external handicaps reinforce each other in these unfortunate families. Rather than trying to answer the conundrum 'Which comes first ... ?' it may be more useful to ask at what point to try to break the vicious circle (West, 1969).

Children in one-parent families

So far there has been relatively little research into the psychological and social effects on children of growing up in one-parent families. These will naturally vary, not only because of individual differences between children, but also because the age when one parent has to take over and the period during which only one cared for the child are bound to have a differential effect. Some of these questions will be examined in the Bureau's ongoing study of one-parent families; and they have already been explored in relation to illegitimately born children in the national cohort.

There is much evidence that a considerable proportion of one-parent families are likely to suffer financial hardship, if not actual poverty (Holman, 1970; Marsden, 1969; Pochin, 1969; Wynn, 1964 and 1970). Less is known about the emotional, social and educational effects. Results obtained from the Bureau's *National Child Development Study* made it possible to show that economic circumstances vary not only in relation to which parent is bringing up the family but also with regard to the reason why this is so. The rates of payment made by the Supplementary Benefits Commission were chosen as the general indicator of a subsistence standard of living.

As many as one in nine children (or 11 per cent) were no longer being cared for by both their natural parents by the time they were eleven years old, according to the results of the Study. Of these, some 5 per cent were being raised by one parent alone; the other 6 per cent were being brought up in more than thirty different types of 'anomalous' family circumstances. Here three particular groups will be considered: those being brought up single-handed by one natural parent; those born illegitimate; and children of divorce.

Single-parent families

The children in the study who – for whatever reason – were living in a one-parent family at the age of eleven years were more likely to have lost their father than their mother. In fact, the proportion of fatherless children was nearly five times as high as those who grew up without a mother. Although the rate of re-marriage was very similar for fathers and mothers respectively (about a third in each case), a further 25 per cent of the motherless children were being cared for by a mother substitute whereas father substitutes were provided for only 5 per cent of the fatherless children (Ferri, 1973).

Thus women are much more likely than men to be left caring single-handed for their families, following the loss of their marriage partner. This probably reflects differences in social attitudes: much greater sympathy is extended to the man who has been deserted by his wife and is trying to look after the children; also grandmothers, sisters or neighbours are more ready to offer help. However, there is perhaps less acceptance of a father staying at home and living on state support. The deserted wife calls out far less concern and assistance. There is a tacit assumption that it is easier and perhaps also more appropriate for a woman to combine the parental and wage-earning role than it is for a man on his own to do so.

The most common single cause resulting in one natural parent being left to bring up a family was marital breakdown; in fact, divorce, separation and desertion accounted for about half the cases. In the remaining families, where there was no mother, this was due to her having died; in households without a father, death was the reason in only a third of cases; the rest consisted mainly of illegitimately born children whose mothers were raising them.

In 1969, when the children were eleven years old, almost half (47 per cent) of the fatherless families had been dependent on state support at some time during the preceding twelve months; this compares with only 6 per cent among intact families. Motherless children were less badly off although their families were twice as likely to have received Supplementary Benefits than two-parent homes. Even single-handed mothers who did not have to rely on state support were probably worse off financially than their male counterparts since women workers are usually paid at a much lower rate. Mothers whose husbands had died were far less likely to have had to rely on benefits than when the marriage had broken down or the child was illegitimate.

Examining the quality of housing in terms of the availability of basic amenities, twice as many fatherless as two-parent families lacked the sole use of a bathroom, indoor lavatory and hot water supply; the situation of motherless children was also less favourable but not quite as bad as that of the fatherless (Ferri, 1973).

Children born illegitimate

A marked increase in the proportion of illegitimate births took place during recent years but this is now possibly being reversed due to easier abortion and the pill; also more unmarried mothers are choosing to keep their babies. Yet until recently little was known about how the mothers and their children were faring, in the short or medium term: or whether illegitimacy continues to present personal and social problems, even though attitudes towards extra-marital sexual relations have changed.

The *National Child Development Study* made it possible to seek some answers to these questions by comparing an unselected national group of illegitimate children, born in 1958, with their peers born in the same week (Crellin, Pringle and West, 1971). The findings clearly showed that to be born illegitimate is to be born 'at risk'.

As in other recent studies, there was no difference in social class background between mothers who have a legitimate and an illegitimate baby. However, the latter were at a potential disadvantage, right from the start, in respect of their mother's age and their own family position. There were five times as many very young mothers among the illegitimate and nearly twice as many were having their first child. Among both these groups, the perinatal mortality rate is higher as is the prevalence of low birth weight. The overall mortality rate and the proportion of low birth weight babies were, in fact, markedly higher among the illegitimately born.

Ante-natal care was also markedly poorer among mothers-to-be of the illegitimate. A higher proportion than among the legitimate did not seek such care or did so later than is advisable; and a higher proportion failed to make an advance booking for their delivery.

About a third of the illegitimately born babies were given up by their mothers for adoption; they were then being brought up in a much more favourable home environment than those who had remained with their own mothers. The development of these two groups, who had had a similar start in life, was compared when they were seven years old.

By that time, the majority of the illegitimately born was living in some kind of two-parent situation (including those who were adopted). However, a considerable number of homes lacked a stable father figure. Only one in four children lived with both their natural parents.

The most outstanding feature was the much more favourable situation of the adopted. Among the illegitimate not adopted many had to share household amenities or lacked them completely: in fact, this was twice as prevalent as among the whole legitimate group. The same was true of over-crowding, despite the fact that there was a high proportion of only children among the illegitimate.

A considerable number of children experienced supplementary or total substitute care. This was made necessary by the high proportion of mothers who worked outside the home before the child went to school, and by their difficult and unsettled family circumstances. Over three times as many illegitimate as legitimate children were placed in day care facilities; and this proportion is certain to be an underestimate. In the first place, nearly two-thirds of the mothers of illegitimate children worked before the latter went to school; yet only a quarter of the children were reported to have had day care. Even allowing for relatives helping out, a sizeable discrepancy remains. Another reason is that information was lacking about child minders, whether officially registered or those with whom mothers had made some private arrangement.

The proportion of children who came into the care of a local authority or voluntary body was five times higher among the illegitimate than legitimate children.

It is evident, then, that the dice are still heavily loaded against the illegitimately born child. What were the effects on his development? In all aspects which were examined, consistent and marked differences were found between the illegitimate, the adopted and the legitimate group. Time and time again, the illegitimate were at the bottom of the league table, whether for general knowledge, oral ability, creativity, perceptual development, reading attainment or arithmetical skills.

Even in the relatively more favourable environment of middle-class homes, the illegitimate did less well than legitimate children in such homes. Over and above social class effects, there were important 'illegitimacy effects'. For example, they account for twelve months' difference in progress between the adopted and the illegitimate groups in reading. In contrast, the progress made by the adopted was similar to that made by legitimate children in the same social class.

Once they went to school the illegitimate also suffered disadvantages. They had more changes of school; their attendance was more irregular; and their parents showed less interest in their educational progress. Marked differences were also found between the three groups of children in behaviour and adjustment in school. The proportion of 'maladjusted' children was nearly twice as high among the illegitimate as the legitimate, while the adopted more closely resembled the latter.

Inevitably, many questions remain unanswered. For example, there was no information on the personality of the child's mother or other members of his family. Soon, however, it will be possible to say whether the problems encountered by the illegitimate differ from those who, for other reasons, live in one-parent families. Meanwhile, it is evident that illegitimacy still brings with it personal and social problems. The children were beset by a multiplicity of unfavourable circumstances; these gave them a relatively poorer start in life which continued to build up into a complex web of cumulative and interacting hardships and deprivations. To be born illegitimate is still to be born disadvantaged, at least for the present.

Can a favourable environment halt or reverse the effects of early disadvantage? To judge from the development of those children who were adopted, the answer is that it can. Of course, it remains to be seen what the later development will be of both those who were and those who were not adopted.

Children of divorce

Every year the family life of thousands of children is disrupted by divorce and the indications are that the number is still rising. 'In 1968, the total number of children affected was almost 73,000 of whom it is estimated some 60,000 were under the age of sixteen; by 1969 the total had increased to over 81,000' (Mortlock, 1972). An even steeper increase occurred in 1971 when, largely due to the Divorce Reform Act of 1969, there was a 55 per cent increase in divorce petitions over 1970; the total number of children involved then rose to 116,726, three-quarters of whom were under sixteen years of age (Gibson, 1973). Indeed, the majority are likely to be quite young, since separation and divorce occur most frequently within five years or so after marriage.

There may well be a link between the rising divorce rate and the increasing trend towards early parenthood which allows young couples little time to adjust to the new relationships and responsibilities of marriage; then financial and housing problems are added with the arrival of a baby. If both spouses are under twenty when they marry the divorce rate (in England and Wales) is about three times the rate for all marriages. 'One of the most striking demographic features associated with divorce is the increased risk among wives who were pregnant at the time of marriage ... marriages are now taking place at a younger age than previously and young brides are forming an increasing proportion of all pre-marital pregnancies so it is likely that a larger number of children than at present will be innocent witnesses of a broken home and family' (Gibson, 1973).

Remarkably little attention has been given to the effects which the break-up may have on children's development. What research there is has largely been confined to self-selected and probably atypical groups, namely those seen in psychiatric and child guidance clinics. 'We do not know whether it damages the child least to grow up in an unhappy home with both parents, or alone with one parent where there is no remarriage, or with one parent and a step-parent' (Mortlock, 1972). In relation to children's reactions to new marriages of either of their parents it has been suggested that 'overall, it seems it is better to have three or even four parents and six grandparents than no father or mother. This pattern of multiple marriages in fact produces a new type of extended family and consequently a variety of people with whom the child can identify and form relationships ... Structurally, the family of the future will be polynuclear' (Benn, 1969).

Financially, there is often a drop in the standard of living since most children will stay with their mother who now depends on alimony which is not only a reduced but may also not be a reliable source of income. Even if she herself is earning a salary, it will be less than the previous joint income; moreover, she may have to incur additional expense in having the children looked after out of school hours and term time.

On the psychological side, it is difficult to help a child to understand the reasons for the marriage break-up, the more so the younger the child, and the more bitter the feelings between the parents. Not uncommonly they vie for the child's affections, blackening each other's character and motives in the process. At worst, the child may become a pawn in their game of mutual hurt and ascendancy which is played out during prolonged battles for custody; an extreme example being 'tug-of-love' children who are whisked from one home, and sometimes one country, to another in the fight for possession. (An even worse situation is a new phenomenon reported from the United States, namely that neither parent is willing to take on custody; such a degree of rejection is bound to have a most damaging effect on a child's sense of personal worth.) Even at best, when regular and frequent 'access' has been agreed so that the child spends some time with the parent who does not have custody, meetings at weekends and during holidays are not readily conducive to maintaining a close relationship.

What evidence there is suggests that a sizable proportion of children whose parents have been divorced show disturbed behaviour. Whether this is due as much, or more, to deteriorating relationships and possibly open quarrels prior to the final break-up of the marriage, or to the child's conflict of loyalties, or to the finality of the divorce itself, has not yet been established. What is agreed by many, including some lawyers, is that custody decisions, in the lower courts at any rate, tend to be arrived at too hastily and with too little attempt to take into account the child's own wishes or needs. If his long-term interests are to be regarded as of major importance, then some reform of divorce proceedings would seem essential.

Belonging to a minority group

In contrast to the various circumstances considered previously, belonging to a minority group is not in itself necessarily stressful. It will, however, become so when prejudice against a group is prevalent. A child belonging to it will become aware of the stigma or discrimination which may make his loyalty all the fiercer or may lower his self-esteem or possibly both. While little is known about the effects on emotional, social and intellectual development of feeling singled out in this way, it is likely to make a child more vulnerable, particularly if there are other stresses too.

One condition will be selected for discussion, namely being coloured. Looking racially different is in our society a most visible means of recognition from birth onwards. The social attitudes towards, and assumptions about, this minority group are complex and highly charged emotionally; also both exert their influence from a very early age parental reactions to the stress of facing prejudice.

Such children are probably the most vulnerable of all groups discussed just because a high proportion of them are affected by a whole range of adverse circumstances. Not infrequently the families of coloured immigrant children are large and have a low income; their housing conditions tend to be unsatisfactory; family relationships may be more often impaired, either because one marriage partner came earlier or the children joined the family later on or because child-rearing patterns here differ markedly from those practised in their country of origin; language and hence educational handicaps are also bound to be more frequent; in certain groups at least, one-parent families are prevalent because unstable relationships and matrifocal households were sometimes enforced in their own country by conditions of slavery. Because of the multiplicity of these various pressures, a relatively high proportion of children come into care or attend special schools for the educationally subnormal.

Such a combination of unfavourable circumstances would by themselves be highly likely to have very detrimental effects on a child's whole development. But, worse still, coloured immigrant children must adapt – to a greater or lesser extent – to quite different cultural, social and climatic conditions, often with little prior preparation. Perhaps worst of all, however, they are living in a society where they are not always wholly accepted and in which they will become aware of racial prejudice.

For coloured school leavers, unemployment becomes a particularly serious problem. In Greater London, for example, 18 per cent of all unemployed young people were black (Hansard, 1973). A recent report by the Community Relations Commission (1973) stressed the seriousness of this situation. Inadequate educational opportunity was seen as one of the strongest links in the chain of deprivation and discrimination facing coloured people; unless broken now, it is likely to lead to unemployment or under-employment for the second and subsequent generations of coloured British children.

Current signs are that the cumulative and long-term consequences of the massive and multiple disadvantages affecting many immigrant children, have hardly yet begun to be identified, let alone constructively tackled.

References

BENN, C. (1969) Marriage breakdown and the individual *Divorce, Society and the Law*, H. A. Finlay (ed) Butterworth and Co New South Wales Australia

BOWLBY, J. (1951) *Maternal Care and Mental Health*, World Health Organisation, Geneva

BUTLER, N. R. and ALBERMAN, E. (eds) (1969) *Perinatal Problems* Livingstone

BUTLER, N. R. and BONHAM, G. H. (1963) *Perinatal Mortality* Livingstone

CENTRAL STATISTICAL OFFICE (1972) *Social Trends* (3) HMSO

CRELLIN, E., PRINGLE, M. L. K. and WEST, P. (1971) *Born Illegitimate* National Foundation for Educational Research for National Children's Bureau Slough

DAVIE, R. (1972) The behaviour and adjustment in school of seven-year-olds; sex and social class differences. *Early Child Development and Care* 2 (1) 39–47

DAVIE, R., BUTLER, N. and GOLDSTEIN, H. (1972) *From Birth to Seven* Longman in association with the Children's Bureau

DAVIES, B. (1969) Non-swinging youth *New Society* 3 July 14 (353) 8–10

DEPARTMENT OF THE ENVIRONMENT (1973) Children at Play *Design Bulletin* (27) HMSO

DEPARTMENT OF HEALTH AND SOCIAL SECURITY (1971) *Two-parent Families* HMSO

DOUGLAS, J. W. B. (1964) *The Home and the School* MacGibbon and Kee

FERRI, E. (1973) Characteristics of motherless families *British Journal of Social Work* 3 (1) 91–100

GIBSON, C. (1973) Social trends in divorce *New Society*, 5th July 25 (651) 6–8

HANSARD (1973) Unemployment among young black people *House of Lords* 25th July column 1926–7 HMSO

HOLMAN, R. (ed) (1970) *Socially Deprived Families in Britain* Bedford Square Press

LEISSNER, A., (1972) Parents and Children in high-need areas *The Parental Role* 22–7 National Children's Bureau

MARSDEN, D. (1969) *Mothers Alone* Penguin

MORTLOCK, B. (1972) *The Inside of Divorce* Constable

NATIONAL CHILDREN'S BUREAU (1972) *The Second Follow-up at the age of Eleven Years of the National Child Development Study* (1958 Cohort) Unpublished

NEWSON, J. and NEWSON, E. (1972) Cultural aspects of child rearing in the English-speaking world. *The Integration of a Child into a Social World* M. P. Richards (ed), Cambridge University Press

POCHIN, J. (1969) *Without a Wedding Ring* Constable

PROSSER, H. (1973) Family size and children's development *Health and Social Services Journal* (4325 (suppl) 11–12

WEDGE, P. and PROSSER, H. (1973) *Born to Fail*? Arrow Books in association with the National Children's Bureau

WEST, D. J. (1969) *Present Conduct and Future Delinquency* Heinemann

WYNN, M. (1964) *Fatherless Families* Michael Joseph

WYNN, M. (1972) *Family Policy* 2nd edn Pelican

4·4 Middle-class teacher and lower-class child

Bruno Bettelheim

A few years ago I met with several groups of grade school teachers, in an effort to help them with their tasks in schools populated mainly by lower-class black children. Each group numbered some twenty teachers at the beginning of the ten-week session; about fifteen at the end. Most of the teachers were female. The meetings were very informal and were restricted to classroom teachers only, though once or twice the local district superintendent attended.

Teachers ranged from beginners with only one or two years in the field to very experienced teachers. By chance, about equal numbers of white and black teachers were present in each group. As far as attitudes to the culturally deprived black children they teach were concerned, there was little difference between white and black teachers; nor was there any difference in their ability to analyse problems affecting these children or in their eagerness to deal with these problems constructively.

There was, however, a marked difference in the reactions of white and a few black teachers to what the meetings forced them to realize about themselves. During the first few sessions of each group, whenever a white teacher brought up some difficulties she had encountered with her black pupils, some black teachers in more or less veiled form would accuse the white teacher of creating her own difficulties because she did not accept children who were black. As the meetings proceeded, however, it became ever more apparent that the inner attitudes of both white and black teachers toward their pupils were quite similar; the real problem then became obvious. It was the clash between the teacher's middle-class attitudes and those of her lower-class pupils; it was her rejection of their lower-class behaviour and had nothing to do with their or her colour. As this realization was forced on them by what transpired at the meetings,

Source: *Rethinking Urban Education* (1972), pp. 3–11.

those few black teachers who were most militant in believing they saw bias among the white teachers stopped attending. Their number was never more than three or four. The rest of the teachers attended regularly; and each group asked for a continuation when the series of ten meetings came to an end. In two groups this could be arranged, and we then met some five additional times.

At the first meeting of each group I tried briefly to say what such meetings can and what they cannot do. I could not possibly tell a teacher what to do or how to handle a particular child in a particular school situation. Instead, my purpose was to help her develop a certain way of thinking about these children and the problems she encounters with them; a method of analysing problems; in short, an approach that might be called clinical. This I would try to teach by helping her think through any situation she was confronted with in her daily teaching experience and which she cared to discuss.

Instead of presenting a résumé of what transpired in these meetings, I shall use some abbreviated examples to illustrate what we talked about. From this the reader may form his own conclusions about what such a clinical approach can contribute to improving the education of underprivileged children in our big-city schools.

One recurrent problem was the teacher's anxiety that if she were to take time away from the teaching of subject matter, she would be falling down on her job. Despite the most elaborate lip service to the fact that these children need socialization more than anything else, and though convinced that it is the school's task to socialize them, these teachers became anxious and resistant whenever it came to letting the momentary learning task ride for a while to attend to the emotional or social needs of these children. It took several meetings and discussions of this problem in its various guises before the teachers could begin to act in line with their stated convictions. An example may illustrate.

One teacher said, 'If you have just one person that is causing trouble, how can you consistently take time away from the rest?' I asked her to give an example. 'Well,' she said, 'I have one boy in my class and he's a show-off. He likes a lot of attention and I found at first that by talking to him and giving him a lot of attention, I could quiet him down. But the rest of the class was suffering because I was giving this boy so much attention, so I stopped doing it.' How did she know that they were suffering? 'Well,' she said, 'I was taking time out from teaching.' 'True,' I said, 'but didn't they learn anything from it? Didn't they learn, for example, how to deal with a show-off, which might be useful knowledge later on in life?' The teacher allowed that this might be possible but was still troubled that it did not seem fair.

I remarked that this problem had come up again and again – that we call certain things 'teaching' and other things not; that if they were to make a list of what they feel is most important for these children, 'socialized behaviour' would be very high on the list. Nevertheless, it seemed that teaching socialized behaviour to this show-off could not be very high on her list because she insisted that she could not take time away from her subject-matter teaching to do it.

Three weeks later the same problem came up in different form. 'I wrote some problems down', a teacher began, 'and it's a long list. These are problems I have a hard time remembering when I'm here because they're so little, but they're so pervasive and so galling. First, there are the children who don't answer when they're called on, but when others are called on, they answer. And then the children who shout out and it's usally the wrong answer. It's very irritating.'

'Why is it so galling?' I asked. 'Well', she said, 'first of all it's usually the wrong answer – though I'm always so gratified with a right answer that I forget to be angry that the right person didn't give it.' 'So it's really not the shouting out so much that annoys you?' I said. 'Probably not', she agreed, 'but it's very galling when it's all wrong.'

I then asked her for an example of a question she had asked and the wrong answers she got. 'Well, for instance', she said, 'I point to the word *the* on the board and one shouts out "my," something like that.' Her reaction was that the children had not learned the word, that they were thoughtless and inattentive.

I now asked her to speculate why anyone would shout out 'my' when the word she asked for was *the*. 'Because they don't know it. Sometimes they just want to answer anything.' 'That's about it', said another teacher; a third teacher thought that the children were just dying for attention and so would holler out anything at all.

'What is wrong with that?' I asked. 'There isn't one teacher for every child', I was told; 'that's what's wrong with it. The teacher just can't tolerate kids shouting out constantly and having the room in a turmoil. Because one thing leads to another, and the first thing you know, they're all talking, and then they're walking around after that, and it's just bedlam.'

By now, though, previous meetings began to pay off and another teacher said: 'I kind of like it, within limits, this kind of response in my classroom; that everybody's jumping in, even if I have a noisy classroom. If I kind of listen, I find it's possible to distinguish who says what, so this isn't one of the things that bothers me.'

'How about when they don't know it and still shout?' asked the first teacher, the one who raised the problem. And the second teacher replied,

'I think this is good, and I'll tell you why: they're contributing, they're part of it, and this is what they want. The answer I recognize is the right answer. But even the children that don't know get the chance of contributing.'

Still another teacher said she wished she could get this kind of enthusiasm. 'To me, this is an enthusiasm for learning, even if it's the wrong thing. By the time you get them older, they've been told in the lower grades, "That's not the right answer, keep your mouth shut and keep still," and then things are bad. I have them in the higher grades and I wish I could just sometimes get them to say anything. But by then they've been so beaten down in the lower grades about "Keep still, fold your hands" that you don't get any response from them at all.'

I now suggested that we try to understand what goes on in the minds of the children while the teacher is writing *the* on the board. 'How many of you know the Greek alphabet?' I asked. 'In parts', said the first teacher. 'Now let's suppose', I said, 'that you know the Greek alphabet, partly. Suppose somebody writes something on the blackboard in Greek letters. Try to visualize and try to feel this situation. You're trying to read it, but you don't quite know the letters. What are you going to feel? What will your reaction be; what will you feel about yourself? We're all very well able to be quiet. We're not going to shout out, and we're not going to shout out the wrong answer. We might even be afraid to say the right answer if we're not sure. But what are you going to think as you look up there, trying to figure it out?'

Teachers began to answer: 'Why should I learn it?' 'What's in it for me?' 'I'd feel I don't know this and I have to go home and study it.'

'That's right', I said. 'Many of us would feel this, or else "Why have I forgotten it; what's wrong with me?" But most of us would think, "My God, what's that, what can that be?" All of these are rather uncomfortable feelings. Have these children learned to deal with their uncomfortable feelings; have we really taught them that? All of us have learned it. We can all contain such moderate discomfort. But the children can't. Children in general, when they're uncomfortable, begin to holler and yell. I'm afraid that you overlook the discomfort you project the children into when you put something on the blackboard that they cannot read.'

From all of this some psychological understanding was gained of what might be going on in these children, but it did not solve the problem yet. So I asked the teachers, 'What did this child who shouted out "my" want to learn?' One teacher replied, 'I don't get what you said. What do you mean, "What did he want to learn?"' 'Well', I asked, 'where was his interest?' And the teacher said, 'With himself.'

'Of course', I said, 'because he shouted "my". 'Now let's think for a moment about what's more important to a kid: to have a boat or to know that there is a boat somewhere?' To which they answered in chorus, 'To have a boat that is mine.'

'So actually', I said, 'this boy gave us a very important clue about how to teach these children; namely, that we have got to personalize the whole thing. While they are not ready yet for abstract learning, they may be ready for personalized learning. In his own fashion he told us how we ought to be taught, if we just listened to him.'

'Well, I always thought that *my* should be taught first in a lesson and *the* later,' said another teacher. 'It was always my feeling that *my* makes more sense to them right now.' I agreed entirely. 'It's another example', I said, 'of how our teaching is geared to the middle-class child. I can't rewrite the curriculum or your textbooks. But I can help you understand what motivates this boy who says, "I can learn only if a thing is very personal to me," who by implication tells us: "I might be interested in *my* boat, but I'm not interested in *the* boat." All these weeks you have complained here that these children cannot distinguish very clearly between what is theirs and what is other people's – quite a difficult thing to learn. You complain about all the pencils they take and the paper they waste. Then we agreed that they feel "What's yours is mine," though they know that "What's mine isn't yours." All I'm trying to suggest is that here, in the simplest reading error, we are right smack against exactly the same problem.'

This was a lengthy example, but I took time for it because it deals with the question 'What is more important than to teach reading to these children?' and also with the difference between what is mine and what is not. My next example deals explicitly with this second problem.

'We have a teacher', I was told, 'who's working with a particular group of lower-class children and we all admired her tremendously for how much she's been able to do with them, how empathetic she was and how well things were going. Then two of those children were picked up for purse snatching. When they came back, the teacher, who had an excellent relationship with them said, "If you needed money, why did you have to steal? You know I always have money in my desk." The following day her desk was cleaned out of money.'

'Well, she asked for it', I said, and the teacher nodded. 'That's just the problem,' she said. 'None of us realized this. When the money was stolen, we were all stunned.'

But things were more complicated than that. 'The teacher meant very well,' I said. 'I'm sure she was ready to give these kids some money if they needed it. The trouble is, she didn't look at it the way it looked to the child. As good a person as she is, she didn't take the trouble to understand how differently these children view the world. Only recently have the sociologists and anthropologists begun to recognize something they call "the culture of poverty." In our example it might be better to call it "the morals of poverty". Within this culture of poverty, it is perfectly all right to take things if you can grab them, but never from the in-group. If you take from the in-group, then you're really a low-down scoundrel. On the other hand, if you take from the out-group and get away with it, you're smart.'

'Like Robin Hood?' said the teacher. 'If you like', I said. 'Now these children snatched purses because they wanted money. It never occurred to them to take money from a good friend. If anything, they might have shared their loot with him. They considered this teacher a good friend, but lo and behold, she tells them they should take it from her, their close friend. That is, she tells them to do something which, in terms of their morality, is the worst thing a human being can do. So when this teacher says "I expect you to come and take from me", it means that she, whom they trusted, thinks they're bad persons. This makes her a stranger, if not an enemy. And if she has such a miserable opinion of us, we're going to teach her a lesson. In my opinion, this teacher's desk was cleaned out as a punishment.'

'But did she really say they should take it from her?' asked a teacher. 'No', I said. 'She didn't ask them to take it. She just said something that to them meant: "I think you haven't even enough knowledge of what's right and wrong to know that you don't take from a friend." As you can see, an essential part of the culture of poverty is that you share with your friends and take from strangers.'

This example shows that these teachers really want to be helpful to the culturally deprived child but that, despite their best intentions, they get bogged down when they cannot transcend their own value system to meet that of the children. What these teachers need is the clinician's help in going beyond their own middle-class mores, a task they find difficult at best, despite their conscious desires. Even more, they need help with their feeling of obligation to push the subject matter. And this grows worse with all the public clamour that everyone needs more education. Subject to this pressure, and side-tracked by it, they push academics at the expense of those emotional problems which, when not handled, prevent learning altogether. Perhaps a final example may illustrate.

'I have a little girl', said one teacher, 'who has been troubling me. She alternates between extremely aggressive and extremely dependent behaviour. She'll understand an assignment, but she'll ask me specifically to help her with it, and I do, because I feel that if this is going to get her interested in doing work, then fine. So I'll sit down and help her with an assignment even though it's obvious that she doesn't need the help.

Sometimes she'll accept this help, and sometimes she'll just get angry instead. And if I'm not looking at her for five minutes, she'll get angry and she'll make a nasty comment.'

'Like what?' I asked. 'Well, she makes allusions to my race all the time.' 'What does she say?' I asked. ' "Oh, you ugly old white woman", or something like that. Or she'll try to hit me, or something like that.'

'And what do you do when she says you're an ugly white woman?' 'Well', said the teacher, 'I think I just probably make an ugly face when she says that.' I was insistent and wanted to know what was the teacher's reaction. So she said, 'I think I try to get her to sit down, or something like that, and actually ignore the problem. I never take her comments personally.'

'Now this is something that's hard for me to believe', I said; 'somebody tells you that you have an ugly white face, and you don't take it personally. How *do* you take it if you don't take it personally?'

'I mean I'm not insulted by the comments, really', she said. 'But why not?' I wondered. 'I have been a student of human emotions by now for more years than I care to remember, and people are always trying to teach me new things, but I'm an old dog and I don't learn new tricks any more. One of the new tricks people are trying to teach me is that if somebody tells somebody "You have an ugly white face," they don't take it personally. You can pretend not to be offended, but that's all. Because if that's really so, then the blacks haven't a thing to complain about. If all the remarks made about them don't hurt, then what's all the screaming about? But I think they have a right to scream, because I believe these remarks hurt.'

'Well, let me put it this way', said the teacher; 'she says enough good things to offset the bad things.' 'All right', I replied, 'so your husband says many good things to you and just one bad one, that the dinner is awful. And that doesn't bother you because he said some nice things two days ago? Good things don't compensate for bad; they still hurt. And if somebody tells you "I hate your ugly white face," I don't see how you can help but be hurt. If you are not hurt, then you don't take the child seriously, and this is what I'm driving at. If we don't take their invectives, their nasty remarks, seriously, that means that we really don't take *them* seriously. It implies, "You're irresponsible, no good, of no account," because if they're of any account, then we must take seriously what they say.'

'But don't children sometimes say something just for the shock value?' asked a teacher. 'Of course', I said, 'But if someone says something to shock you and you don't get shocked, then he's terribly deflated.' 'But if they continually do this kind of thing, you have to be shocked each time they say it,' she insisted. 'That's right', I said. 'I'm shocked each time they do it. And the more shocked I am, the sooner they stop. If you pay no attention, they're driven to keep up or try harder all year long. But if when she says, "You have an ugly white face," you say "Gee, I'm sorry you don't like my face; I like yours," I think the kid would get some feeling. Because she says it to make you angry, or hurt you. And if you're not hurt, then she's a nincompoop.

'If, on the other hand, she can hurt you, then she might think, "Do I really want to hurt my teacher?" and that's what we're striving for. Because then she might realize that sometimes she wants to, but most of the time she really doesn't want to hurt your feelings. Only, if it doesn't hurt your feelings, then she might as well keep it up.'

What it comes down to, as I told them, is that we must have very clearly in our minds what are the educational goals we have for these children. Is it our goal that they learn what we think are the important things in life: not to show off, not to steal, not to hit people over the head; to be able to wait, to stand some small frustration, and still go on with the task? Or is it our goal that they learn to read and write, no matter what?

4.5 The 'problem' of the urban school: some Radical and Marxist formulations

Gerald Grace

The oppositional tradition

Against conservative and liberal reforms for urban schools, there has always existed an alternative and radical tradition of theorising and ideology which has advanced different constructions of the 'problem' of urban working-class schools, raised alternative problematics and outlined radically different courses of action, to those currently accepted in the conventional wisdom of the time. Thus the Chartist leader, William Lovett argued against state provision of education and for an independent working-class system:

> too many of those who stand in the list of education-promoters are but state-tricksters seeking to make it an instrument of party or faction. We perceive that one is for moulding the infant mind upon the principles of church and state, another is for basing its morals on their own sectarianism and another is for an amalgamation of both; in fact, the great principles of human natures, social morality and political justice are disregarded, in the desire of promoting their own selfish views and party interests ... hence we have addressed ourselves to you, working men of Britain ... and we think we have said sufficient to convince you of the necessity of guarding against those state and party schemes some persons are intent on establishing, as well as to induce you to commence the great work of education yourselves.[1]

The recognition that officially provided elementary education would be more concerned with the controlling rather than the liberating of an urban proletariat was continued in later socialist attacks on the content of

Source: *Teachers, Ideology and Control: a study in urban education.*

education provided by the Board Schools, 'the elementary education given today in our Board Schools does no more than prepare the minds of children for the patient obedience to the domination of a proud and haughty middle- and upper-class'.[2] A tradition of socialist opposition to state education was based on the notion that control of the state and of education was in the wrong hands. Another tradition of opposition was based on objection to state control as such, of whatever ideological character. Joel Spring has shown how anarchism as a social and political philosophy concerned with the role and nature of authority in a society 'has since the eighteenth century raised serious and important questions about the very existence of state systems of schooling and the possibility of non-authoritarian forms of education'.[3]

The oppositional tradition has been derived from diverse ideological origins – from working-class movements in the nineteenth century, from socialism and Marxism, from anarchism and libertarianism. As a consequence of these diverse origins and of a tendency to radical sectarianism, this tradition has been, and is, as much characterized by conflict within itself as by conflict with 'the system'. At the same time, it has been united by a common perception of the school system designed for an urban proletariat. This common perception has emphasized that what is being provided for working-class children is schooling rather than education; that the process of schooling is oppressive and manipulative in character; that this manipulative process is being carried on in institutions which are dominating in their bureaucracy, authoritarianism and hierarchy; that the total effect of the schooling process is to control, to domesticate, to make passive and exploitable; that in the schooling process the person is regarded as 'object' rather than as a creatively conscious subject. The central 'problem' of all schools, though most clearly manifested in urban working-class schools, is the problem of liberation. United in this common view of the 'problem' of school, the oppositional tradition is divided in its understandings of what 'liberation' might mean and what programmes or courses of action are necessary for its realization. Among contemporary formulations a broad dichotomy exists between those derived from anarchism, libertarian philosophy and critical sociology, and those derived from the varieties of Marxism. Whereas the former tend to locate a notion of liberation in the achievement of states of critical consciousness and personal autonomy without commitment to explicit political solutions, the latter locate liberation in terms of the overthrow of an oppressive capitalist system of production and social relations by the action of the proletariat.

Ideologies of education derived from these sources have an influence particularly among young teachers who see the 'crisis of the urban school' as but one manifestation of a wider social and political crisis in industrial society. A new variety of the 'teacher missionary' is thus to be found in some inner-city schools: a missionary concerned not as in the case of nineteenth century elementary school-teachers, with the control and gentling of an urban working-class, but with its liberation from authoritarianism, cultural and political domination and the exploitations of capitalism. The 'missionaries of liberation', although representing only a small section of urban teachers, have the potential for considerable influence in contemporary schools where staff participation and democracy and autonomy in curriculum and pedagogy have any reality.

Anarchism and libertarianism: the death of school

Writers such as Paul Goodman, Ivan Illich and Paulo Freire provide much of the inspiration for contemporary anarchist/libertarian critique of schooling and this critique is popularly diffused in publications such as 'Libertarian Education' and 'The Great Brain Robbery'. With the recognition that 'there will be no libertarian revolution in society unless and until our education system is liberated', the problem of liberation is posed in these terms:

> The problem before us is enormous: we live in an unfree society; our schools are unfree; our teachers are unfree; our students are unfree. Somehow we must break into this vicious circle. It is important to stress that as anarchists we reject authoritarian concepts of education, however they might be used. The educator who sees himself as the possessor of superior knowledge or skills which he 'passes on' to more or less willing disciples, whether this is in the name of a liberal/democratic outlook or a socialist/revolutionary analysis is part of an authoritarian, or at best, paternalistic culture. The libertarian will see education as a sharing of knowledge, skills and experiences and will emphasise the importance of study aimed at understanding the participants' place in society and the nature of the forces acting upon them – with the object of helping to equip the participants to counter oppressive aspects of that society.[4]

The 'problem' of the urban school in a libertarian perspective is a problem of human freedom and dignity both of which are seen to be denied by the 'custodial' school. This in turn generates a problem for the libertarian teacher who faces the dilemma of working within the state system 'where the kids are ... and where the most oppressed of them are likely to remain' or of seeking to establish alternatives in free schools and other non-authoritarian contexts. Thus some teachers committed to this position accept the compromise of working within state schools in order to encourage learning situations which are egalitarian, critical and based upon dialogue and participation, while others, unable to accept a framework of compulsory schooling, work to provide 'alternatives' for urban children. Free schools are only one expression of the possible educational alternatives to the 'authoritarian' urban school but they are valued because they 'tend to be firmly rooted in a neighbourhood so that poor, working-class children have access to their liberating influence'.[5]

The libertarian critique seeks to avoid explanations of the 'authoritarianism' of teachers which locates these in terms of personal characteristics. The problem of 'authoritarianism' is one of role and structure, not of 'personality' and 'attitudes', therefore the liberation of schools can only be found in changes at the level of role and structure and not in the search for 'better' teachers. This thesis is central to the critique.[6]

Urban schools for the working-class were founded as bulwarks against the 'anarchy' seen to be incipient in the social and political consequences of industrialization and teachers in such schools were socialized to become agents of authority (epistomological and political) and agents of imposed social control. Libertarian ideology stands as the antithesis to this enterprise in its rejection of a 'distorted' notion of order, of the need for external control and of the need for the teacher role. Thus it is argued that:

> In the blackboard jungle situation, the teacher is really enforcing chaos, conflict and wear and tear, not order. To promote order he would have to let go of his authority completely. In the short term this would just lead to intensified chaos which everyone would just have to ride out. But gradually the chaos would turn into spontaneous order. From being out of another's control (chaos) the children would come to control themselves (anarchy).[7]

In such situations of spontaneous social control it is envisaged that true education and humanity could be realized without reference to categories such as 'school' or 'teacher' – the whole community becomes the context for education and every member becomes potentially a 'teacher'. The doctrines of libertarian education reformation are clearly reminiscent of the doctrines of earlier religious reformation. In both cases an attack is made on what are seen to be alienating, oppressive and distorting institutions and upon unnecessary 'priestly' roles of mediation. In both cases authenticity is sought among the people in notions such as 'the Church is the people' and 'the priesthood of all believers' – which find their educational expression as 'School is the community' and 'all members are teachers'. The religious metaphor is particularly clear in the writings of Illich and in his attack upon 'the universal church of school'.[8]

The messages of libertarianism, regarded by many established teachers as utopian, impractical or suitable only for non-industrialized and non-urbanized contexts, have, nevertheless, captured the imagination of some young teachers both in Britain and America, who have been repelled by urban schools which they perceive as custodial, authoritarian and alienating. Those who seek to work for 'liberation' within the school system are vulnerable not only to charges of compromise, but also to ideological attack from both establishment and left-wing sources. Regarded officially as subversive and irresponsible, libertarian teachers and writers are accused from a Marxist perspective of taking a romantic and apolitical view of the person and of society. Thus Gintis (1972) argues that Illich 'rejects politics in favour of individual liberation'[9] and claims that he fails to locate his analysis in the sphere of social relations and the mode of production. The libertarian response to such attacks has been to advance different constructions of both 'politics' and 'liberation' to those characteristically employed by Marxist writers. In arguing for solidarity with the young 'as the proletariat of the school system' and identifying with the 'genuinely popular idiom of revolt' which is seen to exist in some urban schools, libertarian ideology claims to be distinctive, 'willingness to ally themselves with their pupils is probably the best touchstone for separating left-libertarians from left-authoritarians and liberals'.[10]

While it is difficult to imagine that libertarian ideology can make a very general impact on bureaucratized urban school systems which are firmly entrenched,[11] it remains an active, fertile and provocative source of alternatives to the conventional wisdom, both in terms of the nature of the educational experience and social relations which it envisages and the contexts within which these might be realized. In its advocacy of 'learning networks', 'culture circles', 'free schools', 'de-centralization' and 'micro-schools', libertarian ideology and its mediators construct an alternative social reality for urban education. If, as many libertarians believe, the 'urban system' and its associated schooling is 'cracking apart at the centre', then this alternative may become a dominant reality in the future.

Critical sociology: the transformation of school

In comparing positivist, interpretive and critical sociologies, Brian Fay (1975) suggests that what is distinctive about the latter is an explicit recognition that social theory is interconnected with social practice. Thus, in its educative role, critical social theory tries 'to enlighten the social actors, so that, coming to see themselves and their social situation in a new way, they themselves can decide to alter the conditions which they find repressive. In other words, the social scientist tries to 'raise the consciousness' of the actors whose situation he is studying.'[12]

Such a description, it can be claimed, would hold true for the critical sociology of education[13] which has been developed in this country since the publication of Michael Young's *Knowledge and Control: new directions for the Sociology of Education* in 1971. Powerfully diffused (and to some extent institutionalized) through publications of the Open University and the widely read, *Tinker, Tailor: the myth of cultural deprivation* it is a critique that has attempted to 'raise the consciousness' of teachers and to encourage them to develop a praxis based upon radically different formulations to those of conventional academic and pedagogic wisdom.

The essential message to urban teachers and to all teachers, has been that they should adopt a stance of 'radical doubt' regarding the familiar and taken-for-granted characteristics of their pedagogic world. That, rather than accepting as 'problems' the official formulations and definitions of educational authorities and 'experts', teachers and others should formulate their own constructions of 'problems'. Such a stance, it is argued, might well locate the 'problem' of the urban school, for instance, more in the practices and assumptions of educational authorities and 'experts' than in supposed deficiencies in urban working-class pupils and their parents. In its encouragement to teachers 'to be their own theorists', the critique celebrates the liberating possibilities which arise from the practice of 'making the taken-for-granted world problematic' and in engaging in 'the subversion of absolutism'. Thus Young (1971) suggests as fruitful, the conceiving of societies 'as products of competing definitions and claims to cognitive and moral legitimacy, rather than as integrated around a core set of absolute values'.[14]

Within a framework of competing definitions, critical sociology of education has generated a host of problematics which many see to be particularly relevant to the 'problems' of urban education. Among these questions of control and autonomy, the social organization of knowledge and the politics of the curriculum are salient.

The simultaneous appearance in English of Paulo Freire's books, *Pedagogy of the Oppressed*, *Cultural Action for Freedom* and *Education for Critical Consciousness* has added a powerful impetus to the critique of conventional schooling raised by critical sociologists of education. In the condemnation of processes of cultural invasion and domination in the third world and the 'culture of silence' which this engenders; in its celebration of the possibilities of 'the people' to achieve a critical consciousness and a critical literacy and in its indications of the means to that end, the work of Freire has provided a world view which some urban teachers see to be as relevant to their world (that of working-class, inner-city schools) as to the world of an oppressed peasantry in Chile.

From the perspective of a critical sociology of education, the 'problem' of the urban school is to be located in its historic function of *transmission* of elements of mainstream culture to a population viewed as essentially devoid of its own culture and understandings and perceived to be deficient in many ways in its capacity to absorb and 'learn' the culture offered to it. Within such an enterprise the consciousness of the teacher becomes preoccupied with questions of transmission, with new strategies (known as curriculum development) for the more effective transmission of 'old' knowledge in new pedagogic forms, none of which challenge the existing status, social determinations or social stratification of existing knowledge forms.

The exponents of critical sociology of education are concerned to change this historic function of the school and its associated assumptions and states of consciousness. This change would involve a conception of the urban school (and all schools) as an arena in which would be realized a variety of cultural traditions and cognitive styles; an appreciation of the various ways in which people 'make sense of the world', a concern with learning as dialogue – participation, rather than as transmission–reception and the recognition of all as 'learners' and 'teachers'. Crucial to such transformation would be changed approaches to the language of urban working–class pupils, white and black, which would involve a full recognition of both cognitive power and the aesthetic of these forms and the rejection of notions of any necessary superiority in white middle-class elaborated English. In this sense, teachers of English, especially in inner-city schools, would be the strategic agents to begin such a transformation.

In addition to raising questions concerned with the transformation of school, writers within critical sociology of education have sought to 'make problematic' the widely accepted notion that teachers in Britain enjoy a high degree of autonomy in their educational activities. Questions of control and of autonomy have always been central preoccupations in the ideological struggles of urban education. Concerned that the teachers of the urban proletariat might become 'active emissaries of mis-rule', the Victorian middle-class created an apparatus of control which encompassed selection and socialization of teachers and effective monitoring of curriculum and pedagogy. The contemporary urban teacher in Britain within the same tradition of popular education appears, in comparison with his American and European colleagues to have attained a degree of autonomy which is unprecedented among 'professional' workers.

This notion of autonomy (the relatively unimpeded right to select appropriate knowledge and skills and to transmit them in a teaching style judged to be appropriate to the situation) is celebrated in the rhetoric of the occupational group; is strong in the consciousness of many teachers; and is seen to be the glorious culmination of the long struggle waged by teacher groups against 'obnoxious interference', 'payment by results' and the prescriptions of an official curriculum code. But this in itself creates an interesting paradox and a whole host of further questions about the reality of teacher autonomy. How has it come about that teachers of the urban working-class, *once so closely controlled* as the strategic agents of social and cultural formation, should, in the context of a modern capitalist Britain, enjoy so much freedom? Is it to be explained in terms of evolutionary progress, the triumph of liberalism and of progressive education? Is it to be seen as the accomplishment of organized teacher power against both the constraints of official prescription and the hostilities of working-class parents? or is it to be explained, rather, in terms of an illusion of freedom?

The varieties of Marxism

Peter Worsely (1975) has reminded us that Marxism is a body of social and political theory and practice which has been realised in a variety of ways:

> Sociologically Marxism does not exist 'in itself': it is embodied in and used by differing groups and milieux, from classes and coteries, with different social characteristics and cultural heritages, different locations in history and society, and is carried by a variety of 'bearers' and mediators.[15]

It seems possible to detect two ways in which the varieties of Marxist thought are mediated to contemporary urban teachers in Britain. The first would be through the writings of academics and theorists who have analysed educational practice from an explicitly Marxist position and whose writings feature prominantly in some courses of further study for teachers. Significant at the present time would be the work of Hoare, Althusser and of Bowles and Gintis – writers essentially located outside the praxis of urban education in school systems.

A second set of mediators may be found among practising teachers within the urban school system (especially in London) who individually or collectively have made available their constructions of the 'problem' of the urban school from an explicitly Marxist position. In the publication of the 'Teachers' Action Collective', 'Rank and File' and 'Radical Education', analysis of 'problems' in education and prescriptions for action are advanced, which, while differing in emphasis, share a common ideological stance. This may be said, also, of the widely read work of one particular inner-city teacher, Chris Searle. Such teachers continue (albeit from an explicitly Marxist stance) the historic tradition of 'resistance from within' which, in the nineteenth century, was always the characteristic of a minority of urban schoolteachers.

In arguing for a socialist theory and practice of education which would contribute to the transformation of capitalist society, Hoare indicates that its central concerns must be the development of critical reason; full acceptance of the social character of man; insistence on the active nature of participation in learning and a dialectical mode of pedagogy. To the achievement of these ends the position of the teacher in terms of consciousness and practice is strategic:

> a central problem is that of the transformation of the teaching body. For the teachers in Britain are overwhelmingly conservative, not merely politically but educationally too. To think in terms of a socialist alternative in education is purely illusory unless this alternative includes the liberation of teachers.[16]

From this perspective the 'problem' of the urban school is located crucially in the presence of a largely apolitical or conservative teachers group whose level of critical consciousness is low and which is not integrated with other workers in the struggle to transform both education and society. The task for socialist teachers is, therefore, to work to increase such consciousness among their colleagues and to increase integration with other workers.

Althusser (1971) identifies the school as 'the dominant Ideological State Apparatus' and schooling as 'the reproduction of the relations of production, i.e. of capitalist relations of exploitation'.[18] The majority of teachers thus act in the role of 'professional ideologists' who transmit as 'normal', or even desirable, the essentially exploitive social relations of capitalism. Only a few are as yet aware that this is the central 'problem' of the school:

> I ask the pardon of those teachers who, in dreadful conditions, attempt to turn the few weapons they can find in the history and learning they 'teach' against the ideology, the system and the practices in which they are trapped. They are a kind of hero. But they are rare and how many (the majority) do not even begin to supect the 'work' the system ... forces them to do.[19]

Bowles and Gintis (1976) call for a socialist strategy for education which involves 'the long march through the institutions', the capture of positions of strength; the democratization of schools and colleges; the undermining of 'the correspondence between the social relations of education and the social relations of production in capitalist economic life'. Teachers, they argue, should abandon their pretentions as professionals, 'pretensions which lead only to a defeatist quietism and isolation'.[20]

In these ways the 'academic Marxists', following the imperative of their ideological position, present not merely an analysis of the 'problem' of the world of the urban school, but proposals for action to change that world. It seems likely, however, that while their work is significant within academic and non-school contexts, only a minority of hard-pressed urban schoolteachers will have had the time (and, in some cases, the stamina) to study it closely.

Potentially a more active element in the day-to-day world of contemporary urban teachers are the productions and activities of the 'teacher Marxists'. The Teachers' Action Collective, a group of Marxist teachers working in London schools, has explicitly set out to provide an analysis of schooling in a capitalist society and the position of the teacher in this process. Made available in a series of collectively produced pamphlets are articles which 'speak directly' to teachers under such titles as 'teachers as workers'; 'the exercise of teacher power'; 'the battle of the working day' and 'teachers and the economy'.[21] In essence, the argument of the collective is that the 'problems' of urban education and of urban schools are derived from the system of economic production in which they are located: a system which requires teachers to shape, grade and discipline the next generation of the industrial proletariat. From this fundamental understanding comes the recognition that urban schools are 'factories'; that teachers are workers and that pupils are apprentice workers and that, together, they should consolidate their power within the work place to oppose an economic system (and its manifestations in schools) which is based upon an exploitive and de-humanising set of social relations.

From the beginnings of state provision of schools for the urban working-class there have always been groups of teachers who have recognized in one way or another the controlling and skilling functions of that enterprise. The Teachers' Action Collective represent a contemporary example of such a group which seeks to make clear to other urban teachers the real nature of the enterprise in which they are engaged:

> We do not accept that compulsory state education is in any way an expression of the benevolence of capitalism towards the working-class. We do not see schools as being malfunctioning machines of enlightenment, institutions in which knowledge is magnanimously presented to the young masses for their intellectual betterment ... Schools are manufactories of labour power.[22]

The 'Rank and File' organization within the National Union of Teachers is another group of largely urban-based teachers which draws its ideological inspiration from the varieties of Marxism, but which expresses both its analysis and its prescriptions for action in terms which distinguish it from groups such as the Teachers' Action Collective or 'Radical

Education'.[23] One of the central 'problems' of the school, from a Rank and File standpoint, is the poverty of, and constraints upon working-class education which arise both out of lack of adequate resources and lack of understanding by teachers of working-class consciousness. These deficiencies, it is argued, could be overcome through the agency of militant union action which would compel the provision of better facilities for urban working-class children and, through the praxis of the struggle, change the consciousness of the teachers.

As the Rank and File pamphlet, *Education and Society*, presents it:

> (Teachers) are in no way fitted to understand what makes working-class children tick and what makes them so rebellious. They have not personally experienced the insults and indignities by those who fail to make it – and their special position in the classroom does not encourage them to make up their deficiency in knowledge. On the contrary, they are expected to crush rebellion. Consequently any feeling of solidarity with pupils is completely absent ... Their way round the problem, socially conscious pedagogues as they are, is to find justification for the pupils' deviance and antagonism to learning, in the sociology and psychology of maladjustment ...

It is envisaged that greater understanding of the working-class would be forged in the context of militant union action:

> Through fighting with the Union against the poor pay, the large classes, the crowded conditions and rotten buildings and the bureaucratic yoke weighing on them, they ... gain experience of the class struggle. Teachers' strikes, demonstrations and other protest actions show that they are learning fast. This lines them up directly with other rank and file workers whose problems are surprisingly similar.[24]

While the various groups of 'teacher-workers' differ in the particular emphasis which they give to the analysis of oppression and in the specific focus which they give in prescriptions for action, they are united in their common rejection of a conventional wisdom which suggests that teachers can be, and ought to be, impartial and neutral transmitters of knowledge and skills. In the words of Chris Searle, 'these hypocritical and shallow dogmas are being challenged by classroom teachers throughout the country, particularly in the urban working-class areas where in every area of public service ... people face systematic underdevelopment and attack.[25]

But while the ideological struggle is clear, its impact upon the majority of urban schoolteachers has been generally unexamined. We know relatively little about how contemporary urban teachers experience their work situation; what constructs they hold of knowledge, ability and the educational process; what professional perspectives or ideologies inform their practice; how they accept, resist or negotiate the prevailing order of the school; of their consciousness of autonomy and of constraint; of how they view the activity of teaching in an urban working-class school. These issues remain to be made explicit.

Notes

1 LOVETT, William 'Chartism: a New Organization of the People' in *The Radical Tradition in Education in Britain* (ed) B. Simon Lawrence & Wishart, 1972, pp. 248–50
2 Quoted in SIMON, B. (1965) *Education and the Labour Movement 1870–1920* Lawrence & Wishart, p. 145
3 SPRING, J. 'Anarchism and Education' in *Libertarian Teacher* No. 9 p. 7
4 *Libertarian Teacher*, No. 9, p. 16
5 *Ibid*. pp. 17–19
6 PATON, Keith *The Great Brain Robbery* Moss Side Press, p. 19
7 *Ibid*. p. 21
8 ILLICH, I. (1973) *Deschooling Society* Penguin
9 GINTIS, H. 'Towards a Political Economy of Education' in *Harvard Educational Review* Vol. 42 (1) Feb. 1972, p. 95
10 PATON, K. *op. cit*. p. 57
11 Where urban schools are in crisis, particularly in inner-city areas, the potential impact of libertarian ideology is enhanced in terms of its claims to provide a realistic alternative when conventional systems have failed. These possibilities might occur in Inner London, New York City or other metropolitan centres.
12 FAY, B. *op. cit*. p. 103
13 Such a description of the 'new' sociology of education is not taken to imply that it has the monopoly of 'being critical', but that the practice of criticism is central to its activity and that it explicitly recognises the need for praxis.
14 YOUNG, M.F.D. (ed) (1971) *Knowledge and Control* Collier-Macmillan p. 60
15 WORSLEY, P. 'The Reification of Marxism: rejoinder to Lazar' in *Sociology*, Vol. 9 (3), 1975 p. 499

16 HOARE, Q. 'Education programmes and men' in *New Left Review* Vol. 32 1967 p. 52

17 The 'overwhelmingly conservative' nature of the majority of teachers is frequently commented upon in radical and Marxist analyses of education. Thus the writer of the editorial in *Radical Education*, No. 2, concerned with questions of racialism in schools, remarks:

'let us not kid ourselves that teachers are an enlightened bunch who would go to the stake rather than implement reactionary, repressive and indeed cruel policies in school. The survey published by the *Times Educational Supplement* (4th October, 1974) indicated that only 30% of the teachers would vote Labour ... put more significantly, this means that 70% of teachers found Harold Wilson and Roy Jenkins too left wing.'

The survey referred to: *Teachers in the British General Election of October, 1974* Times Publication, 1974.

18 ALTHUSSER, L. 'Ideology and Ideological State Apparatuses' in Cosin, B. (ed) (1972) *Education, Structure and Society* Penguin

19 *Ibid.* p. 261

20 BOWLES, S. & GINTIS, H. (1976) *Schooling in Capitalist America*, Routledge and Kegan Paul, p. 287

21 See publications of Teachers' Action Collective, 2 Turquand St, London SE17

22 'Teachers' Action' No. 3 (pp. 1–2)

23 'Radical Education', founded in Autumn, 1974, exists to 'put education-as-radical back on the agenda of the working-class movement' and to serve 'in countering a certain fragmentation which characterizes the radical movement in education'. See *Radical Education* No. 1

24 ROSENBERG, C. *Education and Society* Rank & File Teachers, p. 22

25 SEARLE, C. 'All in the same class' *Times Educational Supplement* 10th October, 1975

Index